Louis Châtellier is Professor of Modern History at the Université de Nancy. His publications include *Tradition Chrétienne et renouveau Catholique dans l'ancien diocèse de Strasbourg (1650–1770)*.

Past and Present Publications

The Europe of the Devout

This book is published as part of the joint publishing agreement established in 1977 between the Fondation de la Maison des Sciences de l'Homme and the Press Syndicate of the University of Cambridge. Titles published under this arrangement may appear in any European language or, in the case of volumes of collected essays, in several languages.

New books will appear either as individual titles or in one of the series which the Maison des Sciences de l'Homme and the Cambridge University Press have jointly agreed to publish. All books published jointly by the Maison des Sciences de l'Homme and the Cambridge University Press will be distributed by the Press throughout the world.

Cet ouvrage est publié dans le cadre de l'accord de co-édition passé en 1977 entre la Fondation de la Maison des Sciences de l'Homme et le Press Syndicate of the University of Cambridge. Toutes les langues européennes sont admises pour les titres couverts par cet accord, et les ouvrages collectifs peuvent paraître en plusiers langues.

Les ouvrages paraissent soit isolément, soit dans l'une des séries que la Maison des Sciences de l'Homme et Cambridge University Press ont convenu de publier ensemble. La distribution dans le monde entier des titres ainsi publiés conjointement par les deux établissements est assurée par Cambridge University Press.

This book is also published in association with and as part of Past and Present Publications, which comprise books similar in character to the articles in the journal *Past and Present*. Whether the volumes in the series are collections of essays – some previously published, others new studies – or monographs, they encompass a wide variety of scholarly and original works primarily concerned with social, economic and cultural changes and their causes and consequences. They will appeal to both specialists and non-specialists and will endeavour to communicate the results of historical and allied research in readable and lively form.

For a list of titles in Past and Present Publications, see end of book.

The Europe of the Devout

The Catholic Reformation and the Formation of a New Society

LOUIS CHATELLIER

Professor of Modern History at the University of Nancy II

translated by
JEAN BIRRELL

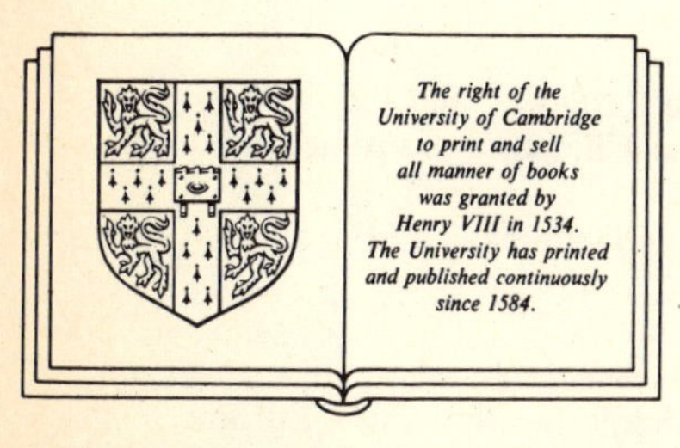

CAMBRIDGE UNIVERSITY PRESS

Cambridge
New York Port Chester Melbourne Sydney

EDITIONS DE
LA MAISON DES SCIENCES DE L'HOMME
Paris

Published by the Press Syndicate of the University of Cambridge
The Pitt Building, Trumpington Street, Cambridge CB2 1RP
40 West 20th Street, New York, NY 10011, USA
10 Stamford Road, Oakleigh, Melbourne 3166, Australia
and Editions de la Maison des Sciences de l'Homme
54 Boulevard Raspail, 75270 Paris Cedex 06

Originally published in French as *L'Europe des dévots*
by Flammarion 1987

First published in English by Editions de la Maison des Sciences de l'Homme and Cambridge University Press 1989 as *The Europe of the Devout: the Catholic Reformation and the Formation of a New Society*

Printed in Great Britain at the University Press, Cambridge

British Library cataloguing in publication data
Châtellier, Louis
The Europe of the Devout: the Catholic
reformation and the formation of a new society.
1. Europe. Catholic communities, 1563–1800
I. Title II. L'Europe des dévots. *English*
305.6′2′04

Library of Congress cataloguing in publication data
Châtellier, Louis.
[Europe des dévots. English]
Europe of the devout: the Catholic reformation and the
formation of a new society / by Louis Châtellier: translated by
Jean Birrell.
p. cm. – (Past and present publications)
Translation of: L'Europe des dévots.
Includes index.
ISBN 0-521-36333-0
1. Catholic Church – Europe. 2. Sociology, Christian – Europe.
3. Europe – Religious life and customs. I. Title.
BX1490.C4613 1989
282′.4–dc 19 88–36549 CIP

ISBN 0 521 36333 0
ISBN 2 7351 0279 3 (France only)

VN

Contents

Figures and tables

FIGURES

TABLES

Preface

For some years now the term 'Counter-Reformation' has been out of favour among historians. By emphasising what was systematically opposed to Protestantism both in the Council of Trent and in its implementation by princes and clergy, it seemed to many to give the vast movement of Catholic renewal in the sixteenth, seventeenth and eighteenth centuries the aspect of a reconquest. There are problems, furthermore, for Catholics in allowing the advantage of priority in the idea of reform to Luther and Calvin, when it was already the order of the day as early as the beginning of the sixteenth century within the old Church.[1] Thus it has become customary to talk rather of reform, Catholic and autonomous, though part, along with Protestantism, of a vast movement which one historian has suggested should be called the 'Age of Reforms'.[2] This approach to the problem is certainly more intellectually satisfying. But it must not be forgotten that theology, though of prime importance, was not all that was at issue in this major sixteenth-century transformation. Society, too, was involved. The partition of Western Christianity was a new reality which churchmen had to take into account, even if they did not accept it. Alongside Protestant Europe, another Europe came into being once the Council of Trent (1563) was concluded. Its emergence forms the subject of this book, which is offered as a study of modern Catholicism as a social phenomenon.

Such a project is not without precedents; it has its roots, indeed, in the works of distinguished authors. But it is primarily Protestantism which has been studied from this perspective. Max Weber, first of all, in *The Sociology of Religion* and above all in his celebrated work *The Protestant Ethic and the Spirit of Capitalism*, explored the complex relationships which exist between religion as lived by the faithful and the way such people behave in society. More precisely, he tried to

[1] Hubert Jedin, *Katholische Reformation oder Gegenreformation?* (Lucerne, 1946).
[2] Pierre Chaunu, *Le Temps des réformes: histoire religieuse et système de civilisation; la crise de la chrétienté, l'éclatement (1250–1550)* (Paris, 1976).

establish how belief conditioned the relations of individuals to money and to work.

The exhortation of the apostle to make fast one's own call is here interpreted [according to the Calvinists] as a duty to attain certainty of one's own election and justification in the daily struggle of life. In the place of the humble sinners to whom Luther promises grace if they trust themselves to God in penitent faith are bred those self-confident saints whom we can rediscover in the hard puritan merchants of the heroic age of capitalism, and in isolated instances down to the present. On the other hand, in order to attain that self-confidence, *intense worldly activity*[3] is recommended as the most suitable means. It, and it alone, disperses religious doubts and gives the certainty of grace.[4]

On the subject of 'asceticism and the spirit of capitalism', Weber further specified:

And even more important: the religious valuation of restless, continuous systematic work in a worldly calling, as the highest means to asceticism, and at the same time the surest and most evident proof of rebirth and evident faith, must have been the most powerful conceivable lever for the expansion of that attitude towards life which we have here called the spirit of capitalism.[5]

Thus the thesis according to which Protestant asceticism permitted the appearance of modern capitalism took shape.[6]

In his fine, though sadly unfinished, *Origines de l'esprit bourgeois en France* (volume 1: *L'Eglise et la bourgeoisie*), Bernard Groethuysen provided a confirmation of the Weber thesis by showing how the 'bourgeois order' in eighteenth-century France was constituted outside the Catholic Church, even sometimes in opposition to it.[7] It is as if there were a contradiction between the bourgeoisie and Catholicism. In both cases, employing different methods, the problem of affinity – or of a lack of affinity – between a social class in the process of formation and a religion was clearly posed and proved rich in insights which assist our understanding of modern society.

It may perhaps be useful, in the wake of these stimulating and

[3] Underlined in original.
[4] Max Weber, *The Protestant Ethic and the Spirit of Catholicism*, translated by Talcott Parsons (London, 1930), pp. 111–12.
[5] *Ibid.*, p. 172.
[6] Philippe Besnard, *Protestantisme et capitalisme* (Paris, 1970), p. 19.
[7] Bernard Groethuysen, *Origines de l'esprit bourgeois en France*, vol. 1, *L'Eglise et la bourgeoisie* (Paris, 1927).

pioneering works, to spell out the method and extend the problematic by applying them to a new field of research. Or, to put it another way, it is no longer enough to examine only the bourgeoisie: we should study the whole social body. We should move on from those societies characterised by reform to those which remained faithful to the old Church.

Of many possible approaches, one seemed particularly appropriate, that is a study of the Marian congregations. These associations of men, established by the Jesuits in their colleges from the end of the sixteenth century, were perfectly adapted to society. There were young men alongside the adults; there were merchants, burgesses and sometimes nobles and clerics alongside the artisans. These *sodales*, as they were called, received instruction appropriate to their condition. They were inculcated not only with pious habits but with rules of life which made a lasting impression and which they transmitted to those around them. It was intended that they should live together in perfect harmony. Ties of brotherhood were quickly established between the congregations of neighbouring and distant towns. Within cities, groups of several hundred, even several thousand, men lived according to the same rule, knew each other and regularly met. By 1600, a dense network extended to various countries throughout Europe without regard to frontiers. It did not, of course, include the whole of Catholic society, but it was its leaven, its leading element and its spearhead. Numerous other confraternities and associations had similar intentions in Catholic countries during the sixteenth and seventeenth centuries. But none had the benefit of a similar organisation on a worldwide scale, or had as its expressed aim, in the words of the founder of the Society of Jesus, to 'reform the world'.[8]

Did they succeed in this aim? Was a Catholic society gradually constituted in the years, or rather centuries, following the Council of Trent? This is the question which we will try to examine through a study of the Marian congregations. It is impossible for a single researcher to work in every archive in Europe which has material concerning these associations. Regrettably, a selection has had to be made, with the emphasis on those areas with which the author is most familiar (Paris, Eastern France, the Rhineland, Switzerland and Southern Germany) and on some with which he is less familiar, but has come to know better (Belgium and Southern Italy). Certain

[8] Father Bouhours, S. J., *La Vie de saint Ignace, fondateur de la Compagnie de Jésus* (Paris, 1758), p. 242.

sacrifices have been particularly painful (Spain and Austria), and it is hoped that these sacrifices will prove only temporary. Such as it is, with all its limitations, the investigation would have made little progress without the great support from which it has benefited. The author owes a particular debt to the archivists who have generously opened their archives and so often given useful advice, to Annik Schon, who has devised the figures, to the Deutscher Akademischer Austauschdienst, whose substantial support at the commencement of the research was so encouraging, and to Louis Audibert, who has greatly contributed by his comments on the first draft, and by the care with which he followed the various stages in the transformation of the manuscript into a book.

Abbreviations

A. B. R.: Archives départementales du Bas-Rhin
A. D. Meurthe-et-Moselle, Nord, Rhône etc: Archives départementales de Meurthe-et-Moselle, du Nord, du Rhône etc
A. H. R.: Archives départementales du Haut-Rhin
A. M. Epinal, Obernai etc: Archives municipales d'Epinal, d'Obernai etc
A. N. Paris: Archives nationales, Paris
A. P. Saint-Martin, Colmar: Archives paroissiales de l'église Saint-Martin, Colmar
A. P. Toulouse: Archives de la province S. J. de Toulouse
A. P. B. M. Namur: Archives de la province belge méridionale S. J., Namur
A. S. J. Rome: Archives de la Société de Jésus, Rome
B. Ars. Paris: Bibliothèque de l'Arsenal, Paris
B. C. U. Fribourg: Bibliothèque cantonale et universitaire de Fribourg (Suisse)
B. G. S. Strasbourg: Bibliothèque du Grand Séminaire de Strasbourg
B. H. Munich: Bayerisches Hauptstaatsarchiv, Munich
B. M. Colmar, Toulouse etc: Bibliothèque municipale de Colmar, de Toulouse etc
B. Maz. Paris: Bibliothèque Mazarine, Paris
B. N. Paris: Bibliothèque nationale, Paris
B. N. U. Strasbourg: Bibliothèque nationale et universitaire de Strasbourg
B. R. Brussels: Bibliothèque royale, Brussels
B. S. Munich: Bayerische Staatsbibliothek, Munich
H. A. E. Cologne: Historisches Archiv des Erzbistums Köln
H. A. S. Cologne: Historisches Archiv der Stadt Köln
M. C. Paris: Minutier central des Archives nationales, Paris
N. P. Cologne: Archiv der Norddeutschen Provinz S. J., Cologne

O. P. Munich: Archiv der Oberrheinischen Provinz S. J., Munich
S. A. Lucerne: Staatsarchiv des Kantons Luzern
S. A. Munich: Stadtarchiv München
U. B. Munich: Universitätsbibliothek, Munich
Z. B. Soleure: Zentralbibliothek Solothurn

PART I *Constructing a model*

On 4 December 1563, the final session of a council which had been meeting at Trent, not without problems, since 1545, was at last completed. The closing decree gave a clear statement of the reasons why it had met and of the spirit in which the participants had worked. 'That is why the holy council believed that it should condemn and anathematise the principal errors of contemporary heretics, and expound and teach the Catholic doctrine, as it has condemned and anathematised the one, and taught the other.'[1]

But how were the decisions of the Council to be put into practice in the daily life of the faithful? How were they to be made to understand that they should henceforward confess regularly, communicate frequently and venerate Christ present in the Eucharist? Like other religious orders, but perhaps rather better since they were first and foremost missionaries, the Jesuits understood the problem. Founded in 1540, and rapidly active on all fronts, the Society of Jesus did not devote itself solely to missions abroad and to education, as is too often believed. Its colleges were, from the outset, very active centres of apostleship, from which preachers, catechists and missionaries left in a steady stream for the various parts of the town and for the neighbouring countryside. They soon began to unite adult and young men in associations under the patronage of the Virgin, and to teach them how to live as good Catholics according to their station in life and according to the principles and spirit of the Council of Trent. Thus were born the Marian congregations.

[1] A. Michel, 'Les décrets du concile de Trente', in *Histoire des conciles* (Paris, 1938), vol. 10, part 1, p. 630.

1. *Foundation*

It was in 1563, according to tradition, that Father Jean Leunis began to gather together, after the evening classes, the best pupils of the Jesuit Roman college so that they might perform pious exercises.[1] This was a modest enough development, but it happened in the very year when the Council closed, and just four years after the death of Ignatius Loyola, at a time when his order was experiencing an irresistible upsurge. Further, Father Leunis came from Liège, and his activities took place in Rome. The conditions were right for this pious initiative by a college regent to assume a European dimension.

FROM NAPLES TO COLOGNE

But in the short run, a number of initiatives which were already well established were more influential. In Rome, the Oratory of Divine Love, founded in 1514, offered an elevated model of the spiritual life and examples to copy in the persons of Bishop Giberti and Pope Paul IV.[2] In Naples, the congregation of the Bianchi, founded in 1430 by Giacomo della Marca in the Church of the Trinity, still enjoyed a high reputation for charity and devotion at the beginning of the sixteenth century. The Society for the Veneration of the Holy Sacrament, founded in 1554 in the church of the Jesuit college, with the approval and blessing of St Ignatius himself, originated here. Its rules already included the duty to 'reform oneself each day, giving a good example and edification to others' by confessing and communicating fortnightly, as well as by serving the hospital poor and attending the regular meetings at the college. Such frequent practice of the sacraments surprised the Neapolitans, who called the brothers

[1] J. Wicki, S. J., *Le Père Jean Leunis S. J. (1532–1584), fondateur des congrégations mariales* (Rome, Inst. Hist. S. J., 1951).

[2] L. Cristiani, 'L'Eglise à l'époque du concile de Trente', in *Histoire de l'Eglise depuis les origines jusqu'à nos jours*, under the direction of Augustin Fliche and Victor Martin (Paris, 1948), vol. 17, pp. 247–8.

'communicants', a name already clearly epitomising the visible activities of the future congregation.[3]

Meanwhile, in the north, in the Rheno-Flemish world which produced Jean Leunis, there developed, thanks to the Dominicans, the confraternities of the Rosary. In 1470 at Douai, in 1475 at Cologne, and subsequently in the towns of the middle and upper Rhine, they foreshadowed, a century in advance, the establishment of the Marian congregations.[4] It was not only in the primacy of devotion to the Virgin that they prefigured the activities of the Jesuits, but also in the character of this devotion. There is more than just a similarity between the *Rosarium mysticum animae fidelis* of the Carthusian Landsperge of Cologne (1531) and the *Cinquante Méditations de la vie et louanges de la Vierge Marie Mère de Dieu* of Father Coster, founder of the Marian congregation in the same town in 1575.[5] The two works were inspired by the same spirit and proposed the same method of praying. Also, as soon as the register of the congregation was opened, almost all the Carthusians of the Monastery of Saint-Barbara in Cologne enrolled.[6] Further, in the first rules prepared for the congregations of Douai (1572) and Cologne (1575), the same father imposed the obligation on every candidate to join first a 'confraternity of the Rosary established by the Dominicans, a confraternity of which we wish this sodality to be a member' (art. 2).[7] And the Jesuits, almost immediately after their arrival in Lucerne, began to promote a similar association before any foundation dependent on their own college.[8]

Nevertheless, although evidently forming part of the movement which, from the *devotio moderna* to the Oratory of Divine Love, served as a prelude to the movement of Catholic reform, the initiatives of Fathers Leunis and Coster were clearly different in nature and quickly developed specific characteristics. Which other confraternity, in the 1570s, imposed on its members weekly confession and monthly Communion, not counting the festivals of the

[3] A. S. J. Rome, province of Naples, 177, fos. 14–15, 98–105.

[4] Jean-Claude Schmitt, 'Apostolat mendiant et société— une confrérie dominicaine à la veille de la Réforme', *Annales, Economies, Sociétés, Civilisations* (Jan.–Feb. 1971), pp. 83–104.

[5] For spiritual life in Cologne in the sixteenth century, see Gérald Chaix, *Réforme et Contre-Réforme catholiques— recherches sur la Chartreuse de Cologne au XVIe siècle*, 3 vols. (Salzburg, Analecta Cartusiana, 1981).

[6] H. A. S. Cologne, Jesuit deposit 52, fo. 57.

[7] *Ibid.*, Jesuit deposit 51, p. 2.

[8] S. A. Lucerne, cod. KK 25/1, p. 36.

Virgin and of Christ? And this was still a minimal requirement. At the Collège de Clermont in Paris, from 1575, the members of the congregation had to communicate 'every fortnight'.[9] At Naples, two years later, it was said in a report sent to Rome that the brothers approached the Communion table every Sunday. Which meant, added the author of the letter, that as a result of the numerous feast days, they took Communion on average at least twice a week.[10] And that was not all; the *sodales* had to learn to serve at Mass. They attended the holy sacrifice every day. Prayer was a constant preoccupation. In the morning, as soon as they got up, they said the Salve Regina, in the evening, the Ave Maris Stella.

> And during the day they should tell their beads to the extent of five Paternosters and fifty Ave Marias. And a further three Paternosters and Ave Marias for the prayers recommended in the congregation. And to this end and in perpetual witness of their good resolution and holy enterprise they should wear their chaplets at all times.[11]

The Neapolitan students added a daily half-hour of meditation on a theme expounded by their director once or twice a week. They also frequently wore hair shirts and did not hesitate to flagellate themselves in public or in private. Everywhere, the Sunday meeting before or after Mass followed in common was the occasion for spiritual enrichment and the most effective means of consolidating the religious life of the group by acts of communal piety.

Public life also was carefully controlled and regulated – no chattering in class for the pupils, no idle banter in the square for the burgesses. With more reason, bars, with the exchanges and the encounters which risked taking place there, were strictly forbidden.

> They should shun bad company, oaths and dirty, false and dishonest talk. By their modesty and their appearance, let them be models for others as is fitting for a true votary of Mary. (Rules of Cologne, 1575, art. 6)[12]

Ideally, since it was a brotherhood, they should meet together as often as possible and constitute a model of Christian society which would serve as an example to the whole town.

[9] B. N. Paris, French MSS, 15779, fo. 2v.
[10] A. S. J. Rome, province of Naples, 177, fo. 4v (1577).
[11] B. N. Paris, French MSS, 15779, fo. 4v.
[12] H. A. S. Cologne, Jesuit deposit 51, p. 3.

They should all take pains to be friendly and familiar together, and when they meet one another, they should discuss and ponder good, holy and virtuous things All in praise of God and our advocate the Blessed Virgin Mary.
(Collège de Clermont, Paris, 1575, rule 12)[13]

The Naples annalist could conclude by writing: 'Our sodality is truly like a seminary of a very holy life' (1577).[14] A seminary – we are a long way from a confraternity; nearer, in fact, to Brothers of the Common Life or a third order.

SANTA MARIA DELLA VITTORIA

This was all the more true since the congregation member began his career by an act of consecration. And like St Ignatius at Montserrat, it was to the Virgin, his Lady, that the postulant appealed:

Holy Mary Mother of God and Virgin, I . . . choose you today for Lady and Mistress, Patron and Advocate, and I order and propose with all my heart, never to forsake you, and never so to say or do that by my deeds anything should be done against your honour; I beseech you therefore most lovingly that it should please you to receive me as your perpetual servant, to assist me in all my actions, and not to abandon me at the hour of death. So be it.[15]

The chivalric character of the act is immediately obvious. It was far more than simply entering the 'service' of the Virgin, as Father Crasset claimed, attempting to explain it a century later.[16] Certainly, the appeal to the mercy and the 'benignity' of the Holy Mother of God was not neglected. In the Rules of Cologne, article 1 stipulated:

This sodality is instituted in honour of the Blessed Virgin Mary in order that the students should be inspired by a special devotion with regard to the Most Holy Virgin Mary, so that they should venerate her and receive from her special help in their studies and their various activities.

But immediately after, in article 2, came the obligation on the postulants to make their 'profession of faith as laid down by the Council of Trent'.[17]

The Virgin at issue here was no longer the compassionate mother in

[13] B. N. Paris, French MSS, 15779, fo. 5.

[14] A. S. J. Rome, province of Naples, 177, fo. 6v.

[15] Quoted from François Coster, *Le Livre de la Compaignie c'est-à-dire les Cinq Livres des institutions chrestiennes, dressées pour l'usage de la Confrérie de la très-heureuse Vierge Marie, mis en français du latin de François Coster* (Antwerp, 1588), in-8o, introductory pieces and 493 pages (not paginated).

[16] Jean Crasset, S. J., *Des congrégations de Notre-Dame érigées dans les maisons des pères de la Compagnie de Jésus* (Paris, 1694), p. 63.

[17] H. A. S. Cologne, Jesuit deposit 51, p. 2.

the long mantle who protects and intercedes, but the *Mariahilf* often represented with sword in hand in the statues carried in processions on feast days. This was a Virgin who gave aid, certainly, but who also fought. It was the Virgin who was seen at the side of the Catholic troops on the day of the glorious Battle of Lepanto (1571), and in whose honour the church of Santa Maria della Vittoria was built in Rome some years after that event.[18] It was the Virgin who gave courage to the Catholics of Vienna in 1579 and who regrouped them when the Archduke Ernest seemed to weaken in the face of the demonstrators who proclaimed the true Gospel. The Marian congregation instituted a few days later under the title of the Assumption appeared almost as a riposte.[19]

In Cologne, the foundation of Father Coster (1575) was contemporary with the schemes of Archbishop Gebhart Truchsess to detach his electorate from the Catholic camp. His failure was seen as due to the zeal of the congregations, supported by Our Lady of Victory.

> In fact, the leaders amongst the Clergy, even many Bishops, even the Most Reverend Papal Nuncio, Barthelemy de Porcie, a very virtuous and very devout person, worthy of eternal memory, with almost all his entourage, having given their names, wished to be entered into the rule and book of the Confraternity; as a result of whose cunning it happened (the Most Holy Mother of God supporting and assisting them) that the Senate of Cologne held very resolutely to the Catholic faith, and most courageously repulsed and surmounted the great perils presented by the enemy.[20]

The Virgin as generalissimo of the anti-Protestant armies appeared nowhere more strikingly than at Antwerp, when the town, subdued by Alexander Farnese, recognised once more the authority of the King of Spain (1585). The first public manifestation of the young congregation of the college, on 7 April 1587, consisted, in fact, of restoring to its old place on the pediment of the Senate House the statue of the Queen of Heaven, the traditional protectress of the town.

[18] Commentary in Victor-Lucien Tapié, *Baroque et classicisme* (Paris, 1957), pp. 77–8; André Chastel, *L'Art italien*, 2 vols. (Paris, 1956), vol. 2, p. 126.

[19] Anna Coreth, 'Die ersten Sodalitäten der Jesuiten in Österreich, Geistigkeit und Entwicklung', in *Jahrbuch für mystische Theologie* (1965), pp. 7–65. See pp. 37–8.

[20] François Coster, *Le Livre de la Compaignie*, introduction (not paginated). Another version of these events is in J. B. Kettenmayer, S. J., *Die Anfänge der marianischen Sodalität in Köln, 1576–1598* (Münster, 1928), pp. 24–5, who shows the role of members of the congregations in the entourage of the Archbishop and their efforts to throw light on his conduct.

Having removed and taken down a profane colossus, and having adorned and refitted her with a diadem and a sceptre, [the town] recognised and received the Virgin Mary Mother of God, oppressed and rejected by the heretics, for its Lady, its guardian and its advocate.[21]

It was a ceremony rich in significance; exaltation in victory and apology were inextricably intermingled, without wholly extinguishing a lingering fear, its roots in the remote past, of the punishment incurred by the whole city as a result of the affront suffered by the holy protectress. The fight of the knight of Mary to defend the honour of his Lady was not unmixed with a strong desire to restore an order whose overthrow was a source of fear and anguish.

As much as a century later, in the tiny, intensely Catholic town of Swiss Fribourg, the passage of French Protestant refugees after the Revocation of the Edict of Nantes made people tremble with fear. Lo and behold, one of them went so far as to insult the Virgin in the street! A congregation member heard him; he rushed to his room, where, on his knees before a pious picture of the Holy Trinity and the Virgin, he prayed to God and his beloved patron 'that they would not leave such a crime unpunished'. His prayer was heard. The next day, when the 'sacrilegious insulter' was in the street, stones miraculously fell off a roof and gashed open his head so badly that his brains spilled out. The Catholics were appeased when they saw their patron avenged,[22] while the heretics were terrified and took good care never to speak ill of the Virgin again.

The Christian knight was also a conqueror. He was a crusader who had enlisted under the banner of Our Lady of Victory and burned to plant it ever further into enemy territory. 'We should work for the revival of the Catholic Church in Germany and for it to recover its place and its eminence', wrote Father Coster to his congregation in Cologne.[23] It was not only Germany which was at issue. The year of the Massacre of St Bartholomew (1572) saw the foundation by Coster himself of the congregation at Douai. Two years later, another Jesuit, Father Jacques Rem, was active in Dillingen. In the same year (1574), it was the turn of Prague. The year 1575 was decisive. Three great towns were involved – Lyons, Paris (where the congregation which

[21] François Coster, *Cinquante Méditations de la vie et louanges de la Vierge Marie Mère de Dieu avec sept méditations sur le cantique Salve Regina* (Antwerp, 1590), introduction (not paginated).

[22] B. C. U. Fribourg (Switzerland), MSS, L. 107, p. 346 (1691).

[23] Kettenmayer, *Die Anfänge der marienischen Sodalität in Köln* p. 36.

had existed since 1562 was completely reorganised) and Cologne. Then came Ingolstadt (1577), Munich, Innsbruck and Lucerne (1578), Vienna (1579) and Swiss Fribourg (1581), all (but especially the two first and the last) strongly marked by the spirit and action of Peter Canisius.

The decade 1570–80 was crucial for the establishment of a network of powerful Marian congregations in the parts of Europe affected by the Reformation. The counter-attack was being prepared. For the moment, certainly, the danger may not have seemed very threatening to the Protestants. The worthy member of the Lyons congregation who ran after their co-religionists as they were led to the gallows to adjure them to convert must have appeared to them both naive and stupid.[24] However, as Peter Canisius wrote to a correspondent towards 1575–80, behind the standard of the Virgin troops were assembling who were preparing great things:

> It seems to me that we can all the more certainly restore the Catholic religion in Germany if a large number of men yearn in their hearts, in the name of Jesus, to defend the cult of the Holy Virgin and to develop the congregation already begun. The heretics may ridicule and mock the children of Christ who sing Hosannas and Ave Marias. The new world which will have restored the honour of the Mother of God with a new zeal in all categories of men will surprise them.[25]

The last sentence is significant. Peter Canisius saw in the Marian congregations not only the instruments of a Catholic reconquest, but also, and perhaps most of all, the means for a transformation of Christian society in its entirety.

ROME ALONE

This is why General Claudius Aquaviva, convinced that the Marian institution could play a key role in the construction of this 'new world', did everything he could to strengthen and extend it. The bulls *Omnipotentis Dei* of Gregory XIII (1584) and *Superna dispositione* and *Romanum decet* of Sixtus V (1587) gave him the means.[26] In the first place, unity – the Roman college's congregation of the Annunciation became the Prima Primaria, to which all existing and future

24 A. S. J. Rome, province of Lyons, 28, fo. 1v (1575).
25 Quoted by Coreth, 'Die ersten Sodalitäten', p. 29.
26 Elder Mullan, S. J., *La Congregazione Mariana studiata nei documenti* (Rome, 1911).

congregations were obliged to affiliate. Next, authority – only whoever was at the head of the Society of Jesus decided which candidatures to accept and which to reject. Lastly, multiplicity – there were to be in every house belonging to or dependent on the Society of Jesus as many sodalities as the General thought fit. Rome directed, and within Rome, the supreme head of the Jesuits. Further, in 1587, the latter revised the rules of the Prima Primaria, which thus became the universal canon, effective throughout Christendom. Locally, in each congregation, a father director was nominated by his superiors without the *sodales* being consulted in any way. Their role was limited to recognising him, honouring him and benefiting from his teaching.

Some good Catholics, however, were uneasy. In the face of these actions apparently designed for the defence, even triumph, of the Church, there were some who went so far as to say that the door was being flung open to heresy. That a fierce Gallican like Etienne Pasquier should be of this opinion is hardly surprising. For him, Ignatius Loyola was the founder of a sect which was a good deal more dangerous than those of Luther and Calvin.[27] But that priests faithful to Rome, even Jesuits, including some of those in the highest positions, should react in this way is more surprising. 'I am extremely grieved', wrote the General to the French Provincial in 1575, 'to hear that anyone is of the opinion, and expresses it, that by means of these congregations an opening has been offered to heresy and I desire that Your Reverence should not only [not] permit such talk, but not allow it to grow in the minds of our fathers.'[28] In fact, at that very moment, reserve with regard to this young institution was visible within the Society in both Flanders and Lyons.[29]

Let us look at the rules of the congregation of the Collège de Clermont in Paris after they had been revised in 1575 so as to be 'as close as possible . . . to the rules and constitutions of the Roman

[27] Etienne Pasquier, *Le Cathéchisme des Jésuites*, critical edition by Claude Sutto, Publication du Centre d'Etudes de la Renaissance de l'Université de Sherbrooke (Quebec, 1982).

[28] Quoted by Emile Villaret, S. J., *Les Congrégations mariales*, vol. 1, *Des origines à la suppression de la Compagnie de Jésus (1540–1773)* (Paris, 1947), p. 52.

[29] 'Porro sodalitatibus externorum hominum, non expediri ut nostri praesint, vel ut eis admisceantur', declared the Provincial of Flanders–Belgium in 1575: see A.P.B.M. Namur, 124,4 (Poncelet notes). There was an identical situation in Lyons, where a congregation of men had existed since 1575; at the time of the provincial congregation the fathers wondered whether it would not be better to transfer it out of the college, and relieve the Jesuits of its direction: see *ibid*.

congregation'.[30] Whilst it was laid down that the father director was chosen by his superiors, it was also clearly stated that the prefect was 'elected and established by the congregation'. The same was true of his two assistants and of the twelve counsellors who headed the twelve 'classes' of brothers. These were very democratic elections. Each 'class' chose three names for the position of prefect. The officers scrutinised them and drew up a list of the three names occurring most frequently, which was presented to the congregation for them, by 'suffrage of the ballot', to indicate which one they wanted as prefect. The other two became his assistants. The counsellors, initially at least, were elected directly by the members of their 'class'. These officers, even though their term of office was, to begin with, short (only three months), played an important role. This was true in particular of the prefect, who presided alongside the father over the fortunes of the congregation. He was not only the head, with all the attendant honours, not only the model whom all should emulate, the supervisor who knew his men, visited them when they were sick and rebuked them if need be, but he was, above all, the person who directed the meeting, said the prayers, intoned the canticles and even contributed to its spiritual quality. It was he, in effect, who chose the brothers who, 'for the discussion session', presented in 'only a quarter of an hour' the Gospel or the Epistle of the day. The letters describing the work of sister congregations all came to him and on him lay the responsibility of replying. The assistants helped him in these varied and onerous functions, and the counsellors acted as links – and singularly effective ones from the fact of their distribution into 'classes' – between the prefect and the simple *sodales*.

It is easy to understand why, when a lay prefect was chosen in 1590 in the very young and already prestigious congregation of the Annunciation in Antwerp, which attracted the élite of the town's clergy and bourgeoisie, the fathers had to face a veritable mini-revolution on the part of the clergy.[31] Was it proper for them to be submitted to laymen, when it was a question of matters of piety and edification? The reply was that nothing in the rules prohibited this, which appears to have appeased them. This seems, however, unlikely, all the more so since it often happened in these early years that the prefect and his deputies took initiatives with potentially far-reaching

[30] B. N. Paris, French MSS, 15779.
[31] A. P. B. M. Namur, Droeshout deposit 23,2, pp. 134–5.

implications. In Cologne, in 1578, a practice of Communion was introduced which, whilst designed to impress the participants with the grandeur of the sacrament, could easily revive memories amongst those who had participated in the Lutheran cult. The members were, in effect, invited to present themselves at the Communion table in procession, candle in hand. Having received the Host, they remained kneeling, waiting for a priest or deacon to offer them the Holy Scriptures, a passage of which they kissed in turn.[32] Bearing in mind that this ritual was not exceptional but happened every Sunday, since the *sodales* had early acquired the habit of weekly Communion, whilst there was certainly something here to edify the mass of the faithful, there was equally some cause for anxiety on the part of a number of ecclesiastics who saw in it an innovation of the reformed-Catholic type, which might foreshadow a certain syncretism.

It is true that the very Catholic convictions of the scholars of Cologne could hardly be called into question when they searched even the libraries of their landlords for heretical books which they promptly tossed on to bonfires hastily erected in the principal streets and squares. It could only have gratified their directors when they asked them to organise regular meetings to discuss the principal points of disagreement with the Protestants, in order to prepare themselves more thoroughly to harangue the crowds of passers-by in the main streets of the town. When they pushed the spirit of reform so far as to try to correct the morals of their landlords, to the extent of taking down, if necessary, paintings and engravings of subjects they deemed licentious, when they urged their parents to say the Benedicite before meals and family prayers at night, and to confess and communicate more frequently, they were acting, after all, in accord with the spirit which they had been taught.[33] It was possible, nevertheless, to find such zeal excessive, and in particular to ask if it was altogether reasonable to abandon to simple laymen, and young ones to boot, tasks traditionally the responsibility of priests. At the very moment when the Council of Trent was carefully distinguishing the simple faithful from Christians invested with the priesthood, and strictly subjecting the latter to the bishops, in particular in their role as teachers, this Jesuit initiative, without calling to mind, obviously,

[32] A. Müller, *Die Kölner Bürger-Sodalität, 1608–1908* (Paderborn, 1909), p. 5.
[33] H. A. S. Cologne, Jesuit deposit 51; Kettenmayer, *Die Anfänge der marianischen Sodalität in Köln*; Müller, *Die Kölner Bürger-Sodalität*.

the universal priesthood, did for some give off a certain whiff of heterodoxy.[34] It was, in any case, to give much more extended functions to the laity. In fact, a new conception of the Church was emerging, which could appear to more than a few as truly revolutionary.

[34] For the sacrament of the Order in the decrees of the Council of Trent, see Michel, 'Les décrets du concile de Trente', pp. 467–505.

2. *Expansion*

The new institution, though operating initially among students, was quick to make itself felt beyond college walls. 'And as at the beginning, it [the congregation] was meant for the young, to make them worthy to become Christian men,' wrote the author of the history of the congregation of Cologne in 1576, 'it seemed necessary to extend it not only to their fellow students but also to the hosts with whom they lodged and even to their families, to confirm them all in the Catholic faith and instruct them in the holy things of the Christian life.'[1] This was a logic entirely in conformity with the intention of St Ignatius, who had wished to make the Society of Jesus into a missionary order, and the college into a centre of apostleship.[2]

FROM COLLEGE TO TOWN

This was the case in Cologne as early as 1576, where the register of enrolments conserved in the town archives reveals the presence, alongside the theology students, of pupils from the 'poetry', 'syntax' and 'rhetoric' classes, distinguished monks from the town's great convents (Carthusians and Dominicans), canons and prebendaries of St Gereon, St Severinus and the Capitol, graduates and doctors, and even important dignitaries from the secular clergy of the Rhenish churches, of the rank of official and suffragan bishop.[3] There were also laymen in these congregations from the beginning. In university towns such as Cologne and Ingolstadt, they were jurists and medical

[1] H. A. S. Cologne, Jesuit deposit 51, p. 32.

[2] I have developed this point in my *Tradition chrétienne et renouveau catholique dans le cadre du diocèse de Strasbourg, 1650–1770* (Paris, 1981). In Fribourg (Switzerland), the establishment of the congregation preceded the opening of classes (1581): see André-Jean Marquis, *Le Collège Saint-Michel de Fribourg (Suisse)— sa fondation et ses débuts, 1579–1597*, Publications des archives de la Société d'histoire du canton de Fribourg, vol. 20 (Fribourg, 1969), pp. 216–17.

[3] H. A. S. Cologne, Jesuit deposit 52.

doctors, or even representatives of families from the patriciate or international trade. One of the most active artisans in the young congregation in Cologne was Jean Stempel, ex-Burgomaster of Gouda, exiled to the Rhineland, and a man whose activities knew no bounds. A few years later, the prefect was Jodoc Van den Cruys, a merchant from Antwerp. It was a good idea, thought Francis Coster, for there to be respectable men amongst the first congregation members,[4] a policy perfectly illustrated by these examples.

At Munich, a little later, the effects of this policy were even more marked. The list of the first enrolments (1584), which the author has had the good fortune to discover, reveals the presence of the papal legate at the head of the ecclesiastics, and of the Duke of Bavaria himself at the head of the laity.[5] An equilibrium was already visible: alongside the 80 students (57.97 %), were 32 members of the clergy (23.18 %) and 26 laymen (18.84 %) (figure 20 pp. 233–5). In addition to the legate and his retinue, the abbots and some of the monks from the great Bavarian abbeys had registered, as had some canons of the Church of Our Lady and some graduate priests. On the part of the laity, the Duke had brought with him certain members of the court and of the nobility, and above all, representatives of the Italian colony which was as active and numerous in Munich at the end of the sixteenth century as in Vienna.[6]

The same process was taking place in Lucerne, Fribourg and Lyons. In the latter, the influx of burgesses was enough to embarrass the fathers as early as 1575. Perhaps they should meet separately? Perhaps a special sodality should be created for them?[7] Nor did the movement stop there. In Naples in 1582, certain brothers adopted the habit of assembling several hundred artisans whom they instructed in the Christian faith and familiarised with attendance at the sacraments.[8] And women, whatever has been said, were certainly to be found in the first sodalities. The congregation of the Holy Sacrament in Naples, founded in the lifetime of St Ignatius, was mixed.[9] So, to

4 *Ibid.*, Jesuit deposit 51, p. 39.
5 *Ibid.*, pp. 159ff., in the letters received by the sodality.
6 Coreth, 'Die ersten Sodalitäten', pp. 12–13. They seem the first to be affected (by 1565) by the movement of the Jesuit sodalities from Italy.
7 A. S. J. Rome, Congr. 42, fo. 102 (1576).
8 *Ibid.*, province of Naples, 177, fo. 21 (1582).
9 *Ibid.*, fo. 60. Indulgences accorded by Pope Gregory XIII dated 1 March 1580 in favour of the Confraternity of the Holy Sacrament for the faithful of both sexes established in the church of the college of the Society of Jesus in Naples.

begin with, was that of the Assumption, founded in Fribourg by Peter Canisius in 1581.[10]

The design, as far as it can be discerned in these first few years, went far beyond the avowed policy of a simple balancing of the student element by mature men of respectable rank. The intention was to create a surge of enthusiasm extending across town and country – from bishop to simple vicar, from abbot to monk, from prince to knight, from merchant to artisan and from men to women, the whole animated, sustained and fostered by the fathers of the college, who were, however, constantly vigilant to the need for limiting as far as possible any direct interference. The whole of society was envisaged from the start; it was this which must be transformed, from top to bottom, even if the stated objective, confined to the spiritual formation of certain good pupils, appeared modest, even negligible.

In point of fact, the method was not yet perfect in the 1580s. It came up against a social reality which was inadequately perceived, perhaps idealised, or understood according to medieval norms, by the followers of St Ignatius. It was hardly practicable to expect nobles and burgesses, or merchants and artisans, to work together – a Utopian dream, indeed, at the end of the sixteenth century! As early as 1593, in one of the great congregations founded by Father Coster, that of the Annunciation in Antwerp, it was decided to restore to the canons their title of Reverendissimi Domini and to the magistrates that of Domini, because, 'although the brothers, who are for the most part lay, desirous as they are to imitate the Christian humility of the Mother of God, can be addressed without any of these honorific titles, it is necessary nevertheless that the constituted authority should always be recognised'.[11] On the other hand, the annals lavish praise on the Prince of Vaudémont, prefect of the congregation at Nancy, for receiving the flower of the nobility of Lorraine into his chapel while at the same time welcoming craftsmen with a highly edifying little speech, in which he said that 'virtue made them noble and that one day the great of the earth would be only too happy to find themselves side by side with them in Paradise'.[12] In the meantime, however, it was made clear that the moment the artisans had a chapel of their own, they were to decamp with all speed.

[10] *Thresor de la Congregation de Nôtre Dame soubs le titre de son Assumption; instituée pour hommes et femmes premierement en la Ville de Fribourg en Suise* . . . (Fribourg, 1655), pp. 478–80.

[11] A. P. B. M. Namur, Droeshout deposit 23,2, p. 138.

[12] Crasset, *Des congrégations de Notre-Dame*, p. 104.

Another reality that the Jesuits had to take into account was the specificity of the sacerdotal quality so strongly reaffirmed by the Council of Trent. The age of the Brothers of the Common Life and of the great confraternities of the Rosary, whose spirit was perhaps present at the start, was long over. There was no suppression, but from the 1590s, and under the impetus of General Claudius Aquaviva, the congregations of clerics were everywhere systematically encouraged – in Spain, in Italy, even in Rome itself.[13]

As for women, Peter Canisius may well not have seen himself as innovative when he welcomed them into the sodality at Fribourg. Nevertheless, with the generalship of Aquaviva, a policy of systematic exclusion was adopted. Not only were mixed congregations no longer tolerated, but congregations of women were rejected.[14] This sudden reversal was symptomatic, and reveals how social realities affected the new project. It was impossible to join a congregation without taking an oath of consecration to the Holy Virgin. How, then, could a woman, who was, as a matter of fact, under the authority of a father or a husband, properly pronounce such a formula which engaged not only her but those who depended on her? Logically, it was for fathers and husbands to engage on their behalf, as they were invited by the terms of the act of consecration. A lesser creature in law, a woman could not dispose freely of her religious life; the embarrassed statements and often contradictory decisions of the generals on this question only express a state of affairs which had nothing to do with religion, but which religion had to take into account.[15]

And this is what happened. Like Luther sixty years before, and in spite of the perhaps unrealistic hopes of some of its members, the Society of Jesus had to accept society as it then was. It accommodated itself, indeed, rather well. Nobles were a fact of life, let them stick

[13] A. S. J. Rome, province of Rome, 2, fo. 210. Letter from the General to the Provincial of Rome (30 October 1610).

[14] A. S. J. Rome, Resp. Gener. ordine alphabetico 1556–1611, p. 290 (letter of 3 July 1586). The women who already had their congregations could continue in this devotion, but they did not share in indulgences because these were only granted to all-male congregations. Further, the Jesuits should not be involved in such associations: 'Nostri tamen ab earum coetibus omnino absint sed externum directorem habeant.'

[15] A. S. J. Rome, Instit. 135, fos. 248–52; A. S. J. Rome, Congr. 21, fo. 188 (reply of Vitelleschi to a demand emanating from the province of the Lower Rhine): 'If other congregations (of women) were not founded, the reasons for this has been given above; however, we have no cause whatsoever to refuse the establishment in our churches of similar associations.' List of the directives of the generals on this subject in Mullan, *La Congregazione Mariana*, pp. 67–8.

together and constitute their own congregation, with their own officers, special chapel, conditions of recruitment, ways and customs and specific areas of activity. It was the same with the craftsmen; and then with the merchants, who were next to form a group of their own. Then it was the turn of the legal profession – *avocats*, *procureurs* and lawyers of every sort. They could hardly be expected to mix with rude mechanicals or base trade; no problem, let them form a special sodality for lawyers. At this stage, the crafts made representations: was it proper to lump together masters and journeymen? The latter ought to split off and form their own congregation. Besides, it seemed to the fathers desirable to separate bachelors from married men, just as clerics and laymen, Latin speakers and non-Latin speakers, adults and scholars were already differentiated. It was not long before the latter, in their turn, began to be separated into homogeneous groups according to age and level of study.

From the 1590s, sometimes even earlier, a stratification is visible. In Naples, in the professed house – that is the establishment where the religious, already priests and with their studies behind them, prepared for the spiritual ministry – it was apparent well before the end of the century. At the head came the congregation of the Nativity of the Virgin, prestigious on account of its two hundred nobles, amongst them many dukes and princes, and admitted in 1587 to the Prima Primaria of Rome. Then came the congregation of the Purification, reserved for clerics, with fifty *sodales* soon after its foundation in 1595. The congregation of the Annunciation, admitted at the same date, was reserved for the legal profession – *avocats*, notaries, *greffiers* – and had eighty members. Artisans and tradesmen, to the number of five hundred, were grouped under the title of the Assumption. And so that the lackeys, coachmen and attendants of the great men meeting in the Nativity neither wasted their time nor endangered their souls waiting about for their masters, they were formed into a congregation of the Virgin of the Angels, where one or other Jesuit priest instructed them in the rudiments of religion. This was the situation in 1595 in Naples in the professed house alone.[16] But in the same town at the same time there was the college, which had seven other sodalities attached to it, including the powerful Assumption which alone counted more than six hundred members, mostly craftsmen, who were dispersed between oratories located in the various quarters of the town.[17] It was soon joined by the Nativity,

[16] A. S. J. Rome, province of Naples, 72, fos. 85–107, 108–112v. [17] *Ibid.*

aimed at apprentices and journeymen. And the scholars too, naturally, had their own various groups.

This concern to adapt to social structure eventually became universal, though varying, obviously, according to the specific activities of a town, the composition of its population and the dynamism of the particular Jesuit establishment. Lyons, it appears, had a congregation of burgesses by 1575.[18] The college at Toulouse had its 'craftsmen' and its 'Gentlemen' by the end of the sixteenth century; so did Dijon and Dôle.[19] At Antwerp, in 1610, there were four sodalities in the professed house alone: that of the Annunciation, divided into two sections, the Latin (for the ecclesiastics and the literate) and the Flemish (also designated 'for married men'), that of the Nativity, for young unmarried craftsmen, and that of the Immaculate Conception, or of the Walloons, intended for craftsmen and merchants who did not speak Flemish but normally expressed themselves in French.[20] Naples and Antwerp were two worlds, poles apart, as the disposition of their congregations immediately reveals. Nevertheless, the concern to adapt a spiritual activity to a milieu is apparent, as is the desire (imposed to some extent, admittedly, by circumstances, as it was apparently lacking at the start) to model the new institution on the changing society of early modern towns.

Did the congregations, by indirectly expressing this change, perhaps themselves exert some influence on it, if only by giving a sort of recognition on the part of the universal Church to a social stratification in the process of consolidation? This may have been what was obscurely felt by the man from Siena who thought it prudent in 1596 to warn the Grand Duke of Tuscany against 'these secret conventicles where the separation of the people and the nobility threatens to ruin the social peace and union of the Republic'.[21] So rapid had been the adaptation of the Jesuits to the social evolution that it appeared in some quarters to have preceded, even perhaps to have provoked, it.

FROM PRAYER TO GOOD WORKS

This all happened so quickly, and often with such success, that it is tempting to see it, like the worthy man from Siena, as the result of

[18] A. P. B. M. Namur, 124,4 (Poncelet notes).

[19] Pierre Delattre, S. J., *Les Etablissements des jésuites en France depuis quatre siècles*, 5 vols. (Enghien, 1949–55).

[20] A. P. B. M. Namur, Droeshout deposit 24, 1, pp. 10–86.

[21] Villaret, *Les Congrégations mariales*, pp. 565–6.

obscure forces working behind the scenes. But what, on the surface at least, could be simpler? The Naples annalist wrote, in 1581: 'Many of these brothers are not content with perfecting themselves, but wish to extend this to their neighbours and lead them as often as possible to confession; they want to oblige them to confess monthly.'[22] The congregation member was thus not only someone who attended to his own interior perfection, but also a Christian who felt himself invested with a veritable missionary vocation with regard to others. 'They instruct the others', wrote the chronicler of Cologne in 1580.[23] The 'others' were their fellow students, on whose behalf they were ready to seek alms, if they were poor, or who they would receive into their own homes, if they were unable to find Catholic lodgings in town. They were their parents, whom, in letters home, they exhorted to a better life and edified during the holidays by their weekly Communion and prayers both before and after meals. They were the burgesses of Cologne, in particular the hosts in whose homes they lodged. The lodgers rapidly transformed their rooms into cells and mealtimes into pious gatherings. The hours of the day so revolved round prayers and acts of piety that life within these bourgeois families was soon regulated as if under the control of one of the college's disciplinary prefects.[24] To be models wherever they went was without doubt the first task of apostleship for the congregation members. This was what impelled them to give to all their acts, and to all their meetings, this distinctive edifying and demonstrative character.

Hence monthly Communion, as we have seen. Hence the great festivities which accompanied the publication of Gregory XIII's brief confirming the sodality of Cologne (1578). The nuncio in person spoke first. Then, next day, after a general Communion, all the brethren came, candle in hand, to kiss the pontifical deed. In the afternoon, in a sumptuously decorated room, adorned with numerous emblems in elegant Latin, the prefect expounded the brief, after which the kneeling gathering sang a resounding Te Deum.[25] The same year saw the first *Römerfahrt*, that is the Christmas pilgrimage to the town's seven great churches. An even more impressive procession, following the same route, was soon organised by the congregation for Holy Week. The members wore the robe of the

[22] A. S. J. Rome, province of Naples, 177, fo. 20.
[23] H. A. S. Cologne, Jesuit deposit 51, p. 34.
[24] *Ibid.*, pp. 31–9. [25] *Ibid.*, Jesuit deposit 52 b.

penitent and processed candle in hand.[26] The arrival of the diploma admitting the new congregation of burgesses to the Prima Primaria of Rome in 1609 was the occasion for great festivities, during which the town of Cologne's reception of the relics of the Three Kings, who had given their name to the new association, was commemorated in a play.[27] Processions, plays and impressive ceremonies provided a means of access to the town, as, indeed, the name of the Three Kings constituted an appeal to an ancient devotion, long dear to the hearts of the inhabitants, which it was hoped to revive.

It was not enough simply to set a good example: the whole population of a quarter, even of an entire city, had to be won over. Thus the noble brothers of Aquileia in the Abruzzi accompanied the missions of the fathers to the villages. They followed the processions chanting the litanies of the Virgin, listened to the sermons, confessed, did penance and prepared for Communion with the greatest devotion; they reconciled themselves to God publicly and gave alms humbly.[28] They showed the peasantry how to follow a mission and benefit from it. They served for these novices, in a sense, as living models.

In Rome, at this period, a congregation of the Pietà established at the Roman college had support for this type of work as its principal aim. Its members acted as assistants to the missionaries. They gathered people into the squares, intoned the canticles, made the responses, said the litanies and led the penitents to the confessors.[29] A programme preserved in the Roman archives is even more explicit. According to this, on Sundays, after vespers, five or six fathers set out, accompanied by fifteen or twenty zealous members of the congregation. They divided the streets and squares of an area of the town between them. Having arrived at his chosen spot, the Jesuit mounted a stool whilst his helpers patrolled the streets calling on the passers-by and idlers to come and listen. When the audience was large enough, the sermon began, always on a very simple theme, such as the example of Christ to be followed (the preacher was equipped with a crucifix) or the necessity of frequent Communion. The instruction over, the *sodales* said the litanies of the Holy Virgin in alternate

[26] *Ibid.*, Jesuit deposit 9, fos. 190v–191; Müller, *Die Kölner Bürger-Sodalität*, p. 10.

[27] H. A. S. Cologne, Jesuit deposit 9, fo. 203v; Fréderic Reiffenberg, S. J., *Historia Societatis Iesu ad Rhenum inferiorem*, vol. 1 (Cologne, 1764), p. 426.

[28] A. S. J. Rome, province of Naples, 177, fos. 257–8.

[29] *Ibid.*, province of Rome, 153, fos. 231–2.

groups, whilst leading the people towards the church. There, a father began to expound the doctrine on confession, Communion or the mystery of faith. Then there was a sermon on one of the points from the first week of the Spiritual Exercises. Finally, the spectators were exhorted to make an act of contrition, whilst the priests, garbed in their stoles, proceeded towards the confessionals to receive the penitents. Throughout the ceremony, the brothers kept a close eye on the proceedings, persuading back to his seat any participant anxious to slip away or leading by the arm anyone hesitant or fearful about approaching a confessor.[30]

In some cases, the congregation members played an even more active part in this apostleship. In Naples, about 1610, they were responsible for the Schools of Christian Doctrine located in the poor quarters of the town, teaching children and young people the rudiments of the catechism, such as how to receive the sacraments and how to live their days and years in a holy manner.[31] The young craftsmen of Father de Pretere were doing the same at this period in Antwerp. Each small group of what was called the 'Legion of the Brave' was assigned a chapel or a quarter where, on Sunday mornings, they gave poor children the elements of religious instruction. The town was soon no longer big enough to contain their zeal and, in groups of ten, they went out into the countryside to teach little shepherd-boys. In each hamlet, every Sunday morning, there appeared a small band of apostles who methodically divided their tasks between them: two taught arithmetic and writing to those who could already read, six explained the letters of the alphabet to the illiterate, two acted as supervisors. This elementary instruction served, of course, as a foundation for religious teaching. Once it was well under way, the young men led the bands of young peasants, a hundred or a hundred and fifty strong, to the nearest town, where the fathers awaited them, to complete their knowledge of the catechism, hear their confessions and prepare them for Communion.[32]

The congregation had at its disposal other, perhaps even more effective, means of influencing the inhabitants of the towns and villages. From the time of the first rules laid down by Father Coster in both Douai and Cologne, charity to the dead and the dying assumed a role of considerable importance.

[30] *Ibid.*, fos. 252–3. [31] *Ibid.*, province of Naples, 72, fo. 166.
[32] A. P. B. M. Namur, Droeshout deposit 24,1, pp. 65–6, 343–4.

Every year, all the *sodales*, wherever they are, should recite the nine vigils of the dead for all the deceased of the sodality.

(article 4 of the Rules of Cologne, 1575)

If one of them falls ill, let everyone commend him every day to Christ and his Mother in Heaven. (article 7)

If one of them dies in a place where there is a sodality, all the local members should recite, on his behalf, the vigils of the dead with the nine lessons and should attend the Holy Mass said for the repose of his soul, as it is laid down for those who are received into that sodality, and remain in it till death.

(article 8)[33]

In practice, this took the form of a series of affecting and generally well-attended ceremonies which could not fail to impress whoever saw them. In Antwerp, at the beginning of the seventeenth century, as soon as a member was ready to receive the last rites, the father director, through the intermediary of the servant, or *Knaess*, alerted all the officers and the local brethren. At the given hour, a cortège formed at the parish church, with the counsellors carrying the twelve torches bearing the insignia of the sodality at its head, and constituted a guard of honour for the holy viaticum borne by the priest. It waited silently in front of the house of the sick man, then returned with the same ceremonial. Signs of reverence and special devotion to the Holy Sacrament, these torch-lit processions, sometimes traversing the town several times in a week, must have appeared to the inhabitants of Antwerp as a tangible proof of the special care shown by the congregation towards the sick, and even more towards the dead. The latter was resoundingly demonstrated by the burials, attended by the congregation as a body, and the Requiem Masses, at which attendance was obligatory, celebrated with great pomp a few days later.[34]

Charity, in fact, in all its forms, clearly emerged from the beginning as one of the major activities of the sodalities. The Naples annalist records as early as 1581 that they sent several brothers into the town's various hospitals every week. They comforted the sick and sometimes, on feast days, provided them with great banquets which they served themselves. Most of all, they taught them to pray and exhorted them to receive the sacraments. A veritable sub-office of the

[33] H. A. S. Cologne, Jesuit deposit 52, pp. 2–4.

[34] A. P. B. M. Namur, Droeshout deposit 24,1, pp. 79–83.

congregation was established at the Neapolitan Hospital of the Incurables at this period.[35]

Around 1590, the institution of the Monte, destined for a great future, was set up in this hospital for the benefit of the sick. The initiative came from the noble brethren whose charitable intentions were frustrated by the rules laid down for Marian congregations by General Aquaviva. In effect, they were forbidden to possess goods or manage capital. To circumvent this prohibition, the Neapolitan nobles constituted an association which was external to the congregation and the college. Between them, the members soon contributed capital to the tune of an initial total of 1,500 ducats. They chose from their members four governors to direct the enterprise, make the money grow, and employ the revenues according to the spirit of the foundation. Patients were certainly the chief recipients of assistance, but the 'shame-faced poor', for whom the knights had a special predilection, were also helped.[36]

The congregation was thus not directly involved. It was nevertheless always present, because all the officers of the Monte, and in particular the governors, had to be *sodales*. Thus a means was established to extend influence and develop new activities. This experiment was destined to be copied repeatedly, and the Neapolitan Monte was seen henceforth as a model.

But the experiment also reveals the extraordinary capacity manifested by the congregations for acting effectively, even though not openly, outside the strictly spiritual domain which was officially recognised as theirs. In Cologne at the beginning of the seventeenth century the congregation of the Three Kings, which was represented in the various guilds, successfully intervened to exclude from their councils those who were suspected of Protestantism. It supported, even inspired, the magistrates in their policy of orthodoxy and the suppression of religious liberty. To this end, the congregation was quite prepared to send certain brethren to keep watch on the houses of people suspected of sympathy towards heresy. They looked for evidence of clandestine preaching or the practice of forbidden devotions, at the risk of earning the nickname, common in the town, of *Schwickelsbrüder* (which could be translated as 'the Sharp-Eyed Brigade'), or of being called, even more contemptuously, 'spies' or

[35] A. S. J. Rome, province of Naples, 177, fos. 19–20.

[36] *Ibid.*, fos. 98–105, 247–8. Definition of the 'Monte' in Giulio Rezasco, *Dizionario del linguaggio italiano storico ed administrativo* (Florence, 1881), p. 649.

'traitors to their neighbours'.[37] Before long, such mockery was no longer possible, as one Cologne merchant learnt to his cost; for having used these terms publicly in a local inn, he was dragged before the courts and compelled to make an apology before the officers of the congregation to avoid going to prison.[38]

It is true that at this epoch, as stated by the annalist, many members of the town council were fervent *sodales*.[39] This explains why measure followed measure not only against the Protestants, but equally against Carnival and those dances described as immoral. The support of a magistrature won over to the ideas of the congregation greatly extended and strengthened the latter's activity. It did not preclude, very much to the contrary, direct action on the part of the most zealous brethren. At Salerno, they attacked widows who ventured out, in their opinion, rather too soon after their bereavement. They took them to the Jesuits, to be taught to live retired lives, remote from the world, as was appropriate to their condition. At Barletta, it was the habitués of taverns who suffered their vigilant and energetic solicitude.[40] Everywhere, people who swore or enjoyed jokes which were a little broad or scabrous were publicly berated and reproved.

Concern for others was taken a long way by the congregations, as far, even, as the establishment, wherever possible, of a veritable moral order and the imposition, when the civil authorities permitted, of social control.

FROM CAPITAL TO VILLAGE

This situation was certainly far from universal at the end of the sixteenth century, but it was beginning to be no longer exceptional. The great founding fathers, in the first place, both Francis Coster and Jacques Rem, increased the number of establishments within their respective spheres of influence, the Rheno-Flemish world on the one hand, Southern Germany on the other. The bull *Omnipotentis Dei* of Gregory XIII in 1584, followed by the 'common rules' laid down by the General for all congregations (1587), facilitated their spread.[41]

[37] H. A. S. Cologne, Jesuit deposit 9, fo. 222; Müller, *Die Kölner Bürger-Sodalität*, pp. 20–2. [38] H. A. S. Cologne, Jesuit deposit 9, fo. 271 (1621).
[39] Müller, *Die Kölner Bürger-Sodalität*, p. 22.
[40] A. S. J. Rome, province of Naples, 72, fos. 54–65, 68–82v (1592–3).
[41] Mullan, *La Congregazione Mariana*, pp. 5–10, 24–42.

From then on, they were to be set up in every college, more or less rapidly according to the region, the quality of the men charged with this task, and circumstances.

Already, through the intermediary of active brethren, congregations established in colleges had sometimes expanded beyond the town, and founded 'daughters' in the larger surrounding villages. The congregation of Cologne was trying to found similar groups in its vicinity before 1580. A curé in the Ardennes, evidently trained in the school of Father Coster, introduced into his parish the exercises he had seen practised in college.[42] When a Jesuit replacement was sent to a benefice, as at Kempten in 1609, he established a sort of prolongation of the mother association in Cologne.[43] This proving successful, the curés of the surrounding area, in this case secular, did the same.[44] In Alsace, the fathers of Molsheim, in the course of their missions, revived an old confraternity of the Virgin at Obernai, reformed it, directed it, and gave it the character of a congregation.[45] In the kingdom of Naples, a combination of all these different methods produced a situation where Marian associations were found even in ordinary villages. The zeal of brethren returning from their studies or simply on holiday, foundations in the course of missions to the villages and effective promotion by the curés are the most obvious factors. The congregations of priests, in particular, appear to have been of key importance. There was one in Naples, in the professed house, in 1593; there was another in the same year at Lecce; and there were others, soon after, at Cosenza, Nola, Benevento and Capua.[46] Their purpose remained the edification of priests. But it is reasonable to assume that the best of these, once they became town or village curés, were tempted to try, generally with the help of the Jesuits, to give their parishioners the benefit of what had been so successful in their own cases.

Thus the congregation and its ethos spread, though unevenly and even chaotically, sometimes reaching the bigger villages before large towns. The result by the 1590s (see figures 1a, b and c) is not without its surprises. Within the area covered (France, the Germanic world and the Low Countries), certain zones of remarkable concentration

[42] Kettenmayer, *Die Anfänge der marianischen Sodalität in Köln*, pp. 29–30.
[43] Müller, *Die Kölner Bürger-Sodalität*, p. 31.
[44] H. A. S. Cologne, Jesuit deposit 9, fo. 222.
[45] A. B. R. Strasbourg, 2 G 300,6.
[46] A. S. J. Rome, province of Naples, 72, fos. 68–82v, 85–107, 108–12.

are visible. The Rhine–Flanders region stands out, with a strong concentration in the southern Low Countries and on the banks of the middle Rhine. There is another concentration in Southern Germany, extending from Dillingen to Munich and from Reichenhall to Würzburg, and gravitating round the central point of Ingolstadt. Another striking zone is constituted by what René Taveneaux has called the *pays d'entre-deux*, extending from Louvain to Turin, including Alsace and Lorraine, Franche-Comté and Switzerland, the Rhône valley and Savoy. The concentration here is at least equal to that of the two others. Contrary to what might be expected, on the other hand, there are no particularly strong densities in the patrimonial Hapsburg states (Upper and Lower Austria and Bohemia). The kingdom of France, apart from the south-west and the Rhône valley, seems as yet little affected by the wave of foundations. It looks as if, before 1600, the heart of the kingdom, essentially, that is, the Parisian basin, was still outside the great centres of congregation activity found to the north, east and south. Was this the result of war, or of the difficulties experienced by the Jesuits in the French province in the last years of the sixteenth century? These are obviously reasons which have to be taken into account. But are they adequate? Or, more precisely, do they not conceal deeper reasons?

An examination of the most favoured zones reveals certain common characteristics. In the first place, the impact of Rome; there was a papal nuncio in residence, or a papal legate staying, in Cologne, Munich, Vienna, Lucerne and Avignon, all important centres of active congregations, at the time of the foundation. Paris had one too, it is true, but his influence was counterbalanced by other powers, and hardly comparable to what it could be in Lucerne or Cologne. The universities, for their part, whether old or new, were also centres of attraction. This was the case at Cologne, Louvain, Dôle, Toulouse, Pont-à-Mousson and Ingolstadt. There was a university in Paris, too, but it was opposed from the start to any erosion of its monopoly by the Jesuits. In Vienna and Munich, in particular, the nascent congregations benefited from the open support of the prince, who often, as in Bavaria, went so far as to set an example and become head of the movement.[47] In Paris, even when the kings, for example Charles IX and Henri III, were not hostile, their attitude towards the

[47] Coreth, 'Die ersten Sodalitäten', pp. 41, 42; Joseph Pichler, *Die Marianische deutsche Kongregation der Herren und Bürger am Bürgersaale zu München* (Munich, 1910), p. 5.

institution hardly differed from that which they exhibited towards the numerous other contemporary confraternities such as those of the Penitents.[48] In any case, the favour of these two kings, the latter in particular, if it existed, carried with it a strong risk of doing more harm than good. It is clear from the maps that many of the cities remarkable for a precocious development of the congregations were neither important political centres nor seats of bishoprics; this was true of Lille, Dijon, Swiss Fribourg, Dillingen and Douai.

One begins to suspect that what attracted these new associations of the devout, and explains their establishment in one place rather than another, was not so much the presence of a strong power but, on the contrary, its absence or its relative remoteness – thus Dillingen before Augsburg, Ingolstadt before Munich, Dijon, Lyons and Toulouse

[48] Villaret, *Les Congrégations mariales*, p. 91.

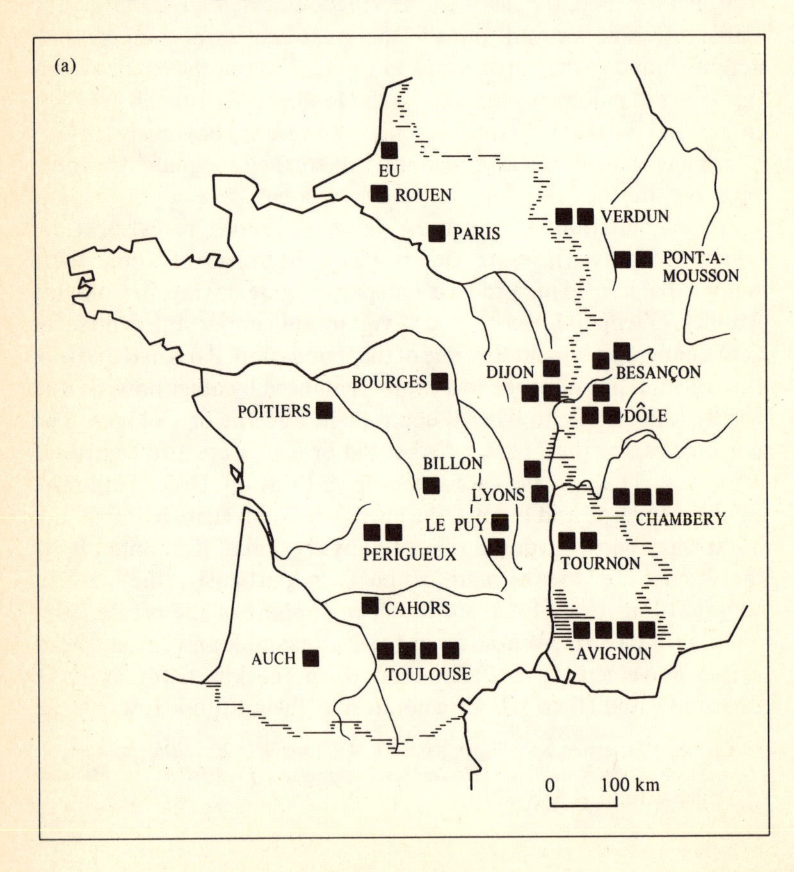

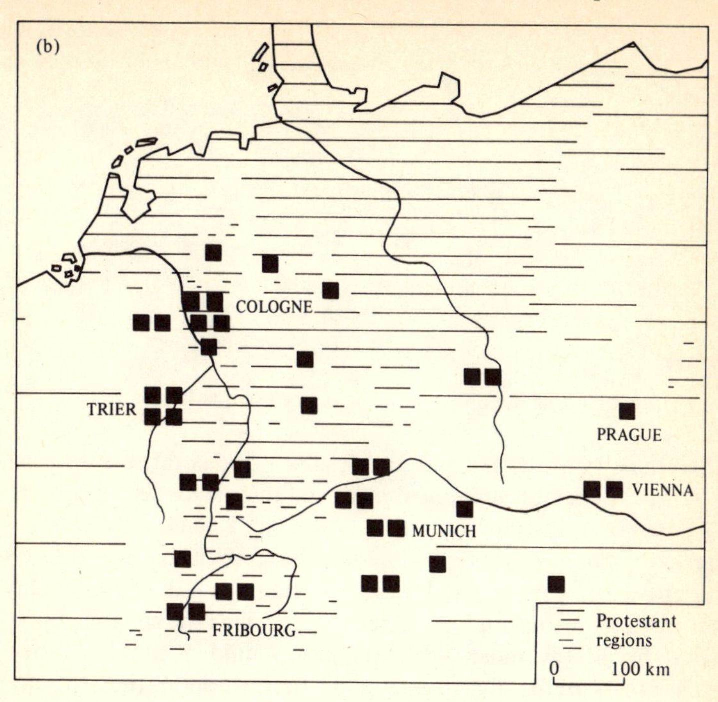

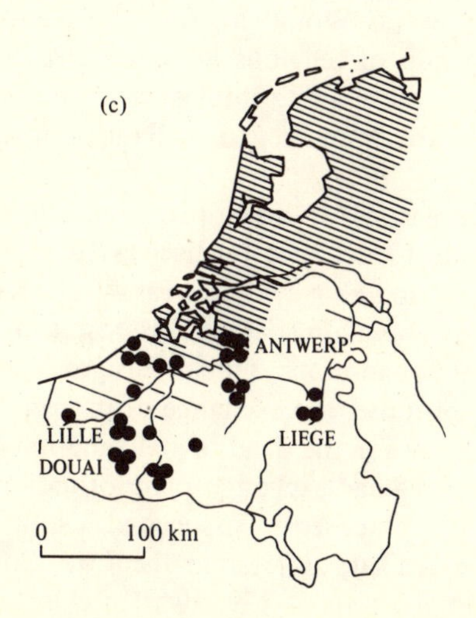

1. The Marian congregations in France, the Germanic world and the Low Countries, 1590–1600

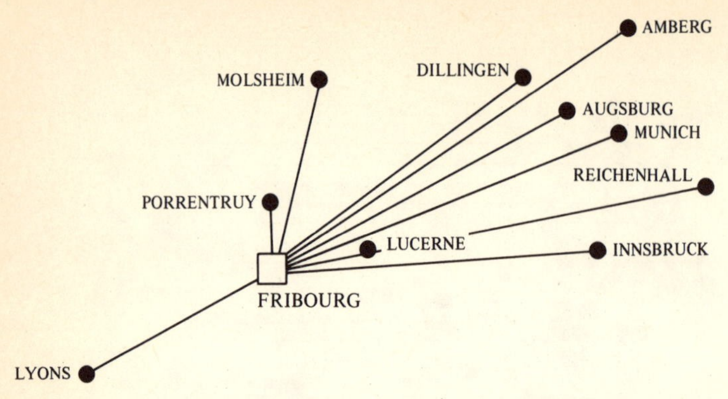

2. Congregations in contact with Fribourg (Switzerland)

rather than Paris. It is as if the Jesuits demonstrated a sort of preference for establishing themselves and their activities, when this was possible and without question of it being a general rule, in the interstices of power, where the remoteness or confusion of authority rendered it less pressing and more uncertain. It was here that the enterprise of spiritual and moral renewal to which the congregations aspired found the most fertile ground. Would a civil authority attached to its prerogatives have found it easy to tolerate these groups of zealous Christians who arrogated to themselves, in both taverns and streets, police powers? Would a proud bishop have viewed without concern a group of religious who attracted to their own church a large part of the male faithful of a town, at the risk of emptying the parish churches and negating all the pastoral labours of their priests?

There are still other reasons for this more or less explicit concern on the part of the Jesuits to distance themselves from authority. A congregation, at this period above all, was rarely isolated and alone *vis-à-vis* Rome. As early as 1576, Father Coster put into practice a plan to unite his first foundations, Douai, Bruges and Trier. This achieved a union of purpose, the exchange of patron saints of the month, common prayers for the dead, a welcome for brethren on their travels, and the regular exchange of information about the devotions and activities practised by associated institutions.[49] This principle was later extended, at least in the Low Countries and Germany. Thus Cologne, around 1590, was in close contact with

[49] Kettenmayer, *Die Anfänge der marianischen Sodalität in Köln* , pp. 33–5.

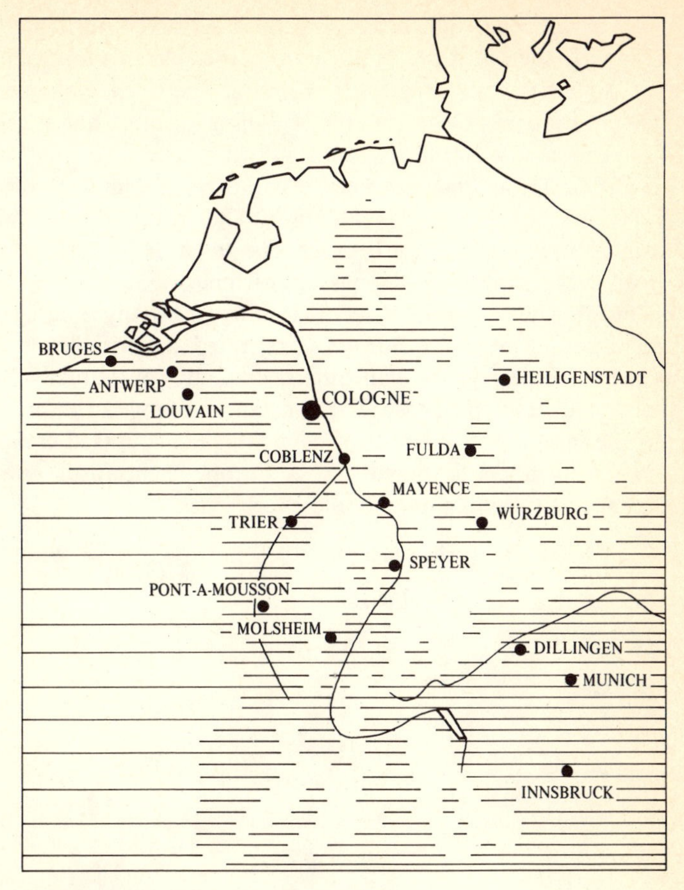

3. Congregations in contact with Cologne

Mayence, Trier, Würzburg, Speyer, Fulda, Heiligenstadt, Molsheim, Coblenz, Innsbruck, Dillingen, Louvain, Bruges, Antwerp, Munich and Pont-à-Mousson.[50] Fribourg, round about 1600, was in close contact by correspondence with Augsburg, Molsehim, Porrentruy, Dillingen, Reichenhall, Innsbruck, Lucerne, Munich, Amberg and Lyons[51] (see figures 2 and 3). The circles grew rapidly, extending beyond neighbouring towns, regions and even provinces. The members of the congregation of Cologne acted to some extent as

[50] *Ibid.*; H. A. S. Cologne, Jesuit deposit 52.

[51] B. C. U. Fribourg (Switzerland), MSS, L 87, fos. 223ff.

guides for those of Munich, advising them and instructing them in the customs. In their turn, the Bavarians kept their elders informed about their activities and progress.[52] Relations between Cologne and Antwerp were very close from the beginning, distance notwithstanding.[53] The same was true of Fribourg (Switzerland) and Augsburg.[54] Francis Coster and jacques Rem, the illustrious founders, were not wholly responsible for this situation. The travels of the various brothers strengthened ties between one town and another, which spread ever further with the passage of time.

Thus, by the end of the sixteenth century, the many congregations established throughout Europe constituted a veritable network, denser in some regions than others, certainly, but already clearly visible and developing fast. The constant exchange of information and the incessant movement of men, which encouraged emulation between members scattered across Europe, henceforth gave the nascent institution an exceptional effectiveness.

[52] H. A. S. Cologne, Jesuit deposit 51.
[53] A. P. B. M. Namur, Droeshout deposit 23,2, pp. 234–5 (1593).
[54] B. C. U. Fribourg (Switzerland), MSS, L 87.

3. *Pioneers*

We now have a map of devout Europe. But the men who pioneered the project remain obscure. We need to know not so much their origins, or how many there were, but what they were, what they did and what they felt in their daily lives. This is difficult not so much because of a shortage of documents as because of their edifying or normative nature. In 1576, the members of the Cologne congregation undertook to give the prefect, each individually, and every week, a detailed account of their good works.[1] Some of these weekly reports have survived, for example those found in the cantonal library of Swiss Fribourg; whilst, also in 1576, Francis Coster, the zealous founder already mentioned, published for the benefit of his congregations a *Libellus sodalitatis*, soon translated into French with the title of *Le Livre de la Compaignie*.[2] This work was the basis for numerous handbooks and directives which succeeded one another right up to the twentieth century, and its first editions constitute a very rich source for those pious habits which the Jesuits wished to inculcate into sixteenth-century Christians. But it tells us little or nothing about how these last responded. It is only by comparing these sources, so inadequate taken separately, by noting differences of emphasis and contradictions, and, conversely, repetition of the same facts expressed in the same words in both, that an attempt at a religious anthropology can be made.

APPORTIONING TIME

'Time should be measured', wrote Father Coster.[3] From morning till night, even night-time itself when awake, weekdays, Sundays, every month of the year, all stages of life and the last moments before death,

[1] Kettenmayer, *Die Anfänge der marianischen Sodalität in Köln*, p. 9.

[2] The French edition was published by Plantin of Antwerp in 1588; see above, chapter 1, note 15.

[3] Coster, *Le Livre de la Compaignie*, p. 103.

all were subjected to rigorous control and an implacable routine. Everyone knew that the devil was always present, on the lookout, ready to seize on the tiniest moment of relaxation or inattention in order to insinuate himself, make his words heard, and lead his victim astray, perhaps for ever. So there should be no more than six or seven hours' sleep, and, once in bed, behaviour as correct, as modest and as holy as that of the Virgin Mary in her garret. If you couldn't sleep, her holy model should again fill your imagination. Thus declared a certain Fribourg *sodalis* who left a detailed account of his activities and his interior life for the edification of his brethren and of future generations.[4] The moment you woke, day or night, you should spring out of bed. 'Because the devil pays particular attention to the first thoughts of the day', wrote Father Coster. You should make the sign of the Cross carefully, dress quickly and hasten to your prayer-desk as the first actions of the day. Then began the long morning prayer. 'Lord, I thank you for preserving me this night', then 'Lord, I pray you to keep me this day from all sin', then 'Lord, I offer you all my actions, beseeching that it should please you to order them to the glory of your name', the whole interspersed with a Pater and an Ave, and followed by the recitation of the Pater, the Ave Maria, the Creed and the Ave Maris Stella. The congregation member was then in a fit state to proceed to church, where he arrived if possible before the Mass the better to prepare himself, especially if he intended, as recommended by Father Coster, and as was the practice of the author of the Fribourg account, to communicate in spirit.

The working day then began, but it, too, was a day of prayer. Both the scholar hunched over his exercises and the craftsman busy at his work-bench were strongly exhorted to utter from time to time some pious exclamation such as *Deus piissimus* or *Deus amantissimus*, or even to sing a canticle. This was not enough for the pious *sodalis* of Fribourg. He usually attended a further Mass, in addition to the one recommended, and sometimes another sermon, too. Fifty Masses and seven 'extraordinary' (on top of those recommended in the rules) sermons, he triumphantly recorded at the beginning of his monthly report! At the first ring of the bell, he was on the alert; at the second, he sped to the church porch, leaving the friends with whom he had been 'honestly' relaxing disconcerted and nonplussed. In compensation, they were treated, immediately the service was over, to a digest

[4] B. C. U. Fribourg (Switzerland), MSS, L 87, fos. 139v–141v.

of the best points in the sermon, which their charitable friend saw it as his duty to engrave on his memory for their benefit. He set aside a few moments of every hour to contemplate the Virgin Mary, commend himself to her and invoke her assistance in attaining a good death. If the evening bells inviting the faithful to say the Hail Mary caught him in the middle of the main square, he would immediately fall to his knees and recite his prayer diligently and with total concentration. He still found time, in the course of the day, to say 'at least twice' the litanies of the Virgin, an entire rosary, which he recited with his arms in the form of a cross, the Little Rosary of Christ, and, in honour of the Five Wounds of Christ, five Paters and five Aves, also with his arms in the form of a cross.

A wandering thought was immediately punished by several strokes of a scourge, vigorously applied. An immodest look merited wearing a hair shirt for several days after. The end of the day was the moment when, having withdrawn to his chamber, the congregation member reviewed, hour by hour, the good and bad acts of his day. This examination of conscience was the indispensable exercise insisted on by every director, Father Coster most of all. He even provided a method in five stages so that it would be practised with profit. You should begin by thanking God for all blessings received, then beseech him for sufficient detestation of all your sins, then examine minutely every act accomplished, however small, and every thought engaged in, from morning to night, then ask pardon for all transgressions committed and make a firm resolve to correct them. Once this examination was completed, the *sodalis* piously recited his evening prayers: the Pater, the Ave Maria, the Confiteor, the Salve Regina and the invocation to his guardian angel.

> When his prayers are finished, he should safeguard his spirit by devout meditation or prayer, and avoid stories, tales and frivolous talk, extraneous thoughts, business matters and anything which tends to prevent union with God.[5]

He can then go to bed, though not without saying before closing his eyes, 'Lord, I beseech you to guard me this night from all the tricks of the devil.'[6]

So the days of the week passed, with for each a theme of special meditation generally taken from the life and Passion of Christ. Thus

[5] Coster, *Le Livre de la Compaignie*, p. 104. [6] *Ibid.*, p. 107.

Sunday was consecrated to a reflection on the humility of Jesus, Monday to his 'good nature and sweetness', Tuesday to his patience, and so on. A day had to be set aside for preparing for and making confession, since the rules stipulated that the Holy Sacrament should be received weekly. The devout young man of Fribourg did not fail in this any more than in his other obligations, and, for good measure, doubled the penance inflicted on him by the priest. He fasted every Saturday and was mindful to scourge himself several times a week.

The congregation of nobles at Aquileia in the Abruzzi gave such mortifications a public character and surrounded them with ceremony. Usually on a Saturday, day of penitence, the brothers gathered in the chapel. Some carried a large cross, some a crown of thorns and others a death's head, whilst yet others held their arms in the form of a cross or prostrated themselves on the ground. The Stabat Mater was intoned and the brothers came, two by two, to stand before the master of the novices, who, with scourges in both hands, flogged them energetically for the length of a Miserere. After which, the penitents kissed the feet of their mortifier and returned to their places.[7]

Communion took place once a month as laid down in the rules. Needless to say, the young man of Fribourg was not content with this minimum. Nor, indeed, was Father Coster. Recalling the words of St Ambrose, who called the Eucharist the 'daily bread', he added that 'it is desirable to be present in spirit each day at the sacrifice of the Mass, and sacramentally once a week'.[8] In other words, Sunday Communion was, from 1585, if not an obligation, at least strongly recommended. Additionally, there was introduced in the 1590s the practice of the monthly distribution of patron saints. At the meeting in the last week, the father director distributed to the *sodales* pictures of saints whose feast days occurred in the following month. Each member was invited to copy his illustrious model and invoke him during the days to come, also to practise his dominant virtue as described in a brief 'maxim' placed below the picture.[9]

All the festivals of the Virgin celebrated during the course of the year were inevitably the occasion for imposing ceremonies and massive Communions. But Lent was also important. In the last years of the sixteenth century, the pious custom of praying for forty hours

[7] A. S. J. Rome, province of Naples, 177, fos. 257–8.

[8] Coster, *Le Livre de la Compaignie*, p. 55.

[9] Mentioned in Antwerp in 1593: A. P. B. M. Namur, Droeshout deposit 23,2, pp. 235, 245–6. They were printed for the first time in 1594.

during the three days of Carnival, modelled on the ostentatious practice of the nobles of the Assumption in Rome, was widely introduced.[10] It was soon followed by the imposing and macabre Good Friday procession through the streets of the town, practised in both Cologne and Munich by the beginning of the seventeenth century.[11] The festivals of Christ were from the start the subject of special attention. It was to celebrate with ostentation the Feast of the Nativity that the congregation of the Immaculate Conception in Naples instituted for the first time in 1580 'the forty hours of prayer'.[12]

The ardent Fribourg *sodalis* gave pride of place to Christmas.[13] He prepared himself from the beginning of Advent, stepping up the intensity during the week immediately preceding the festival. He confessed three times, and communicated three times. He fasted rigorously, barely allowing himself a few scraps of bread for an evening meal. He lived in complete silence, his days and nights dedicated even more than normal to God. He examined his conscience more thoroughly. He got up in the night to devote three whole hours to pious exercises, according to a precise plan (one hour's reading, one hour's meditation on the Incarnation of Christ and one hour of prayer). His meditation was not left to the chance inspiration of the moment. Each day had its particular theme. On day one, he directed his thoughts to the Virgin and St Joseph as they awaited the event. On day two, he followed them to Bethlehem; on day three, he imagined himself in the stable; on day four, he pictured to himself once again 'that vile stable' where the Saviour chose to be born; on day five, he prepared himself for an act of perpetual love, and on day six, he invited the celestial beings to this ceremony, in particular his guardian angel, and prayed with them. The closer the prescribed day came, the more the pious young man felt himself to be transported, overwhelmed by celestial joy, set free from himself, and bathed in sweet tears. And less than ever did he let his mind wander. The mystery of the Incarnation was the sole object of his meditation. At eleven o'clock in the evening, he prepared himself feverishly.

[10] A. P. B. M. Namur, Droeshout deposit 23,2, pp. 48, 434. Also in Lucerne: S. A. Lucerne, KK 25/1, p. 118, and in Fribourg (Switzerland): B. C. U. Fribourg, MSS, L 107 (1), p. 27 (1594).

[11] Müller, *Die Kölner Bürger-Sodalität*, p. 10 (Cologne, 1600); B. H. Munich, Jesuits 102, fo. 190 (Munich, 1619).

[12] A. S. J. Rome, province of Naples 177, fos. 10v–11.

[13] B. C. U. Fribourg (Switzerland), MSS, L. 87, fos. 139v–141v.

Hardly had I heard the hour strike than I was uplifted by love to such a point that I had to cry out, and I felt my strength, through love, desert me. Whilst tears filled my eyes, my heart leapt in my breast . . . as if I had received the Little Jesus from the arms of Mary.[14]

He felt that having received such blessing he should consecrate himself even more fully to God. At the beginning of the Mass, he gave him his five senses, in the second part, his body and his soul; in the third part, he offered his heart.

At the moment of consecration, my spirit and my body filled with joy, I burst into tears, and, no longer my own master, I cried out *Te Deum laudamus*.[15]

In such a transport, he forgot time and place, thinking only of prolonging his prayers. When the time came to leave the church, he was delighted to find his house cold, so that he could all the better concentrate on the sufferings of Christ after his birth. But this did not satisfy him for long; he soon decided that he, too, would 'freely' be cold that night. He returned through the snow to the church, left his coat in the porch, endured the icy atmosphere, no longer able to feel his hands and feet, and spent the night in prayer. In the morning, he was there for the first office. He heard three Masses sung in succession, during which he renewed the night's act of consecration.

Did this intrepid and devout person, in whom were reborn the heroic virtues of the Saints and the Desert Fathers, celebrate the other feasts of the year with similar mortifications and pious exercises? We do not know. He presented nevertheless to all – or, more accurately, his edifying recital presented to all – the model to imitate. The great festivals of the year were not only commemorations of the great events in the life of Christ and the Virgin which should be observed with piety, they were also occasions for internal renewal. This was clearly understood by Father Coster, who in 1576 arranged a general confession every year at the commencement of Lent for the members of his Cologne congregation.[16]

A rhythm was imposed on the year, as it was on the day. The purpose was not simply to subject piety to discipline, or to observe a liturgical year, but to live differently. The time controlled by the Church should be the whole of time. Thus there would no longer be the tiniest place, or so it was hoped, from morning to night, from one year to the next, for evil.

[14] *Ibid.* [15] *Ibid.*

[16] Kettenmayer, *Die Anfänge der marianischen Sodalität in Köln*, p. 9.

CONTROLLING THE IMAGINATION

It was therefore essential that the mind should not escape and that the imagination, that supremely unpredictable element, should be controlled. The ideal was once again achieved by the model young man of Fribourg who thought of the Nativity when he was pierced by the cold wind of winter and who thought only of baptism and the glory of being a Christian when he was caught bare-headed one day in a rainstorm.[17] But such associations of ideas were hardly the norm, so the good fathers had to guide minds and protect their pupils not only from dubious paths but from simple apathy. Hence the care taken by the best directors to make each pious act and gesture correspond to a precise image. Take first the simplest and most important, the sign of the Cross.

> The Passion of Our Lord can be clearly understood by the Cross, which cross is customarily formed with the whole of the hand, that is to say, with five fingers to signify the five wounds; or with three fingers, that is to say, the thumb and the index and middle fingers, just as in the Passion, truly, the humility of Jesus Christ alone sustained and endured, but the whole of the Trinity was at work . . . Finally, with two fingers, the index and middle, because of the two natures, divine and human, in the one single person of Jesus Christ . . . Further, the remission of sins and the celestial glory is shown when the hand is passed, not from the right shoulder to the left, but, on the contrary, from the left to the right. Because we who were with the goats on the left side, stinking from the filth of our sins, are by the Cross and Passion of Our Lord transported to the right side with the sheep, reconciled to the eternal Father, having received the remission of our sins and the promise and guarantee of the Celestial Kingdom.[18]

With more reason, the Mass, which because of its length and its language risked being little understood by the simple-minded and those unaccustomed to concentrating their minds, should perhaps be accompanied by a pictorial commentary. Francis Coster employed this method in a very original way and managed to present his readers with a succession of scenes which unfolded to make a powerful theatrical impact.

> The priest before the steps of the altar represents Jesus Christ praying to God his Father in the Garden of Olives. Those things which are done at the right

[17] B. C. U. Fribourg (Switzerland), MSS, L 87, fos. 139v–141v.

[18] Coster, *Le Livre de la Compaignie*, pp. 308–9.

side and corner of the altar, at which it is the custom to read the prophecies, represent those things which Jesus Christ suffered in the houses of the Jews, under Annas and Caiaphas. The Gospel side, facing north, whence comes all evil, represents the tribunal of the Gentile Pilate and the endeavours and attacks of the other pagans from which Jesus Christ suffered so much ill because Lucifer, or the devil, who wants to transport his seat into the north and be like the Almighty, is principally adored there by pagans. When the Host is elevated, this signifies Jesus Christ raised on the Cross . . . The Lord's Prayer includes the seven words of Christ on the Cross, the breaking of the Host, the separation of the soul from the body. One part is put on the paten and represents the part descended into hell. The other, also put on the paten, represents the body descended from the Cross. The reception and manducation of the sacrament signifies the sepulchre. For we, who are earth, ought to carry within us the body of the Lord, so that he may after revive in us by our changed habits when with all the strength of our body and soul we adopt another life, and another way of living. The book is brought back to the right side and corner of the altar, since after the death of the Lord, the Jews still continued, some asking Pilate to let them guard the sepulchre, and others, by corrupting with silver and persecuting the Christians, attempted to obscure the glory of Jesus Christ. But finally the priest returns to the north to complete the office of the Mass with the reading from the Gospel; inasmuch as, the Jews being abandoned, the preaching and the grace of the Gospel is transferred to the Gentiles.[19]

This surprising text may appear almost irreverent. Was its author not making a veritable stage production out of the Mass, treating it as if it were a theatrical piece with characters, a progression and a climax? It may also appear rather dubious in relation to the doctrine so firmly laid down by the Council of Trent. The profusion of images and symbols evoked, represented even, the story of salvation more than they gave a clear picture of the sacrifice, ceaselessly renewed before our eyes, of the Son of God – it was more a commemoration than a sacrament. But this detailed description was in no way a spectacle to be watched from the outside. If the action was theatrical, it was not to please or out of pedagogic concern, but rather to enable the faithful to enter in and participate. Just as, by the force of their images, the Spiritual Exercises in a sense constrained whoever made them to follow in the footsteps of Christ, so the Mass described in this way was designed to lead the Christian to live with his Saviour. Thus each act and each word had their value and meaning. Nothing was

[19] *Ibid.*, pp. 69–70.

gratuitous. Carrying the book from one place to another had its significance, replying 'Amen' and making the sign of the Cross had the value of participation. The time, place, acts and words spoken all had a sacred character. Thus this text reveals a baroque piety which, far from being external and frivolous, as is often said, appears, on the contrary, as the practical application of the famous and austere scriptural text: 'Compel them to come in.' It was by the image and its effect on the imagination that they were to be compelled to come in. The demands of piety went straight to the heart of a wholly Christian life, which, in its every detail, could be no other than an imitation of Jesus Christ.

This explains the great importance and enormous seriousness of an act like confession. To be a member of a congregation meant above all knowing how to confess. That is why the *Libellus sodalitatis* began with a study of this sacrament. What was most difficult was to see oneself clearly, to know how to distinguish the nature of transgressions, the connections between them and their consequences.

Envy is vexation at our neighbour's prosperity, conceived out of love of our own excellence. There are four ways of being grieved at another's wealth. In the first place, if we fear that we or others will suffer as a result; and this distress is not envy but fear. Secondly, if we are annoyed, not that another has something, but that we do not have it; that is jealousy. Thirdly, if we are unhappy that another has something of which he is unworthy; that is disdain. Fourthly, if we regret another's wealth because it seems to diminish our excellence; that is envy.[20]

Each capital sin was minutely examined in this way, along with its 'daughters'. Thus for anger:

There are four sorts of angry persons. 1. Some get angry quickly, and quickly calm down. 2. Others are slow to get angry, but remain angry for a long time. 3. Others are slow to get angry, and calm down quickly. 4. Others are quick to get angry, and remain angry for a long time; they are the worst.

The daughters of anger are 'Scorn', 'False Courage', 'Shouting', 'Blasphemy', 'Outrage' and 'Quarrelling'.[21] One can appreciate, in this contemporary of Montaigne, the accuracy of such psychological analysis. But 'self-knowledge' was not an aim worthy of consideration for the religious man. 'He should confess often in order to have greater knowledge of his sins.'[22] This was the desired end, which

[20] *Ibid.*, p. 29. [21] *Ibid.*, pp. 32–3. [22] *Ibid.*, p. 13.

explains the insistence in the rules on the daily examination of conscience.

From a controlled imagination to an analytical spirit applied to self-knowledge, there was an underlying guiding principle which was to make the *dévot* into an 'interior man'.

CONTROLLING THE BODY

The body had its place in this process of change which transformed men from top to bottom. It was, indeed, in a way, its instrument. The simple gesture of hand and fingers in the sign of the Cross was, as we have seen, an education in itself. The body movements of a person who addressed God were already a prayer. Commenting on St Augustine, who wrote that 'those who pray dispose the limbs of their body as is appropriate for a supplicant and petitioner', Francis Coster explained the pious gestures of the Christian. In bending the knee and in lying prostrate on the ground, he signified that he recognised himself guilty of the death of Christ. Erect, he appeared as already risen with Jesus Christ and ready to do whatever he was commanded. If he raised his eyes, it was to show that he thought of heaven. If he lowered them, it was to show his fear of divine severity and shame at his sins. He raised his hands to show that the heart should be uplifted towards God. He joined them to show that his 'spirit was firm and not distracted or transported by diverse thoughts'. He beat his breast to declare his hatred for his sins and his desire to do penance. Those who prayed with their arms in the form of a cross signified that 'they were crucified with Jesus Christ, whose Cross and Passion they represented'.[23] To process in town or country was not only to confess one's faith publicly, and show that God was everywhere, but also to show oneself willing to follow Jesus Christ in perfect obedience, thus commemorating 'the various comings and goings' of Our Saviour on Palm Sunday, Good Friday and Ascension Day.[24]

To emphasise this, in the early years of the seventeenth century, the Augsburg brethren organised a solemn cortège through their town, which was still, at that period, largely won over to the Reformation.

At the head [came] a choir of four children singing canticles, behind whom, the brethren of the Holy Sacrament, clothed in red, carried a picture of the

[23] *Ibid.*, pp. 87–8. [24] *Ibid.*, pp. 89–90.

Saviour in the Garden of Olives. The next group, to the sound of solemn music, represented Jesus at the column; they were followed by members of the same confraternity of the Holy Sacrament scourging themselves till the blood ran. Then came the crowning with thorns, followed by the Ecce Homo. Fifthly, came a tableau vivant of the Saviour carrying his Cross, escorted by an officer and soldiers, followed by Mary and St John. The congregation of the Holy Virgin marched behind, clothed in black; four of them carried a cross, raised high, beside which five children representing angels sang a lament; behind the cross came the flagellants, then a picture of the Lady of Sorrows. One last image followed: Jesus in the tomb, surrounded by angels intoning hymns. To complete the procession came another line of flagellants, but these struck themselves so cruelly that the leader of the procession ordered them to cease before they had gone half the distance.[25]

The pilgrimage, especially the distant pilgrimage, was the act of piety *par excellence*. Are we not all 'Pilgrims and travellers on earth'? To take one's staff and set off for the Holy Land was to say 'goodbye to the temporal pleasures and things of this earth for things of the spirit', according to Father Gretser.[26] It was, to use the apt phrase of Father Richeome, 'to reach heaven by travelling on earth'.[27] The body suffering on the road thus became a veritable instrument of redemption, the means to draw near to God by imitating his Son toiling on the road to the Cross. It is hardly surprising that, from the beginning, pilgrimages were held in such honour among the congregations, as at Naples, as early as 1582, and amongst the clerics of Aquileia some years later.[28]

The body was penitent, but also magnified, already almost in its state of glory in the case of the priest at the altar. In his curious work *Le Pèlerin de Lorète*, already noted by Henri Brémond, Father Richeome wrote that 'the Mass [is] the epitome of all ancient sacrifices and all acts of devotion'. Because, he added, 'in the Mass the priest has an attentive ear, eyes raised, then lowered'. The same was true for the hands, the arms, the knees and even the mouth, the tongue, the sense of smell and of taste. In brief, all the senses, the body in its entirety, were part of the sacrifice.[29]

In consequence, how could the least spot on what was given to man by God to serve him, on this sacred body, be tolerated? After

[25] From Villaret, *Les Congrégations mariales*, pp. 385–6.

[26] Jacob Gretser, *De Sacris et religiosis peregrinationibus* (Ingolstadt, 1606), p. 2.

[27] Louis Richeome, S. J., *Le Pèlerin de Lorète* (Lyons, 1607), p. 63.

[28] A. S. J. Rome, province of Naples, 177, fos. 21 (Naples, 1582), 72, 116–20 (Aquilea, 1607).

[29] Richeome, *Le Pèlerin de Lorère*, p. 256.

Christmas, which he celebrated with the heroic virtue we have observed, the pious *sodalis* of Fribourg grappled with the demon who wanted to re-enter him. But he did not weaken, and vigorously resisting the Prince of Darkness, cried, 'You are ignorant, brute, of the fact that my ears were given me by God, also my heart, that I have nothing which does not come from God, thus nothing with which you can do anything!'[30] Such strong words were not enough. Gesture and deed must be added to speech. 'Love I shun with chastity', he exclaimed emphatically. He fled women 'like the plague', especially if they were beautiful. And as this principle of selection seemed not always to function as intended, he protected himself by thinking that 'if the creature is so beautiful, how much more beautiful must be her creator!' It is true that desire sometimes caused him to go and look a little closer at these works of his creator, but it was 'solely' to talk to them about God, while he looked the other way. The nakedness of his own body, even simply that of his feet, much more so that of the arms and legs of his college friends, was for him an object of scandal, and of fear and trembling for his chastity.[31] It was better, once again, to avert the eyes from all such opportunities for sin. In Bavaria, at Ingolstadt, Jacques Rem taught his congregation that perfect service of Mary demanded immaculate purity on the part of her servants. Amongst the *sodales*, he distinguished an élite, that of the first 'Children of Mary', who undertook to live always in internal purity and sanctity.[32]

Thus is visible from the beginning the obsession with impurity which occupied a large place in the rules, edifying stories and models to copy of the Marian congregations in the following century.

FEAR OF THE WORLD

Purity of self, purity in others; these were the aims. The devout young man of Fribourg toiled tirelessly to persuade his comrades, friends and acquaintances to cease to frequent dances and masquerades. 'I have also prayed God to inspire the Magistrates to forbid altogether the Carnival, the masquerades, the dances and other such things', he said.[33] After example came force. In Naples, the congregation, barely established, attacked prostitution. Brothers bought back young girls

[30] B. C. U. Fribourg (Switzerland), MSS, L 87, fo. 141.
[31] *Ibid.*, fos. 139v–140.
[32] L. Delplace, S. J., *Histoire des congrégations de la Sainte Vierge* (Lille, 1884), p. 93.
[33] B. C. U. Fribourg (Switzerland), MSS, L 87, fo. 139v.

who had been sold to matrons anxious to teach them the trade of love. In 1593, they even managed, thanks to substantial gifts, to found a first version of what would eventually become the institution of the Refuge, whose aim was 'to shelter the modesty of girls from the lewdness of men'.[34]

In Switzerland, the danger was not so much lewdness as the heresy always present in the vicinity, even in the same town or village. Thus, within the Fribourg congregation, there was constituted as early as the 1590s an association of young men who were more morally demanding and not satisfied with the communal rules alone. They swore to observe throughout their lives a number of articles amongst which were found, in addition to the obligations of mutual aid, frequent Communion and strict celibacy for the future priests, the necessity to help each other to defend Catholicism.

> He who deserts the Catholic faith is anathema and a victim of the devil. He should pay 100 écus to the others. (article 1)
>
> The members should help each other against the heretics. (article 4)
>
> When it is a question of defending the Catholic religion, no one should keep silent or flee the danger whatever it is. (article 6)
>
> One should prefer Catholics and strive to promote them. (article 7)
>
> The members should make every effort to shield others from heresy. (article 8)
>
> He who marries a heretic and has his children baptised in the Catholic religion should not send them into the places of the heretical religion. (article 9)[35]

The world was a dangerous place. Emerging from college, the congregation member risked falling prey to the devil. Temptation was everywhere – of the senses in the form of dissolute women, of the soul in the form of heresy. For better protection, some *sodales*, in Fribourg for example, decided to bind themselves together more closely with an oath. Others, in Naples, desirous of greater perfection, obtained authorisation to meet on Sunday afternoons to practise additional pious exercises, to spend some time each day in mental prayer, and to withdraw from time to time to perform, under the guidance of their masters, the Spiritual Exercises.[36] A few years later, comparable associations were to be found at Douai and

[34] A. S. J. Rome, province of Naples, 72, fos. 53, 54, 68–82v (1592–3).
[35] André-Jean Marquis, *Saint-Michel de Fribourg*, p. 219 (1593).
[36] A. S. J. Rome, province of Naples, 177, fo. 21 (1582).

Louvain, and then at Ingolstadt, with the Colloquium Marianum instituted by Jacques Rem.[37] Was this not the first indication, as early as 1582, of what were to become the secret assemblies, the famous Aas?[38] One senses amongst the brethren from the very beginning a desire to unite more closely and increase their strength so as to protect themselves against an external world which they feared but did not reject. If society was bad, it was because it was abandoned to evil and because no one did anything about it. It would be the task of the congregations, well prepared, consolidated in their faith and in their habits of piety, to attempt to change the world. Was this not what those who publicly attacked blasphemy, or who tried to get Carnival prohibited by the public authorities, or who offered a refuge to girls at risk of living in sin, were trying to achieve?

The ambivalent relationship with the world entertained by the Knights of Mary was already visible before 1600. Feared and sought after at the same time, was the world amenable to becoming what the *dévots* wished to make of it, that is a Christian world, organised and managed according to their principles?

In the short term, the question seemed premature. The few dozen burgesses and canons who, in the towns where there was a college, joined with the pupils were hardly capable of transforming society from top to bottom. Neither the new rhythm of life accepted by the few nor the type of piety practised by the many were capable of achieving a rapid change of mentality. However, in Naples, Cologne and Antwerp the initial few pioneers quickly became several hundred. In Munich, the Duke, soon followed by all his family, set the example. In Vienna, Graz and Innsbruck, the Hapsburgs, in their turn, participated. In Nancy, the Lorraine family proved welcoming. Even in Paris, the Jesuits entertained solid hopes under Henri III, as it was for his benefit that the work of Father Coster was translated and sumptuously bound.[39] By the 1600s, the change was under way; the movement was spreading. Why, after all, should the model not become reality?

[37] Alfred Poncelet, *Histoire de la Compagnie de Jésus dans les anciens Pays-Bas*, Académie royale de Belgique, vol. 21 (1 and 2) (Brussels, 1927), vol. 2, pp. 331–2 (in Douai and Louvain under the title of 'Tous les saints'); Burkhart Schneider, 'Pater Jakob Rem S. J.', *Bavaria Sancta*, vol. 3, pp. 312–20 (1973).

[38] See chapter 5.

[39] The splendid example in the store of the Bibliothèque Nationale in Paris has a binding which is very similar to that of another work of piety dedicated to the king and described by Franz Anselm Schmitt, *Kostbare Einbände, seltene Drucke aus der Schatzkammer der Badischen Landesbibliothek* (Karlsruhe, 1974), pp. 54–5

PART II *Putting it into practice*

The seventeenth century was the century of the *dévots*. They were everywhere: on the throne, in the persons of the Emperor Ferdinand II, victorious at the White Mountain and thus over heresy, and the Dukes of Bavaria, who took care to head the Major congregation in Munich.[1] But they were also to be found in the poor quarters of Naples, where street-urchins, fishermen, young domestic servants and *Staffieri* were brought together in pious associations. Even prisoners, particularly numerous in this great southern metropolis, and even Turkish slaves, did not escape.[2] The *dévots* were found not only in Naples, Vienna, Munich, Madrid and Antwerp, but in Louvain and in Paris, a town long unenthusiastic about the Jesuits and their activities, but which suddenly opened up to them and followed the general trend. In its own fashion, it must be said; the 'Messieurs' of the Rue Saint-Antoine seem pretty remote, in their behaviour and practices, from the *Akademiker* of Ingolstadt, just as the Flemish 'married men' of Antwerp were very different from the merchants of Lyons. And when, in the course of the century, the ruling classes of the Holy Empire changed, and workers gradually replaced independent artisans in the industrial towns, the composition of the Marian congregations changed too.

This extraordinary adaptability to period, prevailing trends and society may explain the success enjoyed by the work of Fathers Leunis and Coster in the seventeenth century. But was such flexibility compatible with unity and with the pursuit of the initial project to reform the world?

[1] Crasset, *Des congrégations de Notre-Dame*, pp. 100–28.

[2] A. S. J. Rome, province of Naples. 72, fos. 202–10, 247–53; 73, fos. 51–2v, 76^{II}, fo. 370.

4. *The townspeople*

We have already seen how the Jesuits' first priority, as soon as they settled somewhere, was to concern themselves with the townspeople. And this was a practice not only appropriate to countries on the 'frontier of Catholicism'. 'Must we not ask', said Father Demoustier, in his study of the province of Lyons at the beginning of the seventeenth century, 'whether the order had not come to regard its teaching establishments as apostolic bases oriented to the outside world just as much as centres of pedagogy?'[1] We must examine how, in practice, the Society of Jesus conceived this mission to the towns.

THE JESUITS IN TOWNS

Specialists in seventeenth-century architecture have perhaps paid too little attention to the sites of Jesuit colleges and their associated buildings.[2] For, when one looks at the college in Lucerne and its majestic church situated at the other end of the town, almost opposite the old collegiate church of Saint-Léger, and linked to both it and the centre by the fragile, old wooden bridge, or when one sees the college of the Trinity extending along the Rhône in Lyons, or when, near the Neuhäuser Tor in Munich, one passes in front of the austere building which still serves as a Jesuit residence, it is difficult not to believe that a specific policy lay behind the selection of these various sites.[3] Close to the water-course, on the edge of the town, or, even more often, where old and new towns met, as at Lucerne, Cologne, Antwerp and Naples, the sites do not look to have been chosen at random, even to

[1] Adrien Demoustier, 'Les catalogues du personnel de la province de Lyon en 1587, 1606 et 1636', *Archivum historicum Societatis Iesu*, vol. 42 (1973), pp. 3–105; vol. 43 (1974), pp. 3–84.

[2] There is some information, however, in Jean Vallery-Radot, *Le Recueil de plans d'édifices de la Compagnie de Jésus conservé à la Bibliothèque Nationale de Paris* (Rome, Inst. hist. S. I., 1960).

[3] For Munich, see M(artin) Z(eiller), *Topographia Bavariae . . . durch Matthaeum Merian* (Frankfurt, 1654), pp. 8–9, 48–9.

someone who has just learned from the archives that in this or that particular case a gift or an allocation of land by the magistrates explains the location. Access to the town and its suburbs, often less pastorally favoured, and sometimes to the surrounding countryside, seems to us a factor which needs to be taken into account. It also explains the size of churches whose dimensions seem disproportionate to the functions of a simple college chapel, especially when situated in small places like Eichstätt or Molsheim. But the same is true of Lucerne, Fribourg in Switzerland, and even of Antwerp and Cologne, all places where the sanctuary erected by the Society of Jesus took on the character of a second large church, intended to relay to the suburbs and the environs the sometimes rather half-hearted message of the cathedral, collegiate or parish church.

The large size of these buildings is due, in part, to the congregations which had their chapels there, or even, as at Cologne and Molsheim, their meeting rooms in the galleries. Not all were possessed of the means, like the Gentlemen of Grenoble or Chambéry, to build their own chapels, or decorate them, as at Aix, with costly works of art by artists such as Puget.[4] At Antwerp, a whole complex surrounded the Church of Saint-Charles, and today still endows the little Place Conscience with great charm: on one side stands the church, enclosed in the old professed house, on the other, housed in a splendid little Renaissance building, the municipal library, which has replaced the congregations for whom the building was constructed in 1622. The Latinists and the married men took turns in using the great chapel and meeting room on the ground floor. The same arrangement was replicated on the first floor for the Walloons and the young craftsmen. There is marble everywhere: on the altars, walls, the door and window surrounds. Sculpture and paintings abound, gifts of *sodales* such as Rubens and Van Dyck.[5]

There was always a need for more space. In Antwerp, the married men who numbered 320 in 1612, had increased to 700 twenty-five years later, and nearly 1,000 in 1664; in Cologne, their numbers doubled between 1608 and 1654; in Lille, they increased tenfold in less

[4] Marie Girod, *Notice sur la grande Congrégation de Notre-Dame de l'Assomption dite des Nobles ou des Messieurs erigée dans le collège des jésuites à Chambéry en 1611* s. l. s. d., pp. 279–376; The Reverend Father J. Pra, *Les Jésuites à Grenoble (1587–1763)* (Lyons–Paris, 1901), pp. 305–13; André Schimberg, *L'Education morale dans les collèges de la Compagnie de Jésus en France sous l'Ancien Régime (XVI–XVII–XVIIIe siècles)* (Paris, 1913), p. 350 (Aix-en-Provence).

[5] A. P. B. M. Namur, Droeshout deposit 24,2, pp. 143–7.

than twenty years (from 93 to 964).[6] The congregations of Cologne, counting all the sodalities together, numbered 2,000 in mid-century, as they did in Lille, both towns having populations of about 45,000.[7] In Antwerp, in 1664, there were nearly 4,000 congregation members in a population of 55,000.[8] Thus, in these three large towns, about a twentieth of the total populations belonged to congregations. Bearing in mind that these members were, for the most part, active men or fathers of families, the proportion is considerable. In smaller towns, the figures are even more striking: 2,500 in the congregations of Douai, 3,000 at Ingolstadt, including 1,500 in the Civica alone, 2,000 in Swiss Fribourg, of whom 900 were women, 1,000 in Nancy.[9] The two last towns had populations of at most 5,000 and 7,000 respectively in the mid-seventeenth century.[10] In other words, as the chroniclers frequently asserted, in Ingolstadt, Fribourg and Molsheim every family was represented in a congregation. On a regional scale, the progress of the congregations was even more spectacular.

The Jesuit province of Champagne (in practice the whole of north-eastern France) was far from being a particularly favourable zone, as a result of the destruction caused by the Thirty Years' War as well as the existence, at an early stage, especially in the west, of centres of resistance to the influence of the Society. Nevertheless, its success is undeniable, above all in the case of the bourgeois and artisan congregations, which alone outnumbered scholars by the end of the century. As early as the 1660s, all the sodalities together added up to more than the college population. These figures alone clearly reveal the place that apostleship in the towns occupied in the designs of those running the colleges and how this function only increased in importance during the seventeenth and eighteenth centuries.

So the churches were not too big to receive these ever larger throngs, especially when, on the festivals of their name saints,

[6] *Ibid.*, 24,1, p. 126, 24,2, p. 509, 24,3, p. 533; Müller, *Die Kölner Bürger-Sodalität*, p. 27; Poncelet, *Histoire de la Compagnie de Jésus*, vol. 2, p. 334.

[7] H. A. S. Cologne, Jesuits 9; Poncelet, *Histoire de la Compagnie de Jésus*, p. 334.

[8] A. P. B. M. Namur, Droeshout deposit 24,3, p. 533.

[9] Poncelet, *Histoire de la Compagnie de Jésus*, p. 334 (Douai); B. H. Munich, Jesuits 108, fo. 335 (Ingolstadt); B. C. U. Fribourg (Switzerland), L 107 (1), p. 288 (Fribourg); Elisabeth Vaujour, *La Congrégation de l'Immaculée Conception of Nancy (1639–1693)*, Masters thesis, University of Nancy II (1982), p. 75; A. S. J. Rome, province of Champagne, 11 (Nancy).

[10] Franz Kuenlin, *Dictionnaire géographique, statistique et historique du canton de Fribourg* (Fribourg, 1832), p. 263; *Histoire de Nancy*, under the direction of René Taveneaux (Toulouse, 1978), p. 181.

Table 1. *Numbers in the Jesuit houses in the province of Champagne (Champagne, Burgundy, Lorraine, Alsace) in the seventeenth and eighteenth centuries.**

Year	Pupils	Congregation members	In burgess and artisan congregations	% in burgess & artisan congregations	% congregation members from Alsace and Lorraine
1630	5578	3541	1701	48.03	51.42
1665	4454	4624	2985	64.55	53.90
1700	3818	6001	4101	68.38	61.02
1755	3639	9832	7452	75.79	69.77

* Based on A. S. J. Rome, province of Champagne, 10, 11, 13, François de Dainville, S. J., has studied the scholarly population of this region in a famous article, 'Effectifs des collèges et scolarité aux XVIIe et XVIIIe siècles dans le nord-est de la France', *Population*, vol. 10 (1955), reprinted in *ibid., L'Education des jésuites (XVIIe–XVIIIe siècle)* (Paris, 1978), pp. 81–149.

families, friends, the official bodies and representatives of the clergy and the other religious orders came to join the *sodales*. In fact, on very special occasions, the normal place of worship would not suffice, and the whole town was taken over by the festival. This was the case at Antwerp, for example, on Sunday, 24 July 1622, the day when the canonisation of St Ignatius and St Francis Xavier was celebrated with special pomp.[11]

Preparations started early. Every college student and congregation member had his role. All the corporations, the armed guilds and the magistrates had been solicited and had promised their support. In the morning, along the whole of the route which the procession was to follow, the houses were covered with hangings and tapestries, even pictures and precious objects, and the streets were strewn with flowers and greenery. Even greater care was taken with the squares and church forecourts where the procession was to halt. Trestles were hastily erected, along with the scenery and even machinery of a dozen theatres, where the most dramatic scenes from the lives of the two saints were to be portrayed. At four o'clock in the afternoon, the

[11] A. P. B. M. Namur, Droeshout deposit 24,2, pp. 20–80.

procession left by the great portal of the cathedral. It made an impressive sight. At the head came the twenty-six guilds, from boatmen to barbers, each with its coat of arms, the insignia of its craft and its officers in ceremonial dress. They were followed by the six armed guilds. Then came the scholars divided into four groups. First came the guardian angels under the protection of three splendid mounted men, magnificently attired. Then came the triumphal float of Francis Xavier, preceded by catechumens clothed in the manner of the various evangelised peoples, and followed by three converted kings, each on his float. Most admired was that of the Emperor of China; it represented the sea, from which rose sirens holding back their long hair, two Tritons taming sea-calves which were said to be life-size, and finally the Emperor seated on a throne and clothed in a rich cloak which fluttered in the wind. There followed, naturally, the triumph of St Ignatius, preceded by the group of sciences and the procession of the sovereigns of Europe. The fourth and last group of scholars represented the honours rendered to the two saints by the Roman court and the blessed of heaven; it was followed by a float depicting the apotheosis. Behind the scholars marched the congregations, who formed a 'procession of light', each member carrying a lighted candle of white wax. They processed two by two, grouped by sodality, holding their banners and followed by their respective high officials. Behind them, in all their dignity, came the town officers, with the two burgomasters, the magistrates, the counsellors, and, at the end, those townspeople who had joined the procession.

The route was chosen so as to encompass the different quarters of the town. From time to time the procession halted to watch a scene from the life of the saints performed in the open-air theatres. In the main square, next to the Hôtel de Ville, the conversion of St Ignatius was enacted. In the centre stood the citadel of Pamplona, with, on either side, houses hung with the arms of France and Spain representing the two camps with their armed soldiers, music and canons. Hardly had the procession entered the square when battle was furiously joined. To the sound of fifes and drums, musket and canon fire was exchanged and blows were struck with side-arms accompanied by clouds of powder smoke, the cries of the combatants and the cheers of the crowd. Suddenly, the valiant Spaniards gave way before the French troops. The curtain then rose to reveal Ignatius Loyola, wounded, and stretched out on a bed, a book in his hand. The sky opened above him to reveal St Peter who announced that he was cured. The hero was seen to start up from his couch, revealing by his gestures and his facial expressions that he had already resolved to change his life.

The procession resumed and saw, in succession, the appearance of Our Lady to Ignatius, the retreat at Montserrat, the Vision of Our Lord, the approval of the Institution by Paul III, Ignatius at Antwerp, then Ignatius chasing out the devils, and protected against the assassins, the Fountain of the Holy Name of Jesus, St Francis Xavier, Apostle of the Indies, his death and, finally, the apotheosis of the two saints. To keep the audience in suspense and startle it with unexpected events, strikingly bold stagings were devised. Thus the scene representing the killers on the point of assassinating St Ignatius was shown twice, once with automatons, once with actors. Music, too, had a role in the spectacle, as did the declamations of a chorus which took up and repeated such and such a verse, rather like the choruses of Antiquity. It took four hours for the procession to complete its journey. At eight o'clock in the evening, it entered the church of the professed house, where a vibrant Te Deum was sung. After that the armed guilds signalled the end of an impressive day by repeatedly and noisily discharging their muskets into the air.

This festival of the canonisation, which was celebrated not only in Antwerp but simultaneously, with more or less pomp, in all the colleges of the Society of Jesus, may appear baroque in spirit and manner. But it was also the clearest expression of a desire for an apostleship which extended to the whole town, to all its quarters (as shown by the route taken by the procession), and to all its social categories. The attractions of the Flemish Kermesse, with its gigantic floats, combining a taste for exoticism and the most modern refinements of theatrical production, were employed to provide instruction for the populace. The festival of the canonisation of St Ignatius and St Francis Xavier was an open-air mission to the whole town, or, rather, it was the first shock which, as with the Spiritual Exercises, was destined to shake the citizens of Antwerp out of themselves, to impel them into leading a better life. And the role of the thousands of congregation members who, with grave expressions and modest bearing, followed the gaudy procession in a 'procession of light' was to show the example to follow and the path to take.

There can be no doubt that such festivals, which the Jesuits learned to repeat as and when they were needed, had a considerable effect on the population. But such impressive and periodic manifestations had to be backed up by persistent, day-to-day activity, which could only be undertaken in their street or in their trade, by journeymen, artisans and ordinary burgesses.

ADAPTING TO URBAN STRUCTURES

To this end, a whole organisation was established. The number of officers responsible for the direction of the congregation was increased, and their duties were more clearly defined. And they were chosen according to minutely laid-down rules which were not totally dissimilar to those which governed the election of the magistrature in the large towns of Flanders and the Rhineland.[12] Indeed, the group in charge of the sodality was often called the 'magistrature' and its members were proud to number in their ranks, as at Antwerp and Cologne, several magistrates and sometimes a burgomaster.[13] The structures of the congregation, too, while seeking to remain faithful to the intention of their founders, were increasingly modelled on urban institutions. Alongside the prefect and his assistants, the advisers, each responsible for a quarter, assumed more and more importance. 'The sodality', wrote the compiler of the register of the Walloons in Antwerp, 'was divided not by nations, but by the main sections of the town . . . like other sodalities. And this the better to undertake charity, to allow the Advisors to care for their men, to summon them more easily to funerals or to the administration of the Holy Sacrament.'[14] And the historian of the Jesuit houses in Antwerp, Father Droeshout, commented:

> One can readily understand what power of action and what promptness of execution such an organism put at the disposal of each sodality. All the fellows were known to and were under the direction of their respective leaders. Their mobilisation for each service was certain and speedy. The whole Congregation resembled a vast army; each sodality, like a military body, consisted of a dozen legions which were divided between an equal number of districts of the town, with their own leaders and deputies. And if we may continue the comparison, each army corps had its general staff, composed of the chief dignitaries of each sodality, with its meeting place on the premises of the Congregation under the vigilant eye of the chief Directors.[15]

[12] For Antwerp, see *ibid.*, pp. 153–60.

[13] Müller, *Die Kölner Bürger-Sodalität*, p. 28; A. P. B. M. Namur, Droeshout deposit 24,5, pp. 80–1. [14] *Ibid.*, 24,1, p. 78 (1610). [15] *Ibid.*, pp. 78–9.

And to show that this was not simply a rhetorical image, the author inserted in his manuscript a little drawing, extremely rare for the 1630s, in which the congregations can be seen, ranged in perfect order in front of their premises, company behind company, under their respective banners.[16]

It is clear that to achieve this rapid 'mobilisation' the advisors had to know their men well. Thus they had a little book, in which, street by street, were inscribed names and addresses (in the form of 'at the sign of . . .') and trades. When the members living in one district became too numerous, the advisor drew on the assistance of 'adjutants' who were made responsible for one or two streets.[17] What worked so well in Antwerp in 1610 soon existed, in even more perfect form, in numerous other towns. One such was Cologne: a register from the sodality of the young craftsmen contains several pages headed 'Very excellent means easily to maintain and develop the sodality'.[18] These instructions, which are certainly in the hand of a father director, specify that the congregation should be divided into as many sections as there were districts (six, to begin with, then a dozen). Each section, or 'decury', was allocated a certain number of benches in the chapel, each with a bench leader, who sat at the pulpit end and supervised his men, signalling to them when to stand, when to kneel, and when to leave in procession.

At the head of each district was a *zunftmeister*, whose title is also reminiscent of the leaders of the craft guilds who sat on the councils of Imperial towns. Living in his area, he had to know it intimately, and, to this end, he drew on the assistance of subordinate officers called the *Rottmeister*. They patrolled the street allocated to them, keeping the list of members up to date, watching over their morals and their behaviour at work, settling any quarrels which arose, and enquiring into the reasons for any absence from an office or a Sunday meeting. When young workmen arrived in the district, the *Rottmeister* found out their addresses and called on them. They told them about the congregation and endeavoured to persuade them to introduce themselves. Everything was reported to the *Zunftmeister*, who recorded, encouraged, made decisions and eventually reported to the magistrates, who, in any case, gave him very detailed directives which had to be carried out point by point.[19]

[16] *Ibid.* [17] *Ibid.*, p. 156.
[18] H. A. S. Cologne, Jesuits 56, fos. 127–30. [19] *Ibid.*, fos. 142–60.

The *Zunftmeister* also had to keep a close eye on everything which went on within the guilds and in the life of the crafts in general. If there was any unrest in the heavily working-class districts, he promptly despatched his *Rottmeister* to find out the reasons for the disturbances, observe the behaviour of the members in such circumstances, and, if need be, call them to order. His moment of glory came on the day of the *Römerfahrt*, the long procession which traversed the town at Christmas and on the Feast of the Annunciation, with stations at the seven principal churches, as in Rome. On these occasions the *Zunftmeister* divided the men under him into three sections under the banners of Jesus, Mary and Joseph. Thus his task, at all times and in all places, was to watch the inhabitants of his district zealously and to know them intimately, so as to be able, when any member decided to leave Cologne in search of work, at once to award or refuse him the 'patent', the certificate of good conduct which permitted a travelling workman to procure admittance to the sodality of the town where he wished to stay.[20]

What can be seen so clearly in Antwerp and Cologne was also found elsewhere. The artisans of the Grand Collège at Lyons included amongst their officers 'Dizainiers' who 'to perform their Office faithfully . . . had to watch over everyone in their districts and when they knew of people who fell into scandalous faults, or who had vices which they did not correct, they were failing in their duty if they did not inform the Father'.[21] In Munich, in mid-century, the fathers stated that the zeal of the 'district leaders' was the reason for the growth in membership which the sodality of young artisans had for some time been experiencing.[22] These officers seem to have added to their functions within the town quarters the role of representatives of the sodality in their guilds, or *tribus*, as they were called in the Germanic world. Or, as is highly likely, only masters who already enjoyed a certain prestige in their craft had been chosen for these posts. This would explain how in Lucerne in the 1640s every arrival of a workman from elsewhere was at once signalled to the *sodales* of his trade, who came to greet him, converse with him, and without further delay, take him to the father director.[23] The links between the crafts,

[20] *Ibid.*, fos. 127–76.

[21] A. D. Rhône, Galle deposit, *Heures à l'usage de la congrégation des Artisans du Grand Collège de Lyon, sous le titre de la Visitation de la Très Sainte Vierge* (Lyons, 1749), p. 51.

[22] B. H. Munich, Jesuits 108, fo. 179v. [23] S. A. Lucerne, cod. KK 25/1, p. 172.

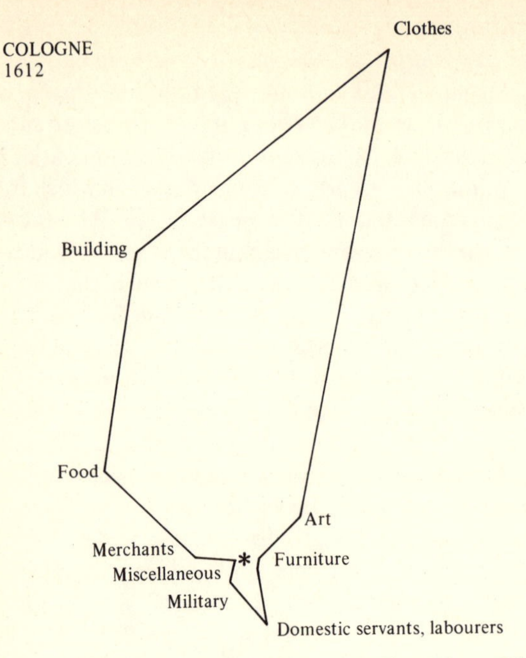

4. Occupations of congregation members. (a) The 'Three Kings' of Cologne

whatever their structure in each town, and the congregations were extremely close.

ADAPTING TO URBAN SOCIETY

It is very often difficult to know what was the exact composition of these congregations because of the very small number of registers of members which have either survived or are accessible, or, when they exist, because of their frequently incomplete nature.[24]

The list of the first members of the congregation of the Three Kings founded in Cologne in 1608 has been preserved in the Jesuit deposit in

[24] This arises from the tribulations undergone by these archives at the time of the suppression of the Society of Jesus, and also from the fact that they were often private archives as the prefects and secretaries – and this till very recently for those congregations which have continued to the present day – were in the habit of keeping the archives in their own homes.

the municipal archives.[25] It is a well-kept list, with, opposite each name, a note of the address, the accredited confessor, and, in 240 out of 392 cases, the trade (see figure 4a). The manufactured goods sector (cloth, leather, metals, wood and glass) was easily the largest, accounting for two-thirds of the trades recorded (64.16 %). Textiles were clearly preponderant with 28.75 % of those mentioned. In contrast, lawyers (*greffiers*, notaries), merchants and tradesmen (1.25 %), magistrates and burgomasters (only one!) were almost non-existent, though reading the *Annual Letters* would lead rather to the conclusion, given the satisfaction with which the membership of 'illustrious' persons was recorded, that they were numerous. It was the small craftsmen of the college quarter and its neighbouring streets who, at least to begin with, made up the membership. The composition may well, of course, have changed completely with the passage of time.

This gives particular interest to the registers found, incorrectly titled, in the Bibliothèque Royale in Brussels.[26] They contain the names of the members inscribed in the sodality of the Flemish 'married men' of Antwerp from its origins up until almost the end of the eighteenth century. A first sample taken for the years 1590–1625, that is at the very beginning of the congregation, gives results comparable to those obtained for Cologne (see figure 4b). The various cloth trades, from silk manufacture (one of the specialities of Antwerp) to simple linen-weaving, easily come first with a third of those trades recorded (31.26 %). The manufactured goods sector amounts to exactly half of the group studied (49.57 %). There is one slight difference, however, compared with the Rhineland metropolis, that is, a greater diversification, including diamond workers and goldsmiths (4.7 %), workers in the book trade (2.35 %), artists (painters, engravers and sculptors: 3.36 %) and, above all, merchants and tradesmen, who alone constitute 15.96 % of the total. However, this more even distribution between the different socio-professional categories seems not to have been maintained throughout the

[25] H. A. S. Cologne, Jesuits 55, pp. 5ff.

[26] B. R. Brussels, MS 20088 erroneously catalogued as 'Registre de la Congrégation de la Sainte Vierge érigée chez les jésuites de Bruxelles'; see Van Den Gheyn S. J., *Catalogue des manuscrits de la Bibliothèque Royale de Belgique*, vol. 6, p. 427. Internal analysis of the catalogue, as well as the reconstruction of the career of the editor (Father François Guebels), who was *praeses* of the sodality of the married men in Antwerp at the time of the edition (B. R. Brussels, MS 20204), shows clearly that the register belonged to the latter congregation.

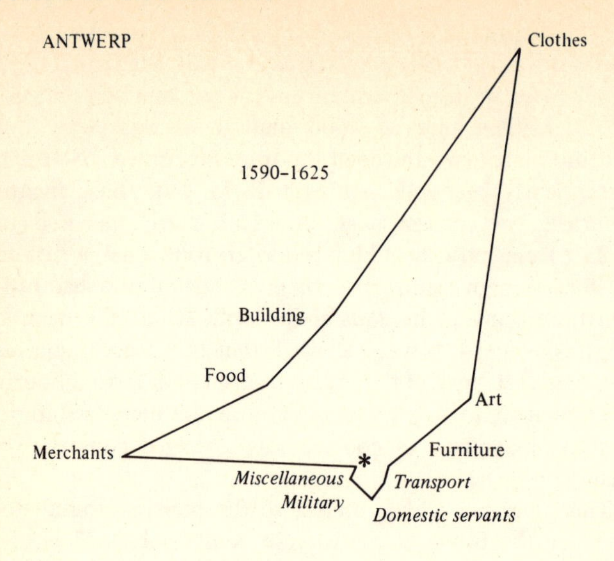

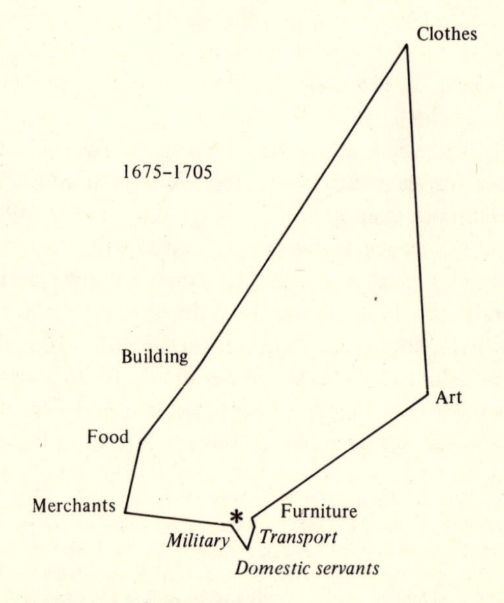

4(b) The 'Flemish married men' of Antwerp

century. In the years 1675–1705 a very large majority of workers in the cloth, glass, leather, wood and metal trades joined the congregation (57.48 %), with a clear preponderance of the first of these (35.19 %). Merchants and tradesmen accounted for only 7.2 % of the entries. The number of registrations in this period was a third higher than in the earlier period (929 as against 595). This is significant: the sodality of Flemish married men in Antwerp was growing rapidly round about 1680, but it was assuming more and more the character of an association of small craftsmen. And, though the names borne by these last had hardly changed (*Caffawercker*, *Zydereeder* and *Boratwercker*), it is by no means certain that they described exactly the same functions and qualities as at the beginning of the century.[27] This seems doubtful in the light of the work of Belgian historians who emphasise the great crisis experienced by the industries of Antwerp round about 1680,[28] and also in the light of what was happening in Lille.

The Lille congregation bore the not unambiguous title of the 'great artisans' (*grands artisans*).[29] It is hardly surprising, therefore, that the manufactured goods sector, with 77.64 % of registrations, enjoyed an overwhelming majority and that, in this large city which employed at the end of the century, according to the intendant, more than 20,000 workers in sayette and wool (*sayetteurs* and *bourgeteurs*), cloth-making constituted the occupation of 60.29 % of the first members (1628–37) (see figure 4c). This last activity must have been overwhelmingly predominant between 1657 and 1666, accounting for 66.71 % of the identifiable newcomers, but losing its preponderance to some extent in the years 1698–1707, with only 53.4 % of those registering. It is true that the total number employed in manufacturing remained surprisingly stable in relation to what it was at the beginning of the century, accounting for 74.35 % of the entrants. But this stability was only apparent. There was visible, in fact, in Lille at the very beginning of the eighteenth century, what we already suspected for Antwerp at the same period, though without definite proof. The word 'worker' followed by *sayetteur*, *bourgeteur* or

27 The *Caffawercker* was a silk worker, the *Zydereeder* made silk for sewing and the *Boratwercker* worked with coarse homespun.

28 Clément Van Cauwenberghs, 'L'industrie de la soie à Anvers depuis 1532 jusqu'à nos jours', *Bulletin de la Société royale de géographie d'Anvers*, vol. 12 (1887), pp. 105–46; Alf. K. L. Thijs, *De Zijdenyverheid te Antwerpen in de Zeventiende eeuw.* (Brussels, 1969).

29 Register preserved in A. D. Nord, cumulus GH 16749.

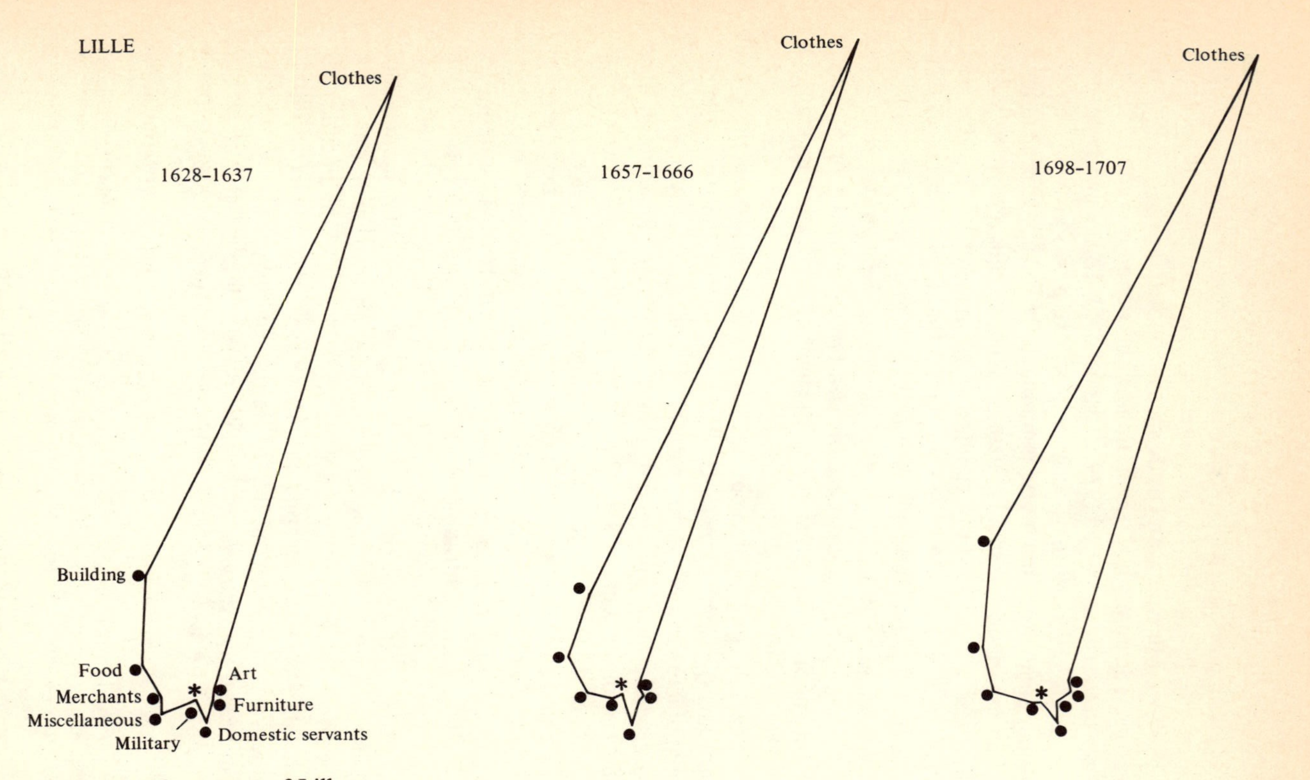

4(c) The *grands artisans* of Lille

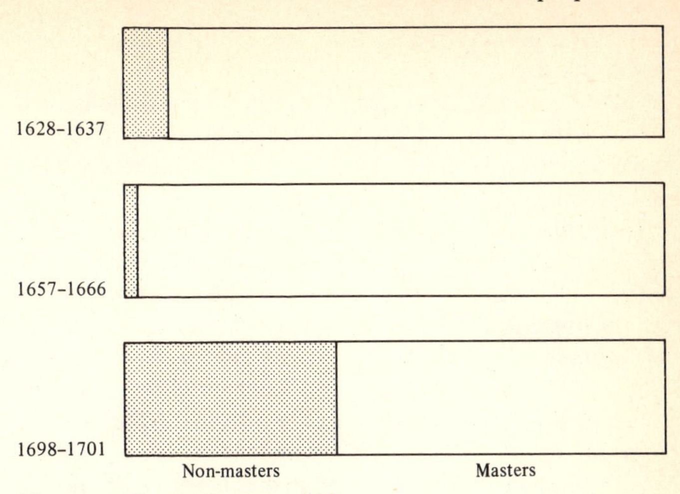

5. Masters and non-masters at Lille

'weaver' appears in the lists and occurs increasingly frequently. From 1698 to 1701, out of 1,013 mentions of occupations, 398, that is 39.28 %, of the craftsmen recorded were 'workers', as against 212 'masters'. Forty years earlier, the letter M (Master) was found after every name entered as a matter of course. Only 2.95 % of the total did not conform to what seemed to be the norm (see figure 5). In Lille as in Antwerp, in considerably enlarging its enrolment at the end of the century (1,410 entries to the 'great artisans' between 1698 and 1707), the congregation of married men underwent a profound transformation. There was a shift from the artisan workshop to the damp cellar of the worker, from the trading street to the poor court.

But it is perhaps in Nancy that the internal transformation of a bourgeois congregation was most marked. To begin with, and to an even greater extent after its re-establishment in 1639, this congregation was, indeed, very bourgeois: merchants, artists (among them, Jacques Callot), *avocats*, judges and, above all, officials of the Duke as well as highly illustrious representatives of his court constituted its most numerous elements. This is to be explained by the last years of the Thirty Years' War. Things began to change about 1650, and, by 1675, the distinguished sodality of courtiers and lawyers had become a congregation of artisans, dominated, as in so many other places, by workers in the cloth, wood and leather trades.[30] By the end of the

[30] Vaujour, *L'Immaculée Conception*, pp. 87–102.

century, tailors and shoemakers, registering in large numbers, had replaced ducal officers.

Such a convergence of elements gives cause for thought. How are these expansions in total numbers and these profound changes in the social composition of the congregations during the second half of the seventeenth century to be explained?

The explanation may be sought in the evolution of the towns in question between 1650 and 1700. Nancy, which lost its Duke in 1634, but got him back soon after 1661, only to lose him once again in 1698, was no longer the brilliant political and cultural capital it had been at the beginning of the century. It was no more, after the Thirty Years' War, than a small town under French tutelage, recovering with difficulty, thanks to the industry of its artisans and its various trades, from the wounds caused by the conflict.[31]

In the case of Antwerp, recent studies have shown that, far from sinking into irreversible decline at the end of the sixteenth century, it knew real splendour once again during the first half of the seventeenth century. The maintenance of international commercial relations thanks to the Flemish diaspora, the function of major port of the southern Low Countries, and, above all, the effects of a strong industrial revival, due, in particular, to the established speciality of its artisans in the manufacture of luxury goods (cloth and silk manufacture, glassworking, cabinet-making, diamond-cutting and the goldsmith's craft) were the basis of this wealth.[32] It was only threatened round about 1650 by the consequences of the war and the reversal of the economic trend. This brought about a collapse in the number of brokers, who numbered no more than fifty in 1680, when in Amsterdam, at the same time, there were several hundred prosperous operators in this trade.[33] The cloth industry had to adapt and restructure if it was to survive. The crisis which came to a head in 1684 between a certain Tréseniers, supported by the governor, and the magistrates, prompted by the masters, reveals a conflict of mentality as much as a change in working methods. The latter wanted to restrict the number of looms in each workshop to eight; the

[31] Taveneaux, *Histoire de Nancy*, pp. 177–86.

[32] Roland Baetens, *De Nazomer van Antwerpens welvaart: de diaspora en het handelshuis De Groote tijdens de eerste helft der 17de eevw.* (Brussels, 1976), 2 vols.

[33] Emile Dilis, *Les Courtiers anversois sous l'Ancien Régime* (Antwerp, 1910), pp. 57–82.

entrepreneur, unable to 'put to work as many looms as he wished', insisted, nevertheless, on operating twelve or thirteen and 'also on having the power to sack obstinate valets and take others in their place'. The victory finally won by Tréseniers foreshadowed the imminent disappearance of many independent workshops in favour of veritable factories bringing together between two and five hundred workers, which were already appearing at the turn of the century.[34]

This conflict seems to replicate, but twenty years later, that which had taken place in Lille from 1663 to 1666 between several innovative masters supported by the merchants and the entire body of sayette workers. There, too, despite certain purely formal satisfactions conceded by the magistrates in times of crisis, and in spite of massive and violent demonstrations organised by the victims of the changes, the movement towards concentration was well under way by the end of the century. It did not, however, prevent a catastrophic decline in cloth production as well as in the number of masters and workers.[35]

One can see, therefore, the social composition of the great congregations of workers and burgesses as a reflection of the urban population in its structure and in its changes over time. But this situation should certainly not be regarded as the simple mathematical result of the mode of recruitment. A more specific intention is visible, which consisted of establishing a true proportional relationship between the socio-professional categories present locally and the groups composing the congregation. This last became, therefore, a microcosm of the town, established in its image, and changing as it changed. Rather than a consequence, the social structure of a congregation was a construct; a willed and carefully considered construct, whose purpose was the conversion of the whole town by the means clearly outlined by the founding fathers, that of the apostleship of like by like.

Obviously, the crises that occurred during the century, the shifts in the Society's policy, and, simply, the intentions of the men concerned, disrupted this grand overall scheme.[36] How, during the crises which devastated the textile industry from the 1660s, could artisans who feared unemployment, or journeymen travelling from town to town

[34] Van Cauwenberghs, 'L'industrie de la soie à Anvers', pp. 105–46.

[35] Alain Lottin, *Chavatte, ouvrier lillois: un contemporain de Louis XIV* (Paris, 1979), pp. 85–97, 119–35.

[36] See below, chapter 7.

in search of work, be prevented from joining congregations in large numbers in the hope of receiving support or alms? In vain did prefects and assistants protest and multiply the regulations to prevent what they saw as an abuse:[37] a change was under way. But it did not always and everywhere conceal what was the essential spirit and intention of the urban congregations.

[37] Müller, *Die Kölner Bürger-Sodalität*, p. 28.

5. *The clergy*

Concern for priests or future priests very quickly became an issue for those Jesuits who were involved with the Marian congregations. The latter would not have been a work of the Counter-Reformation had it been otherwise. At a period when seminaries were still in their infancy, even non-existent in most dioceses, the congregations acted as substitutes, alongside the colleges and the universities where clerics received instruction in theology. They brought to candidates for the priesthood a complement in spirituality and in initiation into clerical life without which there could be no priests, according to the doctrine and spirit of the Council of Trent. They thus made their mark on intelligences and sensibilities at a time when these were still very malleable. They subsequently maintained their hold throughout individual careers thanks to the various ecclesiastical associations. This meant they had considerable influence not only on the Tridentine Church and its cadres, but also on the mass of the faithful. However, this influence was not everywhere the same; it took different forms according to region. These variations concealed different conceptions of the priest and of his place in society.

CREATING CADRES

In the sequence of congregations destined to accompany men from the age of reason to full adulthood, the Major held pride of place. After the Angelica and the Minor, it was a further stage reserved for students (and former students), and more particularly for those completing their theology studies. The lists conserved for two large university towns as different as Ingolstadt and Toulouse make it possible to trace the evolution and nature of their membership throughout the seventeenth century.[1] The rapid increase in regist-

[1] U. B. Munich, MS 543 (Ingolstadt); A. P. Toulouse, CA 124, 125, 126, 127 (registers of the congregation of the Annunciation of Toulouse).

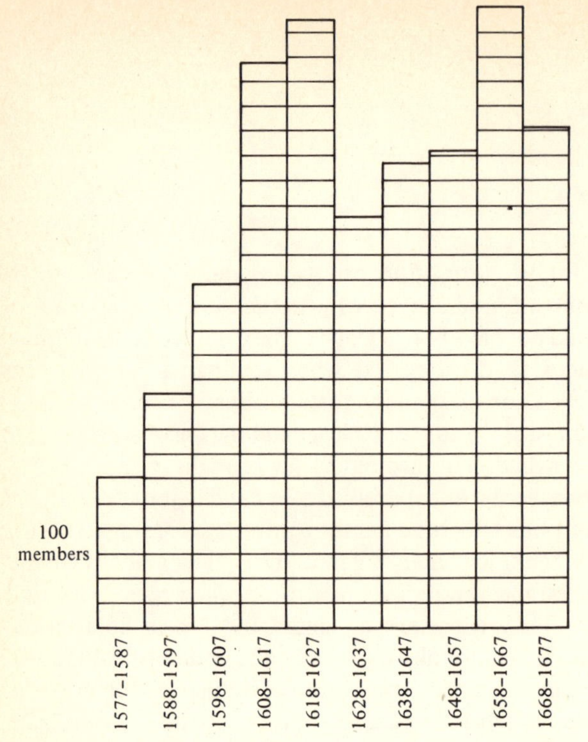

6. Entries to the Major of Ingolstadt in the seventeenth century

rations in the early years of the century is striking. It began very early in Ingolstadt, and the period 1605–20 was one of exceptional growth (see figure 6). In Toulouse, as far as one can judge given the scanty nature of the information available, the period of growth began a little later, about 1630. It then became unstoppable, with 703 registrations between 1628 and 1637, 916 between 1631 and 1650, and an average of 200 young men, most of them theologians, associated with the congregation between 1670 and 1678 (see figure 7). In the Bavarian university, the Thirty Years' War caused a lull after 1630, but it was noticeably less marked than in other places (such as Pont-à-Mousson and Molsheim), and the recovery was not long in making itself felt, effective even before the 1660s. One can see in this large membership and rapid growth a consequence of the dynamism of the

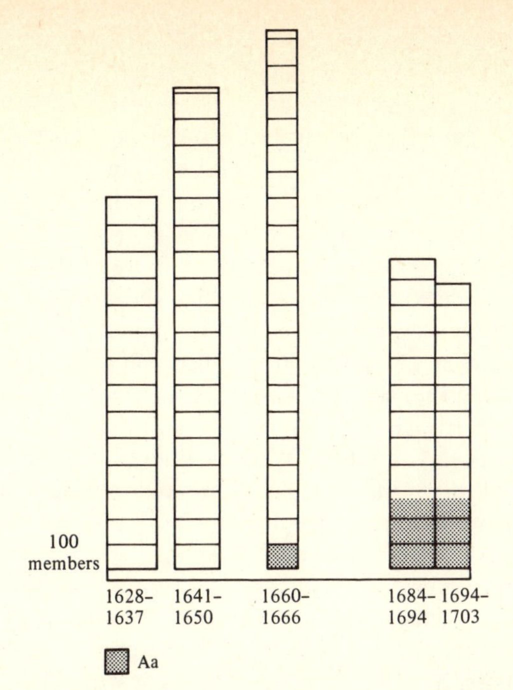

7. Membership of the Annunciation and the Aa of Toulouse in the seventeenth century

Society of Jesus in the early years of the seventeenth century. It is evidence also of its prestige, demonstrated by the presence of many nobles, including the son of the Duc d'Uzès, in the congregation of Toulouse, whilst at Ingolstadt the entire nobility of the Holy Empire was to be found, from the Wittelsbachs to the House of Lorraine, from the Fuggers to the Königseggs. The congregation also attracted people from a wide radius, with *sodales* from Trent to Mayence and from Nancy to Prague flooding into Ingolstadt.

The enterprise was not confined to students. Congregations of priests were found from the beginning, at Cologne and Lucerne, for example.[2] In Munich, the Major, which included 32 (23.18 %) priests in its ranks when it started in 1584, had 166 (30.68 %) in 1673 and 856 (54.59 %) in 1727. By the beginning of the eighteenth century, it had become primarily a sodality of priests (figure 20 pp. 233–5). But it was

[2] Müller, *Die Kölner Bürger-Sodalität*, p. 5 (Cologne); S. A. Lucerne, cod. KK 25/1, pp. 198–9 (Lucerne).

in Italy above all that such sodalities flourished from an early date. There was one in the professed house at Naples in 1593, soon supplanted by that established in the college by Father Francis Pavone in 1611.[3] From then on, every mission to the villages and small towns of the environs was accompanied by foundations. There were 20 outside Naples in 1640, 135 at the end of the century.[4]

Did, however, this very success not perhaps risk killing the institution? Were these very numerous congregations of students or priests, often established in places so small that the direction of the fathers could only be sporadic or exercised through intermediaries, not perhaps in danger of rapidly losing their initial fervour? At Toulouse, where spiritual support was, in fact, plentiful, the most perceptive of the brethren of the Annunciation recognised such a falling off in zeal as early as 1650. 'We have noticed for some time now', wrote one of them, 'that laxity has imperceptibly affected our congregation and we have often resolved to apply some remedy.'[5]

But what remedy? The one, no doubt, which had been discovered and put into practice in Naples by the end of the sixteenth century: the secret congregation.[6] This, as one of the officers in Toulouse stated, was simply 'the cream and quintessence of the congregation' intended to stimulate the latter by acting on it from the inside without making itself known.[7] Because, wrote a Parisian brother, 'the spirit of unity and reciprocal charity constitutes the essence of our devotion, which has no other aim than fidelity to the essential practices of the Congregation and a closer and more intimate Liaison between the members'.[8] We have here the three distinguishing features of the secret associations or Aas: a strengthening of the spirit of the congregations, close union between members, and secrecy.

These principles were being put into practice in Aquileia by 1607, in the sodality of priests founded by Father Pavone in the college at Naples in 1611, and among the members of the Assumption in Rome from 1637.[9] By this date, some students of the Collège de La Flèche

[3] A. S. J. Rome, province of Naples, 72, fos. 202–7.
[4] *Ibid.*, 74, fo. 5v (1640), 76^{II}, fos. 349–50v (1705).
[5] A. P. Toulouse, CA 101, vol. 1, pp. 1–2. [6] See above, chapter 3.
[7] B. M. Toulouse, MS 277, fo. 12.
[8] A. P. Toulouse, CA 101, vol. 1, pp. 3–4.
[9] A. S. J. Rome, province of Naples, 72, fos. 108–12, 202–7; province of Rome, 153, fos. 181–200.

were imitating these examples under the guidance of Father Bagot.[10] The society of the Bons Amis, directed by the same father, was recorded in Paris in 1645. It brought together in one house in the Saint-Marceau quarter young men from the Collège de Clermont, who together led an almost monastic life while preparing for the priesthood. They included François Pallu, Pierre Lambert de La Motte, Henri-Marie Boudon and Vincent de Meur, all destined to play an important role in the history of spirituality or in that of the missions at home and abroad.[11] One of them, Vincent de Meur, helped, in 1658, to found the Aa of Toulouse, a town where it had been shown that several congregation members were in need of renewal.[12] What happened in the largest town in Languedoc was soon copied in Lyons, Aix-en-Provence, Bordeaux, Poitiers and Dijon. Toulouse, in its turn, had its 'daughters' at Auch, Cahors and even amongst the chaplains of the Pilgrimage of Garaison.[13]

There was an active exchange of correspondence between these various French Aas, in which each newcomer was soon involved. It was as if they had returned to the early days of the Marian congregations or joined those (as in Swiss Fribourg, for example) which had preserved intact the spirit of the founders. This correspondence must have been abundant, and a splendid collection of it still survives in the archives of the Jesuit province of Toulouse; it includes advice from the old associations to the new, decisions taken within various associations, the most remarkable 'good works' which had been accomplished, encouragement, remonstrations, recommended pious works, information about foreign missions and news of the death of brethren. By 1660 a veritable network covered the whole kingdom, giving tangible expression to the spirit of unity between brothers, near or far, living or dead, which was to be the touchstone of the Aa. It perhaps also gave additional grounds for the rule of secrecy, since, at the start of Louis XIV's personal rule, it was difficult to envisage the civil and religious authorities tolerating this society which existed on the margins of the official bodies, and was composed

[10] Y. Poutet and J. Roubert, *Les 'Assemblées' secrètes des XVIIe–XVIIIe siècles en relation avec l'Aa de Lyon: edition critique des Annales d'une Aa lyonnaise* (Plaisance, 1968), pp. 123–4.

[11] *Ibid.*; Alphonse Auguste, *Les Sociétés secrètes catholiques du XVIIe siècle et H. M. Boudon* (Paris, 1911), pp. 48–9. [12] A. P. Toulouse, CA 167, pp. 8–9.

[13] *Ibid.*, CA 101, vols. 1–7 (correspondence).

of seculars who behaved as if they were regulars, who were united by rules which remained clandestine, and who, in order to strengthen their unity, kept in constant touch with one another from one end of France to the other.[14] Even the superiors of the Society in Rome seem to have been uncertain what attitude to adopt. 'The good Father Pavone', wrote one critic, '. . . had the intention of vulgarising our exercises and rules and things of the Institute and making them common and secular.'[15] These initiatives, wrote another critic, on the subject of the events of 1607 in the college of Aquileia, amounted 'to mixing our people with the seculars and even with large numbers of seculars and having them make our devotions and exercises, which goes against the spirit of our religious [order]'.[16] We must now look more closely at what actually happened within the secret congregations.

TRAINING

In practice, what Father Pavone was teaching the clerics of Naples in 1611 seems very far removed from the thorough training received by young Jesuits in a seminary. It consisted only of the simple rudiments of the priestly life, intended for men who were, apparently, more or less untutored and till then had been largely left to themselves. How to read a breviary, what words to use in confession, what rites to celebrate, why one should preach and what to say in the pulpit – such were the subjects of the meetings of the public association. In the secret sessions reserved for the more advanced, members learned how, by means of daily meditation, to reflect on the Christian doctrine and the sacraments. They were initiated into prayer. Before the assembled brothers, they did not hesitate to accuse themselves of shortcomings, and seek from the meeting and the father a means of self-improvement. A rule, lastly (and it was perhaps this in particular which made Rome uneasy), bound the secret brethren together and

[14] *Ibid.*, CA 113, p. 17: 'That those who are and will be absent from the town shall take care to keep up, by means of letters, their union and friendship with those who remain in the town, employing great discretion in their method of despatch and never mentioning therein the association or anything that could reveal its existence if these letters were to be intercepted' ('Livre du substitut', 11 December 1670).

[15] A. S. J. Rome, Jesuit deposit 662, fos. 125–31, information kindly provided by the Reverend Father Edmond Lamalle.

[16] A. S. J. Rome, province of Naples, 72, fos. 122–3.

led them to spend every moment of the day in holiness.[17] It goes without saying that for the congregations of priests in the isolated villages and small towns, often founded in the wake of missions, the programme was even more modest. In fact, in Naples and in the countryside, it consisted only of a simple apprenticeship intended as a preparation in the most urgent matters and effected, for the most part, at the request of the bishops themselves.

In time, as the culture of the participants, in the towns at least, left less to be desired, the public and secret meetings assumed the character of 'academies', of moral theology for the *sodales* as a whole, of dogmatic theology for the members of the Aa. The timetable of the meetings was strictly laid down. After a half-hour's talk given by one of the participants on a subject decided in advance, the director and the brothers discussed the subject together for one hour; there was then a reminder of the scriptural foundations (quarter of an hour), their practical application to the work of apostleship (half an hour) and private prayer (quarter of an hour). The Jesuit emphasis on a primarily pastoral orientation is clear. It shows also in the desire not to be limited to spiritual discussions, however much these may be directed towards a practical application. Father Pavone's clerics regularly visited the sick in hospital, and they taught the Christian doctrine every week to the women and children of the poor districts and the environs. During Lent, they toured the prisons. Between Palm Sunday and Whitsuntide, they went in groups into the villages assigned to them to prepare the faithful for Easter Communion. In the summer and autumn months, they went on missions, accompanying the preachers from the college.[18] This communal work was an essential element to which the texts constantly refer, as was the unity it encouraged, and which was desirable amongst the brothers. Even more than in Naples, concern for the latter dominated the practices of the austere secret congregation of the clerics of Aquileia.

These met regularly in a house where, in default of living together, they gathered three times a week, went to perform their penances and, on Fridays and the vigils of festivals, ate together a very frugal meal. This was also where they made their retreats and where they waited for death, surrounded by their brothers. The intellectual training provided by the 'discussions' was here of secondary importance, after initiation into the spiritual life and, above all, asceticism. The quality

17 *Ibid.*, fos. 202–7. 18 *Ibid.*, 72^{II}, fos. 349–50v.

of the latter is demonstrated by one of the most common mortifications offered as examples – sweeping with one's tongue the floor of the room where meetings were held, all covered with spit and filth; others consisted of being hung on a cross, hands and feet tied, or being tied to a column with a crown of thorns on one's head and a cane in one's hand; or one might prefer, the better to get into the spirit of one's last moments on earth, to lie on the ground, stiff as a corpse, eyes fixed on heaven, listening to a companion read the antiphons and responses of the office for the dead. It was, of course, only the most elementary charity to scourge one another fraternally at least three times a week. Meals, taken together in the refectory as often as possible, consisted only of a morsel of bread and some vegetables. Some found this too lavish and instead licked up with their tongues the crumbs which fell from the table. Whilst eating, they kept their minds occupied with prayer and meditation on death, judgement and hell, or fixed on the contents of some spiritual work.[19]

Such self-abasement was deemed excessive by many members of the Society. It continued to exist, nevertheless, and not only in Italy but in the French Aas as well. In Toulouse, the association founded in 1658 by Vincent de Meur seems to have drawn inspiration from both antecedents equally. Asceticism and concern for spiritual progress were both present, and, in a sense, they counterbalanced each other. Everything was done discreetly, cloaked in the secrecy which determined that, even in the reports, words were chosen with extreme care, as if to draw a veil over reality. Besides, those who wrote the reports were careful to state that the exercises of the Aa 'are the same as those of the Congregation, the only difference being that they are more numerous'.[20] We must look more closely, therefore, to understand the association in its specificity and also, occasionally, to identify correspondence written by its members, or a book intended for them.

It is perhaps in the care exercised in the recruitment of brothers that a first distinctive sign appears. Recruitment was a constant preoccupation. 'And as each one should always attach himself to someone', one reads in the *Pratique de Devotion et des vertus chrestiennes*, 'and work skilfully in order to win him for God, the *Commis* will ask what success he has had, without necessarily naming names.'[21] But at the

[19] *Ibid.*, 72, fos. 108–21. [20] A. P. Toulouse, CA 167, p. 110.

[21] *Pratique de Devotion et des vertus chrestiennes suivant les Regles de la Congrégation de Nostre-Dame, suivi de Pratique des vertus chrestiennes propres à la Congrégation*

same time, the criteria for selection were strict. Those chosen had, of course, to have been members of the congregation for some time and to have proved themselves there. Later, it was even specified that, in order to preserve the homogeneity of the group, they must be in the second year of theology.[22] They should also be judicious, prudent and very moderate in their sentiments and ways of acting. 'Those ardent spirits, who always go to extremes, should be suspect, because one observes that contact with such people worries others more than it helps them.' They must have a liking for charitable works:

They must above all be of a very loving nature, and inclined to act cordially and candidly. It is, nevertheless, advisable to see that the amiability of their nature does not render them open to the world at large, and that they are not one of those who make friends indiscriminately, and who tell their innermost thoughts to everyone they meet. Such people are incapable of the secrecy which is necessary in all matters of importance.

Finally, it was advisable for their age and condition to be 'suitable' in relation to the other brothers, 'for fear that too great an inequality might prevent the perfect friendship which should exist between them all'. If disparities of this sort emerged, different associations, 'according to the diversity of the people', should be established.[23] This done, it was necessary to test those under consideration. Had they heard talk of this sort of association as they existed in Rome and of the good that they did? What did they think of them? Their behaviour and way of life had to be scrutinised, not by one but by five or six people. After which came deliberation and a secret vote. This took place on three successive occasions, at intervals of several weeks. 'And no one should be admitted until everyone agrees.'[24] The opposition of one person alone was enough to prevent the entry of a new brother. In such circumstances, it is hardly surprising that the Aa of the theologians in Paris counted hardly more than forty members at its peak (between 1660 and 1670) and that the Aa of Toulouse, one of the most important in France after Paris, consisted of twenty to thirty persons at the period of its most intense activity, in the years 1670–80.[25] These figures were almost too high for some, who saw in

Nostre-Dame (Paris, 1654), p. 45. This very rare work, especially in the first edition preserved in the A. P. Toulouse, CA 109, exists in manuscript in the Bibliothèque Mazarine, Paris, MS 1266. [22] A. P. Toulouse, CA 167, p. 111.

[23] *Pratique de Devotion*, pp. 47–8. [24] *Ibid.*, pp. 50–1.

[25] A. P. Toulouse, CA 101, vol. 1, CA 113.

them a threat to the secrecy and preservation of the strictness of the rules.

The exercises may well have been those of the wider congregation, carried out more rigorously, but they nevertheless present to an attentive reader several specific features. These arise primarily from the fact that the special piety of the Aa was nourished by a book which contained, in a sense, the kernel of its spirituality. This book, disclosed initially in extracts and then in its entirety to newly accepted brothers, was the *Pratique de Devotion et des vertus chrestiennes suivant les Regles de la Congrégation de Nostre-Dame*, which first appeared in Paris in 1654. Appearing in the guise of a simple handbook for congregation members, it is quickly revealed as bearing a message intended for a narrower category. Chapter 1, after a brief history of the Marian congregations, goes on to say:

> But as all things with the passage of time degenerate from their initial foundation into a laxity which impairs their purity, some members of a Congregation, fearing this misfortune in the case of the one in which they have the honour to be, take a serious resolve to preserve, by the practice of the rules, that initial spirit which animated it in the beginning.[26]

This was precisely the purpose of the Aa. The second part, entitled *Pratique des vertus chrestiennes*, was intended to 'serve as a subject for those pleasant conversations' which were the *raison d'être* of the meeting. Aa members met every week for about an hour which they spent in discussing together the pious exercises which they were going to perform. And since to become virtuous was their supreme goal, they applied themselves to the study of one or other virtue.

> That is why this association takes every month a virtue, the most appropriate possible for the devotions and mysteries which the Church practises and celebrates at that time, and in order to proceed more methodically with this study, the virtue is divided into as many particular practices as they wish to spend exercising it.[27]

Thus Advent was devoted to cultivating the virtues of chastity and humility. Week one: how impurity enters the heart through the senses; week two: to preserve purity, the imagination, the understanding and the will have to be controlled; week three: what is humility? week four: external humility must be distinguished from internal humility. The period from the Purification of the Virgin to

[26] *Pratique de Devotion*, pp. 3–4. [27] *Ibid.*, p. 40.

Lent was devoted to the virtues of respect, submission and obedience. Week one: what is the spirit of respect and submission?; week two: 'obedience, lovely virtue of the Saviour'; week three: 'the study of the hidden life'; week four: Jesus, growing in years and in wisdom, 'advises us to work assiduously towards our perfection'.[28] The whole liturgical year was apportioned in this way. Nor were these exercises to be left to improvisation. Each meditation was divided into three parts; the first consisted of a clear and distinct expression of the virtue, the second 'furnishes some fairly pressing reasons to inflame our hearts "to the love of this particular virtue"', the third 'determines some particular actions, internal or external' to perform during the day to maintain us in its study and practice.[29]

Thus not only the content but the method of these weekly discussions was determined. The officer elected by the brothers, who led the sessions, had only to refer to what was in his handbook in order to expound 'the virtue of the week'. He was sometimes even content just to read aloud. 'Then each one, having pondered it alone, proposed a theme and also one or two practices, taking them always from the [liturgical] time, the place and the other circumstances which should be considered.'[30] The leader then summarised, in a few words, the essence of what had been said. Next, in imitation of the Paris brethren, a 'password' was chosen, a verse from the Bible which summarised or illustrated the spiritual topic.[31] This was repeated throughout the week whenever they met, unless the presence of strangers constrained them to say, while shaking hands, only 'Monsieur, remember you know what'.[32]

The meeting was continued in the daily pious exercises. In the morning, in addition to his duties as an ordinary member of the congregation, the brother had to reflect on the means of putting into practice during the course of the day 'the virtue of the week'. In the evening, after a reading from the Holy Scriptures or the Imitation of Christ, he had to examine his conscience on this subject. In spite of its importance and the care with which it was conducted, the spiritual topic did not take up the whole of the weekly meeting. The distribution of alms and other charitable works also occupied the attention of the participants.

[28] *Pratique des vertus chrestiennes*, pp. 7–17, 33–40.
[29] *Ibid.*, pp. 5–6. [30] *Pratique de Devotion*, p. 40.
[31] A. P. Toulouse, CA 101, vol. 1, pp. 38–9 (letter from Paris, June 1669); B. M. Toulouse, MS 277, fo. 4 ('Livre du substitut', Toulouse, 1678).
[32] A. P. Toulouse, CA 113, p. 16.

They concerned themselves with the sick and with prisoners from an early date. In hospitals, they swept the floors, made the beds and consoled the patients. In prisons, they prepared men and women for confession and the Easter Communion, heard them recite their prayers and distributed alms or provisions. For greater efficiency, the brethren were divided into 'bands'. One recited the office of the dead whilst another went to the Basilica of Saint-Sernin to communicate for the Aa, and yet another visited prisoners, and the remaining one went to the Hôtel-Dieu.[33] Each week, the 'band' had its service changed, so that in the course of a month each brother undertook all the various tasks. Very detailed instructions were given as to the spirit in which these good works should be undertaken. Those destined for the hospital recited the four prayers during the meeting which preceded their departure.[34] When, in the rather longer monthly meeting, accounts were rendered of alms given and those to be given in the coming weeks, 'one sees what sort of poor should be visited that month, and above all, it should be remembered to join the spiritual to the temporal in all these holy visits, and make each serve the other'.[35] Thus in summer, when, in that mild climate, it was unnecessary to make the beds of the sick, it was emphasised that the brothers should go to the hospital all the same 'to carry out instruction on holidays' and 'that every Saturday they should not fail to attend, as they did in winter, to instruct the poor wretches in those things of which they were ignorant'.[36]

It is true – as the episode just described reveals – that the zeal of the brothers, however carefully they were selected, needed periodic reawakening. This explains the renewals which, in the Toulouse Aa, took place twice a year. Preparation started ten days or a fortnight in advance, in the form of more numerous prayers, fasts, mortifications, and a redoubling of care and attention to the sick. On the day of the ceremony, the celebrant was usually a former brother dignified by some office in a chapter or responsibilities in a bishopric. At the beginning of the Mass, he intoned the Veni Creator and the Ave Maris Stella. After the Elevation came the moment of the renewal proper, when the officer recited the four prayers with the new recruits and when all the members of the association repeated, candle in hand, the prayers and the act of consecration to the Virgin. After the Mass,

[33] *Ibid.*, CA 167, p. 14; CA 113, pp. 76–7. [34] *Ibid.*, CA 167, p. 22.
[35] *Pratique de Devotion*, p. 46. [36] A. P. Toulouse, CA 113, pp. 237–8.

the brothers embraced each other lovingly, pronouncing the words which were like the 'device, image and epitome of the whole Aa': C. U. E. A. U. (*Cor unum et Anima una*). 'It was quite common for the eyes of many brothers to shed tears at this stage.' The celebrant or the director then gave a short speech on the necessity for renewal, which was followed by the reflections of former brethren returned to immerse themselves once again in the spirit of the Aa which had formed a part of their experience. Then all together raised their voices in a resounding Te Deum.[37]

An impressive ceremony intended to convince one and all to make a fresh start, the renewal was also a tangible demonstration of the vitality of the Aa. This is why the reports concerning it occupy such a large place in the surviving accounts and in the correspondence exchanged between towns. It was also the most concrete testimony to the unity which reigned between the brothers, from the youngest to the oldest, from the former member now elevated to a bishopric to the newly recruited sub-deacon.

There were other means of maintaining unity. These included the 'walks' which took place twice a month, and which allowed the brothers, whilst getting exercise, to take stock of works undertaken, or of the methods to be employed in such and such a type of apostleship. In July 1671, for example, they discussed 'the topic we should deal with in the hospital and the prisons and ways of impressing ourselves on the minds of the persons whom we wish to win for God'.[38] In the archives of the S. J. of Toulouse, there are sixteen volumes filled with accounts of these walks from the eighteenth and nineteenth centuries! Another means employed to maintain the spirit of unity amongst the brothers was to make periodic pilgrimages to the sanctuaries, large or small, in the vicinity. 'Experience tells us that these little journeys do much to reunite our hearts in the same designs', wrote the Gentlemen of Paris in 1663.[39] They, in fact, went regularly to Mont Valérien, Montmartre and Our Lady of Boulogne. Some of them took advantage of their holidays to pay homage to Our Lady of Liesse, a journey 'that they made on foot in spite of its length, which was more than sixty leagues there and back, spending the time in prayer, spiritual discussions and in reciting

[37] *Ibid.*, CA 167, pp. 98–101; numerous accounts also in the 'Livre du substitut', A. P. Toulouse, CA 113, and B. M. Toulouse, MS 277; for Paris, A. P. Toulouse, CA 101, vol. 1. [38] *Ibid.*, CA 113, p. 31.

[39] *Ibid.*, CA 101, vol. 1, pp. 11–13.

together the office of Our Lady, her chaplet and her litanies'.[40] Others (or possibly the same ones) went to Chartres, working out in advance a few rules, choosing a theme for reflection, which in 1670 was salvation, giving alms, visiting the Holy Sacrament in the churches and instructing children along the route. They marched to the rhythm of the recitation of the rosary or the singing of hymns. This, at the beginning of the reign of Louis XIV, was the first version of the student pilgrimage to Our Lady of Chartres.[41]

The theologians of Toulouse did not fail to follow the example set by Paris. From the 1670s, they regularly made the pilgrimage to St François de Paule, to the house of the Minims, in the week after Easter, in order to strengthen the resolutions taken during the retreat in Holy Week. They made another pilgrimage, in July, to the Chapel of Saint-Bonaventure kept by the Recollects, to 'find a way of passing their holidays in holiness'.[42] During this, in imitation of the Gentlemen of Paris, a visit was arranged to Our Lady of Garaison.[43] And, a few years later, 'they ceased to make the pilgrimage to Bruyères on the Thursday before Whitsuntide'.[44] These journeys to holy places were the occasion, if not for missions, at least for reflections on 'the means which should be employed to instruct the peasantry in the countryside'.[45]

There is a world of difference between Father Pavone's congregation of priests founded in Naples in 1611 and the Aa of the theologians in Toulouse as it appears around 1670. Preparation for the priesthood was common to both, but the training was no longer the same: to begin with, we see the rudiments of a primarily 'professional' character, which were indispensable for a largely ignorant clergy; by the end, the training was a supplement of an essentially spiritual nature intended to accompany the high-level teaching which the theologians received at the university or in the upper college classes. This did not exclude the initiation which students accustomed to the methods of thought and action of the Aa might receive indirectly to help them accomplish their future pastoral tasks. The transition from 'spiritual upkeep' as it was conceived by the Jesuits to the classical sermon was imperceptible – they had the same framework, the same progression and a similar content. The

[40] *Ibid.*, p. 88 (1666). [41] *Ibid.*, pp. 92–5 (1670).
[42] *Ibid.*, CA 167, p. 19. These places of pilgrimage were located in the suburbs of Toulouse. [43] *Ibid.*, CA 113, p. 134.
[44] *Ibid.*, p. 253. [45] *Ibid.*, p. 112.

works of apostleship among the poor and the sick which the young clerics had to accomplish whilst instructing children or in the course of rural missions were not the least of these preparatory works. But this was not the essence of the Aa. Its essence lay in the method it transmitted for learning to master oneself, live one's religion and constantly unite thought and deed, pure spirituality and practical application. It was also a way of life, a behaviour learnt almost unconsciously within the bosom of the Aa, which meant that, seeing the priest some years later, people in the know could not help but think 'He was trained by the Jesuits.'

TWO CONCEPTIONS, ONE AIM

This did not prevent some people, though totally committed to the Society of Jesus, from wondering whether it was really necessary, in order to have good priests, to construct such a complicated system; if, indeed, it was healthy and in conformity with the spirit of St Ignatius to maintain within communities these secret conventicles which operated in the shadows. Was there not a risk of sowing discord, or, at the very least, of creating confusion? And, in a Society which held in such high regard the duty of obedience, was it permissible to let many of its religious advise members of the Aa to conceal their membership from their confessors?[46] When, in 1615, a secret meeting, no doubt established in imitation of the Italian (Naples) or Bavarian (Ingolstadt) models, was discovered amongst the pupils of the top class of the college in Lucerne, the Father *praeses* and the rector did not hesitate: they forbade it outright.[47]

It was perhaps to avoid a similar incident that the 'discussion' was established at this period amongst the various Antwerp congregations. Every Sunday afternoon, at the oratory, an hour-long spiritual colloquy took place, to which the *sodales* of two or three out of the dozen sections comprising the association were invited. The father discussed, in the form of a lecture or a less formal talk, a spiritual issue proposed by the audience. The aim was to 'maintain charity between the brethren and teach them to know themselves'. It was also to instruct them and lead them to deepen their spiritual life,[48]

[46] *Ibid.*, p. 11. 'it was also decided not to name the association either in letters or elsewhere, and not even in confessions, since there was no need to do so.'
[47] S. A. Lucerne, cod. KK 25/1, pp. 129–30.
[48] A. P. B. M. Namur, Droeshout deposit 24,1 p. 254 (1615).

that is to say, exactly what the secret meetings aimed to do. The daily meditations on the sufferings of Christ which the Antwerp congregations practised in their oratory, with their director as guide, during Holy Week are not without echoes of the closed retreat which was held in the Toulouse Aa.[49]

The work of Father Scribani, published under the title *Meditation*, an adaptation for ordinary people of the *Spiritual Exercises* of Ignatius Loyola, which was widely diffused at the beginning of the seventeenth century amongst the great Northern congregations, responded to the same need.[50] Here, in any case, books played a key role from the beginning. In Cologne, a library had been established by and for the congregation of the Three Kings by 1609. Anyone could borrow and take home spiritual or polemical books.[51] Antwerp followed suit. One, then several, libraries were soon established in a brand-new building which had just been built for the sodalities opposite the professed house. They already benefited from a modern organisation, with a responsible officer helped by assistants, and a large stock of pious books (six hundred volumes for the Major in 1656), carefully looked after.[52] As it was sometimes advisable to encourage rather indolent readers once the novelty had worn off, various procedures were adopted. In the Antwerp Major, after a Mass of the Holy Spirit, they resorted to drawing lots for the books and their readers.[53] In Cologne, books were distributed willy-nilly.[54]

More or less everywhere, but particularly in the Germanic and Rheno-Flemish world, the habit developed from the mid-seventeenth century of compiling annually a gift book and distributing it to all the fully registered members of the Major. The library of the great seminary at Strasbourg possesses an almost complete collection of those distributed by the academic congregation of Molsheim between 1670 and 1790. Works of spirituality or meditations for every day of the year, on the pattern of the celebrated work of François Nepveu, easily predominate. Amongst the first titles are a *Vademecum ou le Raphaël du voyageur chrétien*, *La Manière de toujours jouir de la vraie paix de l'âme* of Sarasa, the *Sagesse des saints enracinée dans la crainte et l'amour de Dieu*, a collection of prayers, *Le Prix inestimable de la*

[49] *Ibid.*, 23,2, p. 113. [50] *Ibid.*, 24,1, p. 195.
[51] H. A. S. Cologne, Jesuits 9, fo. 203 bis.
[52] A. P. M. B. Namur, Droeshout deposit 24,2, p. 275 (1627), p. 384 (1632); 24,3, pp. 377–8 (1656). [53] *Ibid.*, 24,3, p. 378.
[54] H. A. S. Cologne, Jesuits 9, fo. 257v.

Grâce divine, a guide for conversing well (and piously) with one's neighbours, devout thoughts for calling on people to imitate the love of God, and, of course, the *Spiritual Exercises*.[55] In a few years, Alsatian curés, and canons, even seigneurial bailiffs or clerks, who could get themselves registered at the 'Academic' as easily as clerics, had access to a collection of spiritual works in which were discussed and developed at length those same themes that were being debated by the brothers of the Toulouse Aa under the seal of secrecy.

There were two opposing conceptions, then, underlying the common aim of the congregations. For some, zeal could only emerge from a tiny group, carefully selected and then initiated; for others, dynamism was the consequence of an active spiritual life and a sound religious culture freely offered to all. On the one hand, the little coterie, on the other, the big battalions. It was more, in fact, than just a matter of tactics. Behind these divergent attitudes amongst the officers of the congregations lay two different conceptions of the priesthood. In the Major of Molsheim, as in those of Munich, Lucerne, Cologne and Antwerp, clergy and laymen, young students and grown men, rubbed shoulders. In Toulouse, when the question of admitting adult men to the Aa arose, whether priests or the pious bourgeoisie of the town, the brothers, on the advice of their director, preferred to opt for the creation of a second association.[56] The desire to isolate the young cleric from the world, as a prelude to the isolation of the curé in the village, was a factor operative in this French example, which was much less influential in Germany and the Rhineland. The analysis can be taken further, and we may wonder whether these two models of associations do not, in fact, reveal two forms of Tridentine Catholicism.

Let us return to the study of the register of entries to the congregation of the Annunciation in Toulouse. A sharp decline in the number of enrolments is visible at the end of the century (see figure 7, p. 69). There were only 598 between 1685 and 1694, and 520 between 1694 and 1703, as against 916 between 1641 and 1650. The average number of annual registrations had fallen by almost half in less than fifty years. Is this evidence of a decline of the sodality? This is by no means certain. The geographical origin of the members, which can be

[55] Châtellier, *Tradition chrétienne et renouveau catholique*, pp. 164–5, 390–2.

[56] A. P. Toulouse, CA 113, pp. 56, 80–2, 131: 'There were lengthy discussions on the necessity for creating two associations due to the differences in age and status which were beginning to harm the unity which ought to exist between the brethren.'

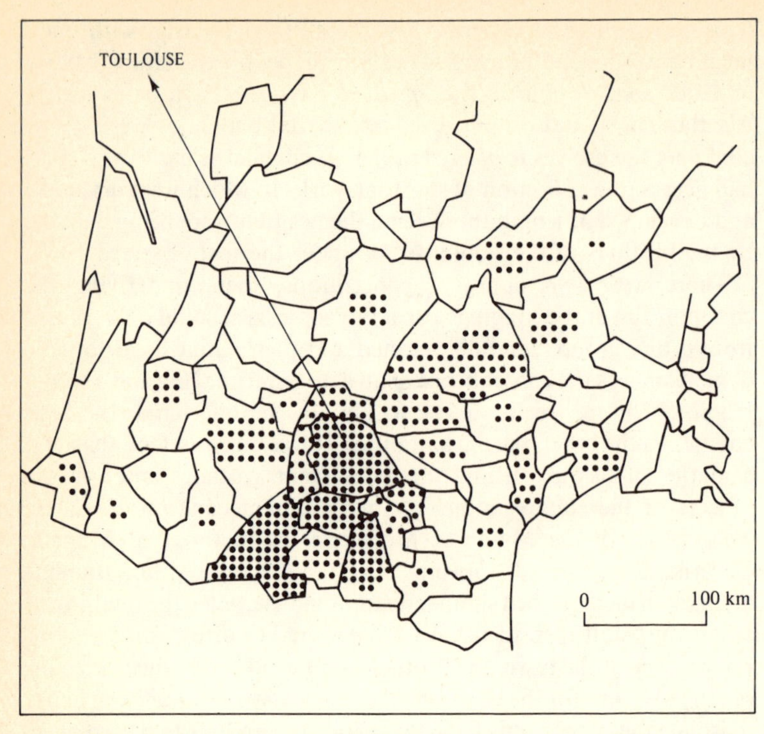

8. Distribution of members of the Toulouse Annunciation in the seventeenth century

established for the very end of the seventeenth century, though unhappily not before, reveals a very curious situation (see figure 8). The little bishopric of Saint-Bertrand-de-Comminges, with 81 entries, almost equals the archbishopric of Toulouse (85). Pamiers (37) and Rieux (26), equally small, are also very well represented. With the archiepiscopal town providing only 15.34% of the members, the vast majority came from the multitude of small dioceses of the south-west. A closer analysis reveals that 59.2% of the recruits to the congregation came from elsewhere than the episcopal town, that is to say, in most cases, from large or even small villages. The recruitment, then, was largely rural. At the same time, the nobility and, even more, the great families of the region provided far fewer recruits than at the beginning of the century, if any at all. It is difficult to say what it was like fifty years earlier, but, at any rate around 1700,

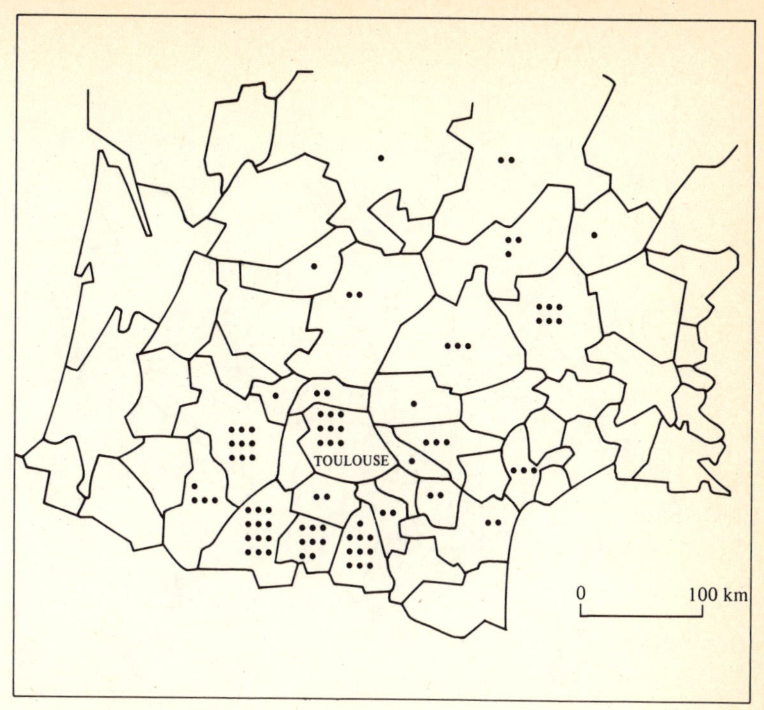

9. Origin of members of the Toulouse Aa (1658–67)

the spirit of the congregation had penetrated as far as tiny villages such as Couserans and Comminges. It would be interesting to compare this map with one of candidates for the priesthood (the ordinands) to see whether the evolution of the congregation was similar to that of the new priests, as seems likely. It is certainly the case that recruitment to the Aa, which we can follow closely thanks to the 'Livre d'or', reflects perfectly, even exaggerates, this extra-urban origin of the great majority of the brethren (see figures 9 and 10).[57]

A further point emerges from a study of these statistics: the *sodales* received into the secret association comprised only 3.14% of the total of new registrations in the Annunciation between 1660 and 1666; they were 26.15% between 1694 and 1703, representing, that is, over a

[57] *Ibid.*, CA 102, 'Livre d'or': 'Book in which are contained, at the beginning, the Names, Surnames, Place of origin and diocese of the Servants of Jesus, Mary, Joseph and the Guardian Angel according to date of admission.'

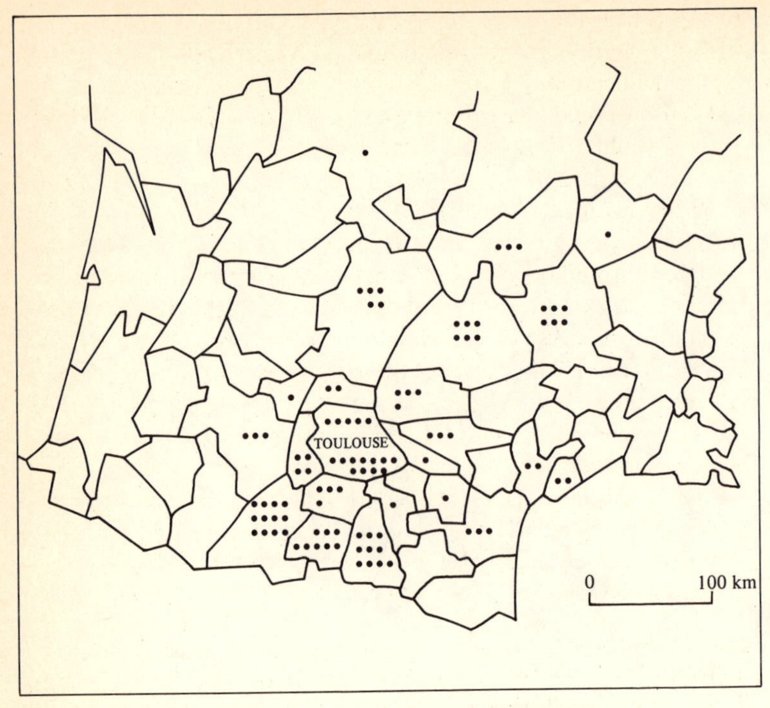

10. Origin of members of the Toulouse Aa (1699–1708)

quarter of the new members of the congregation. When one remembers the care with which entry to the Aa was controlled, it has to be concluded that, far from experiencing a decline, the sodality of the Annunciation instead enjoyed an expansion of its recruitment into social strata and geographical areas where it had previously been unknown, as well as an improvement in the quality of its members. The decline in the absolute number of entries certainly came from an increase in the level of requirements, which, as has been shown in recent studies of the seventeenth-century clergy, eliminated undesirables.[58]

The Aa certainly played a role in this overall improvement. All the more so in that its own archives show very clearly that it controlled the congregation. Following an incident in the election of the officers

[58] See the very pertinent remarks of Marc Venard in *L'Eglise d'Avignon au XVIIe siècle* (Lille, 1980), 5 vols.

of the congregation, 'they resolved further that to avoid these little difficulties in future, they would hold an election eight [days] earlier in the association, and that afterwards the Gentlemen of the association would give their vote to these three so that the three first officers would always be from the association'.[59] It could hardly be plainer. Comparable situations, but with other consequences, ensued when several former Aa members happened to teach in the same seminary or, even better, were at the head of numerous seminaries scattered throughout France. A network of establishments for the training of the clergy, controlled or influenced by the Aa, thus existed in different dioceses of the kingdom, as has been shown by Yves Poutet.[60] The indirect power of these secret associations appeared in all its force at the time when, throughout the France of Louis XIV, the Tridentine reform entered its institutional phase.

However, the question remains, and needs to be answered: did the brothers really need such secrecy in order to carry out these numerous activities with such far-reaching consequences? The reply was perhaps given by a brother from Paris, who, travelling through Toulouse in 1672:

> told us that since our association made a particular point of being attached to the Holy See, so the brethren ought to endeavour to defend the infallibility of the Pope wherever they were, because they were often in the company of people who, with a worldly air and wishing to appear free thinkers, opposed this, that he had heard said to a brother of the true institution of the association which was originally at La Flèche that our Society would not be able to exist if we did not have a total attachment to the Jesuit fathers and to the director of the association and that he had often heard said at the Paris association that they had often tested it.[61]

Papal infallibility and the Jesuits were two things which were far from being accepted all over France, and least of all in the middle of the Regalian crisis and the spread of Jansenism.[62] Were the Aa and its secrecy a response adapted to a particular period and milieu? But we must stop thinking of Catholic Europe in the seventeenth century as a

[59] A. P. Toulouse, CA 113, pp. 216–17.

[60] Poutet and Roubert, *Les 'Assemblées' secrètes*, p. 67.

[61] A. P. Toulouse, CA 113, p. 59.

[62] The litigation between the Pope and Louis XIV over the exercise of Regalian rights had a particular resonance in the region of Toulouse due to the proximity of the two recalcitrant bishops who had taken the matter to the Roman court, Pavillon d'Alet and Caulet de Pamiers.

whole. What the study of the congregations, in particular the congregations of clerics, shows, is that a distinction should be drawn between two Europes. In one, people could declare that they were convinced of the infallibility of the Pope, and of the Immaculate Conception, and show themselves to be faithful to the teaching of the Jesuits without having to fear any criticism on the part of their co-religionists; in the other (France and part of the Low Countries), these opinions were contested by some and the doctrine professed by the Society was often fiercely attacked.

In spite of everything and taking full account of these differences, the desire formulated in 1611 by Father Pavone seemed, by the 1680s, to be on the way to being realised: 'through the congregation of priests, to reform the clergy.'[63] In Ingolstadt and Toulouse alike, this reform was well under way.

[63] A. S. J. Rome, province of Naples, 72, fo. 207.

6. *The ruling classes*

It would be perverse to present the seventeenth-century Jesuits, so often accused of complaisance towards the great, as exclusively concerned with ordinary townspeople and lowly clerics. In actual fact, those in power, whether in small towns or powerful states, were from the beginning the object of special attention. Moreover, the fathers very quickly learned how to adapt their strategy to the various specific situations they encountered throughout Europe. The kingdom of Naples was very different from Bavaria, an Imperial town like Cologne was very different from Rennes and Aix with their Parlements. And Paris, above all, was a sensitive location, where prejudice against the Society was considerable, but which nevertheless became under Louis XIII and Richelieu the crucial base for a revival of Catholic reform; it had to be treated with special care, and demanded imagination, innovation and discretion from those who were entrusted with responsibility for its leaders. But what was the goal to which all these endeavours and so much concern to adapt to circumstances and to men were directed? Was it conquest or apostleship which was at issue?

PRINCES AND BURGOMASTERS

In the first place, everything suggests that, in the first half of the seventeenth century, the Society of Jesus aimed, through the intermediary of the congregations, to exert control over those in positions of power. The famous congregation of the Holy Sacrament in Naples had at its head in 1641 the Emperor Ferdinand III himself, the Viceroy, and the Cardinal-Archbishop.[1] In Munich, the Duke and members of his family always headed the list of enrolments in the Major, and distinguished themselves by their exemplary assiduity and piety.[2] When a congregation of the Sorrowful Virgin was

[1] A. S. J. Rome, province of Naples, 177, fo. 124v.
[2] Joseph Pichler, *Die Marianische deutsche Kongregation der Herren*, pp. 5–25.

established in Neuburg in 1618, the reigning Prince-Palatine, accompanied by several of his family, soon came to enter his name, and became its first prefect.[3]

It does not seem, despite claims to the contrary, that Louis XIII went so far.[4] But he appeared, with the Queen, at the offices of the professed house of the Saint-Paul quarter, communicated there, and accorded effective protection to the congregations and the Jesuits.[5] This was all the more necessary in that in fiercely Gallican France there was no shortage of difficulties for the Jesuits, which crystallised in particular in the Parlements. Did counsellors who were congregation members have the right to report affairs in which the Jesuits were involved? This was the big question in the years 1630–5, which agitated the top legal world, especially in Paris and Rouen.[6] Such significant incidents foreshadowed, more than a century in advance, the great trials of the 1760s. Already, behind the petition objecting to certain magistrates, lay a direct attack on the congregations whose rules were being questioned. The King himself had to intervene, showing both the fierceness of the conflict and the determination of the monarch to involve himself in this affair.[7]

These events also reveal that the world of Parlement, though traditionally mistrustful, not to say hostile, with regard to the Jesuits, was changing. There were magistrates amongst the Gentlemen of Toulouse in the first years of the seventeenth century. They constituted the active and leading element in the similar sodality founded in Rouen in 1615.[8] In Grenoble, the sodality's beginnings in 1624 were presided over by Artus de Lionne, counsellor in Parlement, soon to be Bishop of Gap, and father of the future Secretary of State for Foreign Affairs. He was accompanied by the *président*, Audeyer, the counsellor Sautereau, future Royal Commissioner at the Cinq-Mars

[3] B. H. Munich, Jesuits 102, fo. 162.

[4] Villaret, *Les Congrégations mariales*, pp. 233–4. The letter from the General to the director of the congregation which this author cites appears to leave no doubt. But, as we have found no act of consecration amongst the well-classified collection in the Archives Nationales, nor any other reference, it seems either that the director gave his Superior an impression which went further than the facts justified, or that the General had deduced a consecration to the Virgin according to the rules of the congregation from certain actions of the King, which remains unproven.

[5] A. S. J. Rome, province of France, 33^{I} and 33^{II}.

[6] Villaret, *Les Congrégations mariales*, p. 229; Alexandre Féron, *Introduction à l'étude des Sociétés secrètes catholiques dans le diocèse de Rouen aux XVIIe et XVIIIe Siècles* (Rouen, 1927), pp. 58–61.

[7] Féron, *Sociétés secrètes*, pp.60–1

[8] *Ibid.*, pp. 57–8, 74–114.

trial, the *président* of the Chambre des Comptes, Buffevant de Murines, and the counsellors de Ferran, de Bonet, Baudet and Rosset as well as many other persons from the upper ranks of the lay and ecclesiastical world of the capital of the Dauphiné.[9] For these educated men, old pupils of the college and very probably members of the congregations of scholars, entry to the 'Messieurs' was only the prolongation of a career as *sodalis* begun in extreme youth. The same was almost certainly the case with the members of the urban magistrature, though with the difference that they passed through the sodalities of young artisans before entering the Civica or, less often, the Major. It was not uncommon for an entire council to belong to the congregation, recorded the Cologne annalist.[10] This was certainly not new at the end of the century, or the merchant who was caught in the 1620s in the act of criticising the sodality of the Three Kings would not have been so promptly and so vigorously pursued by the same Senate.[11] As for the little Catholic towns of the Germanic world and the Rhineland, such as Ingolstadt, Reichenhall, Obernai and Molsheim, there was no need, in the seventeenth century, to rely on the opinion of the editor of the *Annual Letters* to know that the majority, if not all, of the magistrates, belonged to the sodality of burgesses.

It is hardly surprising that the membership or protection of the prince or of the most prominent people in the city promoted something of a chain reaction amongst the nobility and the principal members of the bourgeoisie. The congregation of the Veneration of the Holy Sacrament in the professed house in Naples, which had at its head the Emperor, the Viceroy and several cardinals, along with 26 princes, dukes and marquises, that is nearly a third (29.36 %) of the total membership (126) in these two categories alone, assumed in the 1640s the character of an association bringing together all the dignitaries in the Kingdom.[12]

It was to some extent similar in the case of the Major in Munich, whose membership lists make it possible to trace the changes (figure 20 pp. 233–5). The membership was still very disparate in 1584: the Duke and a few nobles rubbed shoulders with merchants and, above all, representatives of the important Italian colony. A century or so later, in 1673, the Elector and his family appeared at the head of

[9] Pra, *Les Jésuites à Grenoble*, pp. 303–4.
[10] H. A. S. Cologne, A 642, fo. 51v.
[11] See above, p. 25.
[12] A. S. J. Rome, province of Naples, 177, fos. 124v–125.

the 71 dignitaries from the court and the provincial administration out of a total of 171 lay members, that is 41.52 %. Fifty-four years later, in 1727, servants of the Prince-Elector (at his court or in his States) amounted to 52.48 % of the lay membership (275). When one remembers that in a century and a half (1584–1727), the latter had grown from 26 to 524, it is reasonable to conclude that this famous sodality, at least in its secular section, had become, at the dawn of the eighteenth century, almost an association of all those who were attached, closely or from afar, to the Prince-Elector of Bavaria. At the same time, the noble section, which was 16.37 % of the laity in 1673, grew to 23.66 %, that is practically a quarter, by 1727.

In Ingolstadt the phenomenon was both more spectacular and earlier. Towards the end of the Thirty Years' War, between 1638 and 1647, a third of the new registrations (32.7 %) were of noble rank, as if the entry of representatives of the very greatest families (Hapsburg, Wittelsbach and Lorraine) into this academic congregation of the first Catholic university of central Europe had attracted the whole nobility of the Holy Empire.[13] But we should perhaps also see in the considerable growth of this category a consequence of political events. After the victory of the White Mountain (1620) and the death of Gustavus Adolphus (1632), the danger of invasion of the Catholic states by Protestant armies seemed remote and, for the same reason, the authority of the Hapsburgs and the Wittelsbachs confirmed. The time was ripe, therefore, for young nobles aspiring to high office, who had hitherto thought it prudent to keep their options open, to make a public demonstration of their Catholic convictions. Membership of the most famous Marian congregation in the whole of Germany offered a means to do this in an unequivocal fashion.

That connections between the sodalities designed for the ruling class and the politics of states existed is not in doubt; the question is rather what form they took.

PARIS: THE COURT AND THE TOWN

Ascension Day, 1641 (9 May) was without doubt a great day for the whole of the Society of Jesus, the day when the King of France, the Queen and the entire court attended the inauguration of the new church in the professed house. Dedicated to St Louis, situated in the

13 See figure 6, p. 68.

middle of the Saint-Paul quarter, on the edge of the Marais and close to the Hôtel de Ville, it turned out to be the ideal meeting place for the court and the town. Only just finished, and hastily covered with hangings and tapestries, the building as yet lacked the sumptuous décor which would attract the admiration of visitors at a later date. But the nave was resplendent with the beautiful clothes and rich attire of those who counted as the most distinguished, titled and powerful in Paris. Beside Louis XIII were the Ducs d'Orléans, d'Enghien, de Conti, de Nemours, de Chevreuse, de Montbazon, de Ventadour, d'Uzès and de Luynes. The Queen, Anne of Austria, was accompanied by the Duchesses de Lorraine, de Condé, d'Enghien, de Soissons, de Longueville, d'Elbeuf, de Ventadour, de Montbazon and d'Aiguillon. The most important men in the government, including Chancellor Séguier and Secretaries of State Bouthillier, Sublet de Noyers, Chavigny and Loménie de Brienne, were present. Most extraordinary of all, in the choir was Cardinal Richelieu, officiating in person, accompanied by bishops, prelates and abbots.

After the Mass, the King, the Queen and the Duc d'Orléans communicated, followed by a throng which included the principal ministers. The Superior of the house then handed the King, as founder of the church, the candle of white wax (hence, perhaps, the erroneous interpretation according to which Louis XIII joined the congregation). Early in the afternoon, the court resumed their places in the church to listen to Jean de Lingendes, chaplain and preacher to the Most Christian King and Bishop-Elect of Sarlat, and attend the musical vespers and the solemn translation from the old to the new site of the cult of the Holy Sacrament, attended by a hundred Jesuits clothed in surplices and each carrying a candle in his hand, surrounded by a guard, fifes and drums. It was a great day, certainly, for the Superior of the house, who could not conceal his joy in the detailed description he sent to the General.[14] It was a success, also, for the members of the congregation, who were present everywhere, in the pulpit, at the altar near the Cardinal, in the nave close to the royal family, or simply mingling with the crowd; whilst they in no way put themselves forward, they could nevertheless be seen as the principal craftsmen of this enterprise and its success.

A congregation of Gentlemen ('Messieurs') was founded in the professed house in Paris in 1630. Significantly, the initiative for it

[14] A. S. J. Rome, province of France, 33^{II}, fo. 266.

seems to have come from the Superior himself, Louis de La Salle, who directed and assumed responsibility for it during its early years.[15] Father de La Salle had completed his noviciate and all his studies in Rome, at the Roman college, where he had been able to see in operation the oldest and most famous congregations; he then went to the Collège de La Flèche at just the time when Father Bagot was teaching there, and experimenting, perhaps, with what later became the society of the Bons Amis.[16] His successor in charge of the Gentlemen of St Louis was Pierre Lallemant, who had undergone a similar, though much shorter, training in Rome.[17] The model of the great congregations of nobles, Roman and Neapolitan, was certainly influential, enriched by the experience gained in a variety of places and tempered by concern to avoid any scandal in a town such as Paris, given the difficulties already experienced there by the Jesuits. This explains why the Superior himself assumed responsibility, at least in the early years.

Who, in particular, was this new sodality aimed at? Preserved in the Archives Nationales, gathered together in tiny, carefully bound volumes, are the acts of consecration to the Virgin signed by the hand of all those who joined the congregation from shortly after its foundation (1631) up to 1760.[18] Altogether there are 970 leaves, bearing names which are sometimes famous though for the most part obscure, but many of which can be identified thanks to the registers in series Y of the Archives Nationales and the genealogical material in the Bibliothèque Nationale. The sample studied consists of the initial group, that of the first 118 to enrol, who pronounced and signed their act of consecration between 1631 and 1640.

There is no shortage of names which catch the eye. One such is that of Noël Brulart de Sillery, brother of Nicolas, Chancellor of France, Commander of the Order of Malta, entrusted with several extraordinary missions by Maria de' Medici, then sent to Rome by Louis XIII, famous for his prodigious wealth and his ostentation, but

15 *Ibid.*, 22, fos. 248, 288. I wish to thank the Reverend Father Bottereau, who has greatly helped me in the work of identifications in connection with Father de La Salle and the Jesuits of the professed house at this period; see also Camille de Rochemonteix, S. J., *Nicolas Caussin confesseur de Louis XIII et le cardinal de Richelieu* (Paris, 1911), pp. 26–7.

16 *Ibid.*; G. Bottereau, S. J., 'Jean-Baptiste Saint-Jure S. J., 1588–1657', *Archivum historicum Societatis Iesu*, 49 (1980), pp. 161–202, especially pp. 165–6.

17 A. S. J. Rome, province of France, 12, fo. 7v.

18 A. N. Paris, MM 649, 650, 651.

also a celebrated convert ('one of the finest conquests of Vincent de Paul') who was, towards the end of his life, involved in all the great charitable and spiritual works of the early seventeenth century.[19] Nicolas Fouquet, the famous *surintendant des finances*, was still relatively unimportant when he registered in 1635. He was no more than a counsellor in the *conseil souverain* at Nancy, and still only twenty years old. He was in the company of his brother, Abbé François Fouquet, who edified his entourage by his assiduous attendance at the Tuesday meetings at Saint-Lazare, before embarking on a brilliant episcopal career.[20] Vaugelas, the grammarian and academician, registered, as well as the powerful protector of the Jesuits in France, Cardinal François de La Rochefoucauld.[21] A murkier and more disquieting figure was Jean Martin de Laubardemont, *maître des requêtes*, known for his leading role in the affair of the possessed sisters of Loudun and for his fierce animosity against the unhappy Urbain Grandier, an animosity manifested in his interrogation of the Abbé de Saint-Cyran, a few months before he joined the congregation.[22]

Louis de Rochechouart, Comte de Maure, was to enjoy a brief moment of fame at the time of the Fronde. Meanwhile, it was through his wife, a *précieuse* well known in the salons and fiercely committed to defending the memory of her uncle, the Maréchal de Marillac, that he was known to the world.[23] The *présidents* de Mesmes and de Nesmond, whose names would also often crop up during the troubles of mid-century, were not men to seek fame.[24] De Mesmes in

19 *Ibid.*, Y 174, fo. 96, 178, fo. 352, 381, fos. 138v, 225v, 427, 180, fos. 399v, 406, 420v, Vincent de Paul, *Correspondance, Entretiens, Documents*, ed. Pierre Coste, 13 vols. (Paris, 1920–5), vol. 1, p. 41, note 1; *Dictionnaire de biographie française*, part 38, cols. 494–5.

20 B. N. Paris, French MSS 32788, pp. 477–8 (family); Pierre Coste, *Le Grand Saint du grand siècle: Monsieur Vincent*, 3 vols. (Paris, 1934), vol. 1, p. 368, vol. 2, pp. 151–3; *Dictionnaire de biographie française*, part 80, cols. 707, 712–18.

21 De La Chenaye-Desbois, *Dictionnaire de la noblesse* (Paris, 1863–76), vol. 7, cols. 796–7 (Claude Favre de Vaugelas); Cardinal de La Rochefoucauld did not register until 1642 and does not, therefore, figure amongst the 118 names studied here.

22 A. N. Paris, Y 184, fos. 34v, 186; B. N. Paris, French MSS 32826, p. 203; Coste, *Le Grand Saint*, vol. 3, pp. 151, 155; Tallemant des Réaux, *Historiettes*, 2 vols. (Paris, 1967), vol. 1, pp. 297, 968; Nicolas Goulas, *Mémoires*, vol. 1, p. 395.

23 A. N. Paris, Y 178, fos. 181, 231v, 183, fo. 79, 184, fo. 330, 186, fo. 368v, 188, fos. 36v, 152v, 193, fo. 145v; M. C. Paris, Studies LXXIII, 389 (18 July 1647), I, 124 (2 June 1649); Vincent de Paul, *Correspondance*, vol. 1, pp. 345, 470–1; Tallemant des Réaux, *Historiettes*, vol. 1, pp. 522–6.

24 A. N. Paris, Y 184, fo. 271v, 187, fo. 178; B. N. Paris, French MSS 32785, pp. 362, 363; M. C. Paris, studies LI, 152 (4 March 1628), I, 105 (16 April 1633), XXIX, 344

particular, one of the first to join the congregation, was involved in charitable works and became one of the most active members of the Society of the Holy Sacrament.[25] François Sublet de Noyers, too, made his act of consecration as early as 1631. Neveu de Marigny, the *surintendant des finances* 'given' to Richelieu by his relative, La Mothe-Houdancourt, Bishop of Mende, was already Controller-General of Finances before shortly becoming Secretary of State.[26] This very influential person was known for his devotion, which some reckoned excessive, and for his compliance before his master, the Cardinal. 'He had', wrote Tallemant des Réaux, not mincing words, 'the soul of a servant.'[27]

Thanks to the famous book of Father Saint-Jure, Gaston de Renty, who inspired the most diverse activities, and was constantly paying with his person for his own austerities and apostolic zeal, was presented to the world at large soon after his death as a model to imitate.[28] One may wonder, nevertheless, whether Monsieur de Renty, who was eleven times Superior of the Society of the Holy Sacrament and who was in contact with so many missionaries, heads of orders and spirituals, was really representative of the congregation in its specificity.[29] The same applies, though to a lesser degree, to *président* de Mesmes and Noël Brulart de Sillery. The strongest personalities of this 'century of saints' cannot, in fact, be appreciated within the inevitably narrow confines of one single institution, however estimable. Conversely, men of the world, whose devotion was not their constant preoccupation, may well have been drawn towards this pious association by a concern to pay court, especially once more numerous and abundant royal favours were being manifested towards the Jesuits of the Saint-Paul quarter. The

(16 April 1636), XVI, 111 (9 September 1655) (Jean-Antoine de Mesmes, Seigneur d'Irval); A. N. Paris, Y 180, fo. 292; M. C. Paris, study XIX, 417 (1634), 427 (1643); B. N. Paris, French MSS 32785, pp. 398–99 (François-Théodore de Nesmond).

25 Henri Beauchet-Filleau, *Annales de la Compagnie du Saint-Sacrement* (Marseilles, 1900), pp. 105, 112, 183, 266, 269 (succeeded M. de Renty as Superior).

26 M. C. Paris, study XXIV, 331 (1631), 337 (1633), 344 (1636, 1637), 416 (1640), study XLIII, 32 (1640).

27 Tallemant des Réaux, *Historiettes*, vol. 1, pp. 297–9.

28 A. N. Paris, Y 175, fo. 15; M. C. Paris, study LXXIII, 393 (1648); Father Jean-Baptiste Saint-Jure, *La Vie de Monsieur de Renty* (Paris, 1651); Reverend Father Bessières, *Deux grands méconnus précurseurs de l'action catholique et sociale, Gaston de Renty et Henry Buch* (Paris, 1931).

29 Beauchet-Filleau, *Annales*, pp. 110, 112, 113, 134, 269; Alfred Rebelliau, *La Compagnie secrète du Saint-Sacrement: lettres du groupe parisien au groupe marseillais, 1639–1662* (Paris, 1908), pp. 65, 68, 69; Coste, *Le Grand Saint*, vol. 1, p. 273, vol. 2, pp. 614–15, vol. 3, p. 9.

presence of a Sublet de Noyers, on the other hand, and even more of expert spies such as Jean Martin de Laubardemont or Monsieur Tardif, also in the congregation, who was to be found with the title of *lieutenant-criminal* searching bookshops after the appearance of Pascal's *Première Provinciale*, may well be explained by the desire of those in power not to leave unsupervised these discreet meetings of influential people.[30]

So, to advance the analysis, we need to study the group as a whole, not simply a few easily recognisable names. This is all the more necessary in that many of the members – Nicolas Fouquet provides the most striking example – did not become famous till long after their entry into the sodality, and we should not allow what we know of the future to distort the reality of the period 1630–40. Therefore to study the group in its dynamic, as far as it is possible to do so, the posts held at the time of enrolment have been distinguished from those held at the end of a person's career (see table 2, p. 98). It has not been possible to identify all the members, it is true, but with 96 identifications out of 118, and 90 references giving indications of career, the table as a whole has some credibility.

The first observation concerns the relative diversity of those enrolled. Drapers, apothecaries and booksellers, usually endowed with the title of magistrate, were not lacking in this old commercial district of Paris. Nor were minor abbés, who could not all, given how many there were, have been expecting a mitre or even a canonry. Three categories, however, predominate: the King's Council, the *cours souverains* and finance. In practice, these headings must be understood as, largely, in the case of the King's Council, *maîtres des requêtes* (10 out of 14); in the case of finance, treasurers of France (8 out of 9); and in the case of the *cours souverains*, the counsellors in Parlement, but with a not inconsiderable number of judges from provincial courts. Further, if certain categories are combined, especially groups 1, 2 and 13, to which can be added, in part, groups 3, 4, 5 and 6, one is forced to conclude that direct service of the King (royal household) was predominant, and increasingly so with the passage of time. It seems as if to become ordinary master of the household was a desirable, and, in general, quite common goal for a treasurer of France.

[30] Sainte-Beuve, *Port-Royal*, 7 vols. (Paris), vol. 3, p. 56 (Tardif); Coste, *Le Grand Saint*, vol. 3, p. 156 (the same informed M. Vincent that a letter of his was to be found in the papers of the Abbé de Saint-Cyran).

Table 2. *The congregation and the court at the time of Louis XIII (the Gentlemen of the Jesuit professed house)*

	Offices at entry to congregation	Offices at end of career
A: Laity		
1. King's Council and Government	14	14
2. Offices at the court	6	12
3. Governors and equivalent	1	2
4. Magnate households	4	3
5. Army	4	3
6. Nobles without office	7	7
7. *Cours souverains*	13	11
8. Financial administration	9+1[a]	8+4
9. Miscellaneous offices	2	2
10. *Avocats*	2	2
11. Trade/business	8	6
12. Miscellaneous	2	1
	72[b]	71
B: Ecclesiastics		
13. Court chaplains	4	2
14. Offices in the dioceses	1	6 (including 3 bishops)
15. Abbés and equivalent	13	11
Total	90	90

[a] The treasurers of France who occupied a post at court. They have been counted in group 2.
[b] The different totals for the beginning and end of career are explained by the entry into orders of one member. He is therefore to be found amongst the ecclesiastics at the end of his career.

This does not, oddly enough, preclude a great diversity in the ties of clientage. The *parti dévot* was represented, hardly surprisingly, by the Comtesse de Maure already mentioned and by René Frotté, former secretary to the Maréchal de Marillac, who remained faithful to him right up to his execution, and was accordingly regarded as a trifle simple-minded by the court.[31]

[31] A. N. Paris, Y 180, fo. 216, 193, fo. 347v; Jean-Paul Charmeil, *Les Trésoriers de France à l'époque de la Fronde: contribution à l'histoire de l'administration financière sous l'Ancien Régime* (Paris, 1964), pp. 106, 131, 269–70; Tallemant des Réaux, *Historiettes*, vol. 1, p. 291, vol. 2, p. 200.

But these reminders of the past were outnumbered by the loyal followers of the princes and powerful men of the present. The house of Gaston d'Orléans was present in the persons of the latter's chamberlain, the famous Vaugelas, and Claude Goulas and Abbé Hallwin, both followers of the Duke by family tradition.[32] So, also, was the Abbé de Lingendes, who had preached so well before the court on that memorable 9 May 1641, but who 'would more likely have been a bishop' according to Tallemant des Réaux, 'if he had not been with Monsieur'.[33] The same was probably the case, at least for a time, with Charles de Besançon, 'Counsellor to the King in his Councils of State and of War, Commissioner-General of his camps and armies'.[34] It is true that one memoirist saw Besançon as a man wholly committed to Cardinal Richelieu.[35] But we encounter here one of those cases of overlapping loyalties which seem by no means uncommon among the members of the congregation of the professed house. The Abbé de Lingendes served the Cardinal after having been with Monsieur.[36] In so doing, he was behaving like his patron and brother in the congregation, Sublet de Noyers, who was attached to the Marillac at the time of their splendour, as was *président* Amelot.[37] Some people could see nothing wrong in occupying, whilst in the service of the King, some important post with one of the princes; one such was Monsieur Le Nain, counsellor in the Paris Parlement, then *maître des requêtes*, but also *chef du conseil* of Madame de Longueville; and another was François-Théodore de Nesmond, Chief Justice, and later first *président*, but also Superintendant of the Household of the Prince de Condé, which cannot but have posed problems of conscience for these worthy judges at the time of the Fronde.[38]

32 B. N. Paris, Hozier collection, 168 (Goulas); Father Anselme, *Histoire généalogique et chronologique de la Maison royale de France, des Pairs, Grands Officiers* (Paris, 1728), vol. 3, p. 915 (Hallwin).

33 Tallemant des Réaux, *Historiettes*, vol. 2, pp. 324, 779–80.

34 A. N. Paris, Y 187, fo. 29; M. C. Paris, study LXXIII, 390 (1647); Tallemant des Réaux, *Historiettes*, vol. 1, pp. 736–7.

35 The Comte de Brienne, *Mémoires*, Collection nouvelle des Mémoires pour servir à l'histoire de France, series 3, vol. 3, p. 32.

36 It was he who introduced the young Abbé de Retz to Cardinal Richelieu: Cardinal de Retz, *Mémoires*, ed. Marie-Thérèse Hipp and Michel Pernot (Paris, 1984), p. 9.

37 Sublet de Noyers was connected with the Marillacs through his uncle M. de Marigny, *surintendant des finances*; through him he knew Louise de Marillac: Vincent de Paul, *Correspondance*, vol. 1, p. 345; for *président* Jacques Amelot, see M. C. Paris, study XXIV, 322 (1628).

38 B. N. Paris, French MSS, 32785, pp. 545–7; Louis Moreri, *Le Grand Dictionnaire historique* (Le Nain); A. N. Paris, Y 180, fo. 292; M. C. Paris, study XIX, 427 (1643); B. N. Paris, French MSS, 32785, pp. 398–9 (de Nesmond).

A further complication lay in the fact that many of these highly placed men also had their network of connections, even clients. François Sublet de Noyers, Secretary of State, did business with *président* de Mesmes and had more or less dependent on him the bookseller Sébastien Cramoisy, also in the congregation, who represented him in many transactions, and also, probably, Jean de Donon, Controller-General of the Royal Buildings (when Sublet de Noyers was Superintendent of the Buildings and Factories of France), whose name appeared alongside that of his patron in many deeds registered by the latter.[39]

Thus little sub-groups are visible within the congregation – a patron (Sublet de Noyers) and his clients, for example, or the house of the Duc d'Orléans – without it being remotely possible to say that it was dominated by one group, or that it was the affair of one clique. The same is true with family relationships. There were inevitably several brothers-in-law. Jean Sevin de Bandeville and Jean-Pierre de Montchal, both *maîtres des requêtes*, had married the sisters du Pré, also daughters of a *maître des requêtes*.[40] The families of de Mesmes, Thiersault and de Lorthon were all closely related.[41] So were the Le Nain and the de Bragelongne families, and the families of de Mesmes and Barillon.[42] This is hardly surprising in this world of top lawyers and Parisian families who often resided in the same district. It is, rather, surprising that family ties were not more common.

Further, it does not seem that all the members of the congregation had been trained, prior to their enrolment, in identical habits of piety. Beside certain families already well known at the beginning of the century for their participation in great charitable works (such as the de Mesmes, Barillon, de Bragelongne, Fouquet, Maupeou, Amelot and Legras families),[43] and those *sodales* who were related to the great reforming bishops (such as Antoine Danès, brother of the Bishop of Toulon, and Jean-Pierre de Montchal, half-brother of the

[39] M. C. Paris, study XLIII, 30, 31, 32 (1640–1, deeds of Sébastien Cramoisy 'acting for' François Sublet de Noyers); M. C. Paris, study XXIV, 418 (1641), numerous deeds in the presence of Jean de Donon; M. C. Paris, study XXIV, 344 (1636), business dealings with J. A. de Mesmes and F. Sublet de Noyers.

[40] B. N. Paris, French MSS, 32788, pp. 369–71, 482–3; 32785, pp. 519–20.

[41] A. N. Paris, Y 187, fo. 178; Y 172, fo. 251v.

[42] B. N. Paris, French MSS, 32785, pp. 545–7: the mother of Jean Le Nain was a Bragelongne; the mother of Antoine Barillon was a de Mesmes: B. N. Paris, French MSS, 32788, p. 356.

[43] See, amongst others, Vincent de Paul, *Correspondance*.

Archbishop of Toulouse and husband of the great-niece of St François de Paule),[44] there were others whose antecedents or ties of friendship come as a surprise. These include Monsieur d'Amours, of Protestant origin, Monsieur Berger, newly converted, as were, probably, Messieurs de Besançon and Tardif.[45] Even stranger are the links of the Comtesse de Maure with the nuns of Port-Royal, with whom her sister-in-law, the Duchesse d'Atri, lived.[46] It is true that the Countess, wife of congregation member Louis de Rochechouart, was generally known by the nickname 'the madwoman'. But Jean Le Nain, 'one of the worthiest judges to appear in the seventeenth century', had anything but a reputation for being soft in the head. Yet his sympathies with notorious Jansenists such as Dugué de Bagnols, a fellow *maître des requêtes*, are documented.[47] Did the influences which marked the piety of the father also determine the vocation of the son, the celebrated Sébastien Le Nain de Tillemont, hermit of Port-Royal and author of the *Histoire ecclésiastique*? It is, in fact, difficult to talk of Jansenism in 1635, before the appearance of the *Augustinus* and the *Fréquente Communion*. It was at most a question of a certain sensibility, or an orientation of thought, either of which, in fact, could easily, at the period in question, be shared by men who were later positively hostile to Jansenism, even, indeed, by Jesuits.

Other contrasts are equally surprising. Alongside saintly men like Gaston de Renty, or Adrien Le Bon, Prior of Saint-Lazare, who resigned from his benefice so as to permit Vincent de Paul to develop his work, or famous 'converts' like Noël Brulart de Sillery and Thomas Le Gauffre, *conseiller-maître* to the Chambre des Comptes, who, after meeting Claude Bernard, 'the poor priest', quit the world

[44] A. N. Paris, Y 200 (1661); de La Chenaye-Desbois, *Dictionnaire de la noblesse*, vol. 6, cols. 752–3 (Danès); B. N. Paris, French MSS, 32785, pp. 519–20; de La Chenaye-Desbois, *Dictionnaire de la noblesse*, vol. 14, cols. 149–51; Coste, *Le Grand Saint*, vol. 2, p. 363.

[45] Haag, *La France protestante*, 9 vols. (Paris, 1846–59), vol. 1, pp. 68–70 (d'Amours); B. N. Paris, French MSS, 32788, pp. 26, 231–2; de L'Estoile, *Journal*, vol. 2, p. 469; Jacques Pannier, *L'Eglise réformée de Paris sous Louis XIII (1610–1621)* (Paris, 1922), pp. 184–7 (Berger); for the others, see above.

[46] A. N. Paris, Y 188, fo. 36v.

[47] M. C. Paris, study LXXV, 95 (1657), will of M. Dugué de Bagnols, who charged M. Le Nain with responsibility for a considerable foundation, though one which remains obscure, in the terms advocated by the Society of the Holy Sacrament in such circumstances; Raoul Allier, *La Compagnie du Très Saint Sacrement de l'Autel: la 'Cabale des dévots', 1627–1666* (Paris, 1902), p. 32.

to live only for distant missions, there were *sodales* who seem to have been inspired only by ambition, or even the search for pleasure, like Martin de Laubardemont and Nicolas Fouquet.[48]

In fact, rather than bringing together men who were already of like mind, the characteristic of the congregation of the professed house, here as elsewhere – and perhaps more in Paris than elsewhere – was to give unity to an association which, when all is said and done, was to a large extent composed of persons from different backgrounds, with different sensibilities, and often belonging to opposed coteries. To unite what was formerly divided, and to bring together those who seemed destined not only not to respect each other, but never even to meet, appears to have been the key idea presiding over recruitment to the Parisian association in its early days.

PARIS: THE FUNCTIONS OF THE CONGREGATION OF GENTLEMEN

To this end, the Jesuits counted on the common devotions and habits of piety acquired over the years. An incident in the life of Nicolas Fouquet speaks volumes about the effects of such practices. When, after his disgrace, the brilliant *surintendant des finances* awaited the verdict which would reduce him to absolute and definitive silence, he could find nothing better to do with his time than consecrate it to the composition of an *Office de la sainte et immaculée conception de la glorieuse Vierge Marie*.[49] Thus those *sodales* who appeared the least zealous, ended up, all the same, at one of life's decisive moments, by adopting the behaviour of devout Marians.

Other activities enabled the Gentlemen to act in common and demonstrate their spirit of unity, amongst them the great charitable works of the seventeenth century – the general hospital, the Hospital of the Incurables and assistance to prisoners. They also assisted St Vincent de Paul in his work, whether this involved missions into the countryside, training the secular clergy, or protecting foundlings. Of the ninety persons identified, at least thirty had some connection with the saint.[50] Many wives of congregation members were amongst the first Daughters of Charity, zealous and effective assistants of Louise

[48] A. N. Paris, Y 173, fo. 329v; M. C. Paris, studies II, 188, VIII, 583, IX, 381, 400 (Le Bon); Coste, *Le Grand Saint*, vol. 3, pp. 313–14; Beauchet-Filleau, *Annales*, p. 92 (Thomas Le Gauffre). For Nicolas Fouquet and Martin de Laubardemont, see above, notes 20 and 22.

[49] *Dictionnaire de biographie française*, part 80, cols. 712–18.

[50] According to Vincent de Paul, *Correspondance*, and Coste, *Le Grand Saint*.

de Marillac. These included Mesdames Barillon, de Bragelongne and Le Roux, Mademoiselle Hardy, who vigorously solicited Vincent de Paul on behalf of orphans, and Madame de Nesmond, who was one of the founders, along with Marie de Maupeou, mother of Nicolas Fouquet, and regarded as 'one of the most admirable'.[51]

Foreign missions also attracted the energies of many *sodales*. Antoine Barillon, Laurent de Brisacier and Jean-Marie Lhoste were amongst those who prepared the way for the establishment of the seminary in the Rue du Bac.[52] Not content with participating in the training of a specialised clergy, and imitating once again the Neapolitan brethren of the Holy Sacrament, who, at the beginning of the century, had proposed the foundation of a Monte for this purpose, they wished to intervene directly in support of the missions.[53] In these years of Louis XIII's reign, when the Jesuits sent numerous fathers, many of whom suffered martyrdom, across the Atlantic, it was Canada which aroused enthusiasm, Sébastien Cramoisy, the bookseller of the Rue Saint-Jacques, trusted agent of Sublet de Noyers, Richelieu and many French bishops, was also in 1633 procurator for the Compagnie de la Nouvelle-France, and, in this capacity, received and transmitted to Canada the large sums which the Duchesse d'Aiguillon intended for the Hospitaller nuns of Quebec.[54] Bertrand Drouart, several times Superior of the Society of the Holy Sacrament, was, from 1634, a member of the Montreal Society, the society inspired by the Jesuits and constituted with a view to the purchase of the island which was to become the site of Ville Marie.[55] At the head of this society, as if by chance, was another Superior of the Holy Sacrament, a man of wide involvement in good works, Antoine Barillon.[56] It was another brother and congregation member, Thomas Le Gauffre (who was involved with both Jesuit missions and those of the Sulpicians), who came to mind when the

[51] Coste, *Le Grand Saint*.

[52] *Ibid*., p. 218; *Dictionnaire de biographie française*, part 26, col. 473 (Barillon); Vincent de Paul, *Correspondance*, vol. 2, p. 484 (de Brisacier).

[53] Edmond Lamalle, S. J., 'La propagande du père Nicolas Trigault en faveur des missions en Chine (1616)', *Archivum historicum Societatis Iesu* (Jan.–June 1940), pp. 49–120.

[54] A. N. Paris, Y 179, fo. 206v, Y 180, fo. 203.

[55] Beauchet-Filleau, *Annales*, p. 56; *Dictionnaire biographique du Canada* (Laval, 1966), vol. 1, pp. 439–41 (Lauson article).

[56] A. N. Paris, Y 199, fo. 282v. Acting in the name of the Compagnie de Montreal in New France 'for the conversion of the savages', donation to the parish church of Notre-Dame de Montreal of the newly cleared lands in the territory of Sainte-Marie de Montréal (1661).

question of nominating a bishop for Canada arose.[57] Six years later, the governor appointed for New France (1651–6), Monsieur de Lauson, former director of the Compagnie des Cent Associés, was one of the first members of the congregation.[58] Thus the congregation members were interested not only in missions, but also in colonisation, though at a period, it is true, when it is often difficult to distinguish the two.

Above all, very strong links bound together from the start the congregation of Gentlemen of the Saint-Paul quarter and the famous Society of the Holy Sacrament. The latter had been constituted at almost the same time as the sodality of the professed house (1630).[59] It had links with the same important persons in the French Church (Vincent de Paul and the Jesuits). It was interested in the same good works: the general hospital, the Hôtel-Dieu, 'Christian charity', 'poor prisoners' and foreign missions. It was organised according to the same principles. Established in Paris, it was not long in spreading to the provinces. Its various societies were in correspondence with one another.[60] In Paris, supervision of the districts was organised according to the model already practised by the *sodales* of Cologne and Antwerp.[61]

And last and by no means least, a comparison of the registers of the two societies shows their close ties and the presence of the same men in both.[62] In addition to Gaston de Renty, already mentioned, we should note Antoine Barillon, *maître des requêtes*, one of the founder members of the sodality and one of the first recorded brothers of the famous Society, of which he was more than once Superior; also Pierre Chomel, former counsellor to the Parlement of Paris, who later became priest and Vicar-General under the Bishop of Saint-Flour; also Bertrand Drouart, equerry-in-ordinary to the Duc d'Orléans, René Le Roux, *maître des requêtes*, Jean-Marie Lhoste, *avocat* in Parlement, and, of course, *président* de Mesmes, who succeeded Baron de Renty as Superior.[63] Of more modest rank, but equally

[57] Beauchet-Filleau, *Annales*, p. 98; Coste, *Le Grand Saint*, vol. 3, pp. 313–14.

[58] B. N. Paris, French MSS, 32788, p. 289; *Dictionnaire biographique du Canada*, vol. 1, pp. 439–41. [59] Allier, *La Compagnie du Très Saint Sacrement*, p. 42.

[60] Rebelliau, *La Compagnie secrète*.

[61] Allier, *La Compagnie du Très Saint Sacrement*, p. 104.

[62] A. N. Paris, MM 649, 650, 651; Beauchet-Filleau, *Annales*.

[63] *Ibid.*, p. 77; Rebelliau, *La Compagnie secrète*, pp. 56, 57, 59, 60–5, 85, 95 (Barillon); *ibid.*, p. 15; *Dictionnaire de biographie française*, part 44, col. 1245 (Chomel); B. N. Paris, Hozier collection, 123; Beauchet-Filleau, *Annales*, p. 56; Rebelliau, *La*

active, were the good and faithful René Frotté, Martin de Bragelongne, whose celebrated piety was still renowned well into the eighteenth century, Jacques d'Amours, Jean Lecomte, Master of Revels to the King, and Abbé Perriquet, attached to the Fouquet, all secretaries or influential members of the illustrious Society.[64]

Other members of the congregation were also members of the Society, such as Guillaume Bidé, *maître des requêtes*, Jean Bardin, *président* of the Chambre des Comptes of Burgundy, Abbé Laurent de Brisacier, chaplain to Louis XIII, Counsellor of State, future tutor of Louis XIV and entrusted with a mission to Rome by the Society, François Fouquet, brother of Nicolas, who also protected the Society and participated in certain of its meetings, Catherin La Fontaine, bourgeois merchant of Paris, Abbé La Verchère, Thomas Le Gauffre, another saintly man, Mathias Marguerie, *maître des requêtes*, Abbé Maupas, soon appointed Bishop of Le Puy, and no doubt others.[65] It is saying very little, and not altogether accurate, to state that the congregation of Gentlemen of the Church of Saint-Louis was the antechamber of the great Catholic secret society. In the number and quality of the superiors it furnished, and in the zealous and ever-ready workers it trained, it appears rather as its reserve army or perhaps even its general staff. As Raoul Allier clearly realised, the congregations served as supports to the Society of the Holy Sacrament and its provincial daughters, and they offered it the means of continuing its activities when it was compelled, at least in Paris, to dissolve.

Thus was established in France, and in Paris in particular, a veritable devout system, at the heart of which the congregations of Gentlemen, that of the Saint-Paul quarter in particular, occupied a privileged position (see figure 11, p. 106). This network of pious

Compagnie secrète, pp. 11–78 (Drouart); B. N. Paris, French MSS, 32785, p. 511; Beauchet-Filleau, *Annales*, p. 198; Rebelliau, *La Compagnie secrète*, pp. 45–54, 75 (Le Roux); A. N. Paris, Y 186, fo. 38v, 189, fo. 307, 192, fo. 440; Beauchet-Filleau, *Annales*, pp. 179, 218 (Lhoste); *ibid.*, pp. 105, 112, 183, 266, 269; Rebelliau, *La Compagnie secrète*, p. 75 (de Mesmes).

64 *Ibid.*, pp. 63, 67–8 (Frotté); *ibid.*, p. 65 (d'Amours); *ibid.*, pp. 75–6 (Bragelongne); Tallemant des Réaux, *Historiettes*, vol. 2, p. 1,289 (Lecomte); Rebelliau, *La Compagnie secrète*, pp. 40–2 (Perriquet).

65 *Ibid.*, p. 85 (Bidé), p. 77 (Bardin); Vincent de Paul, *Correspondance*, vol. 2, p. 484; Beauchet-Filleau, *Annales*, p. 189 (de Brisacier); *ibid.*, pp. 67, 181, 219 (François Fouquet); *ibid.*, p. 261 (Nicolas Fouquet); Rebelliau, *La Compagnie secrète*, p. 78 (La Fontaine); Beauchet-Filleau, *Annales*, pp. 21, 67 (La Verchère); *ibid.*, p. 92 (Le Gauffre); Vincent de Paul, *Correspondance*, vol. 2, p. 28 (Marguerie); *Dictionnaire de Spiritualité*, part 64, cols. 825–6 (Maupas).

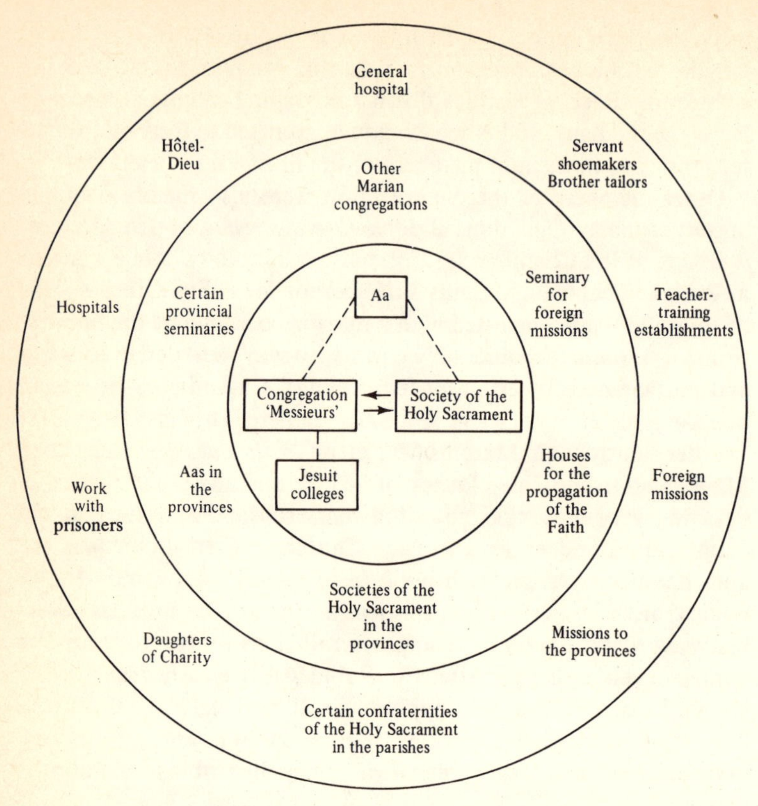

11. The 'devout system' in France

activities, which soon covered the entire kingdom, was clearly created in response to charitable and missionary intentions. But one may wonder to what extent these, in themselves, justified such an organisation. Was the objective perhaps, in reality, much more far-reaching? The study of the occupations of the people who composed the congregation of Gentlemen suggests another interpretation.

Direct royal service, as we have shown, accounted for more than half of those identified. Take the court first: Louis de Rochechouart, Comte de Maure, and Philippe de La Trémoille, Seneschal of Poitou, were the only great lords.[66] Nor was there any powerful minister other than François Sublet de Noyers. At court there were only

[66] Anselme, *Histoire généalogique*, vol. 4, pp. 174–5 (de La Trémoille).

masters of the household, chaplains, a Jean Lecomte, Master of Revels, a Saldebreil de Brullon, usher of ambassadors, and a Barthélemy Rolland, secretary-interpreter of the King in the German language.[67] The Abbé de Brisacier, though tutor to Louis XIV, was only the assistant, and subject to the direction of Monsieur de Péréfixe. The Gentlemen included no or very few of the most important people, but they were men who were in daily contact with the King, the Queen, the Dauphin, the principal ministers and the most powerful lords, whether the Condé or the Duc d'Orléans. This was perhaps what was intended – a continuous, discreet and modest presence, close to those in power, in such a way as to demonstrate in all circumstances, by example and, if need be, by advice, the way to behave.

Father Nicolas Caussin, Louis XIII's confessor in 1637, seems to have put these fine principles into practice rather too enthusiastically, since his stay at court was short.[68] He expounded them at length in a book destined to have a great success, *La Cour sainte*. At the beginning, seized with enthusiasm for the task he assigned to the courtiers and by the prospect of eventual success, he wrote: 'Do you see, O Nobles, what influence example can exercise over the hearts of men? It is up to you to create here and now a new world, and banish vice from the earth, so that a golden age can flourish.'[69] Was it not the aim of the congregation of Gentlemen, thanks to the example provided by its members, and to their constant penitence, to make the Louvre of Louis XIII into a true holy court?

After those in direct royal service came the high-ranking administration, the nobility and the clergy. It is hardly likely to be coincidental that the treasurers of France constituted an important group within the congregation of the Rue Saint-Antoine. In addition to those of Paris, well represented, there were the treasurers of Soissons, Orléans, Outre-Seine and Yonne, Rouen, Le Mans and Amiens.[70] The whole Parisian basin was involved. Among the *maîtres des requêtes* and members of Parlement, there were many who were commissioned in the various provinces of France. Martin de Laubardemont had been

[67] M. C. Paris, study LXXIII, 359 (1640) (de Brullon); A. N. Paris, Y 175, fo. 167 (Rolland). [68] Rochemonteix, *Nicolas Caussin*.

[69] Nicolas Caussin, *La Cour sainte*, 2 vols. (Rouen, 1655), vol. 1, p. 32.

[70] Paris: Hardy (son), Le Gras; Soissons: Bérault, du Fayot; Orléans: Courlay; Outre-Seine and Yonne: Danès; Rouen: Guybert; Le Mans: Hardy (father); Amiens: Piètre, Trudaine.

first *président* of the Cour des Aides of Guyenne before entering the congregation; Thiersault would be intendant of Alençon, de Lauson intendant of Provence, and Barillon, king-pin of the Society of the Holy Sacrament, was intendant at Bar-le-Duc and *président* of the Parlement of Saint-Mihiel at the time of the first French intervention in Lorraine in 1634; nor should we forget Nicolas Fouquet, at that time attached to the *conseil souverain* of Nancy, and Jean Bardin, *président* of the Chambre des Comptes of Burgundy.[71]

The members of the nobility who appear from the sources to be without specific offices were often connected through their lands to more or less distant regions, as, for example, Monsieur de Renty to Normandy. In the case of the abbés, in the years following their enrolment many were nominated to distant episcopal sees, such as François Fouquet to Bayonne, then Agde, then Narbonne, Jean de Lingendes to Sarlat and Henri de Maupas to Le Puy. These people, members of the congregation as well as, in many cases, affiliated to the Society of the Holy Sacrament, occupying foremost positions in their province, not only had a mission to serve as models for their region, but ought also to use the power at their disposal to influence society and its institutions. At court and in town, in the provinces and in the countryside, they aimed to put into practice the Ignation principle of reforming the world.

Thus the twofold aim of the congregations intended for the ruling classes emerges clearly, in Paris and Munich alike, at the beginning of the seventeenth century. After the troubles of the sixteenth century, which had had their effect on society, accentuating its divisions, provoking new dissension both between and within families, and often producing an increase in clientage and warring factions, the aim of the congregations consisted in the first place of uniting men in loyalty to the Virgin and in a religion lived intensely. In fact, in Munich and Paris – with more success, certainly, in the case of the former – one can see an attempt to reconstitute a society, the desire to create at all points a Catholic élite destined to surround and serve the Christian prince. But this could only be a stage towards the achievement of the second objective, clearly visible in the recruitment of the *sodales* (court, nobility, high administration), which was the realisation of the Christian State.

[71] B. N. Paris, French MSS, 32786 (Thiersault); A. N. Paris, Y 175, fo. 82v (Bardin).

Within the space of a few years, Catholic Europe was thickly scattered with Marian congregations. They were everywhere, they involved all social groups and all ages, they overlapped with professional associations. Their success was due, it is clear, to their complete adaptation to countries and their traditions and modes of government, and to towns with their special functions, along with, at the same time, a constant concern for change. But it also corresponded to a clearly defined project which the Jesuits zealously pursued wherever they were. It was not simply a matter of adding a pious association to the numerous confraternities which proliferated throughout the seventeenth century. The intention was no more and no less than to change the relationships which existed between men. In regrouping them, first of all, giving nobles, merchants and craftsmen that spirit of union which they too often lacked, the congregations were a cohesive factor. But they were also intended to be the ferment of a new society. Every congregation member was invited to serve as a model for others, those who remained outside the association and whom it was the intention to influence in their professional, family and worldly lives. Thus, little by little, the global change could be realised.

PART III *The problem of the consequences*

In the light of so much effort, the results may appear modest. Did the Thirty Years' War, the popular revolts and the French Fronde perhaps compromise, sometimes irrevocably, the early results achieved? In any case, the princes, the Church and the interested parties themselves did not always show much enthusiasm for collaborating in the great project that had been put before them. They often, indeed, viewed it with suspicion. Worse, they were ready to divert the institution away from its aims. Princes saw in it a means to consolidate their power; nobility, clergy and bourgeoisie saw in it an opportunity to advance themselves in the world; craftsmen and journeymen, the possibility of reconstituting within the crafts the prohibited unions. As for Christians of only average zeal, some were no doubt tempted to seek in the congregations an assurance of Paradise, at a late stage and little cost. Pascal's *Provinciales* (*Provincial Letters*) and Molière's *Tartuffe* serve to show that the *dévots* provoked the disapproval of strict Catholics, and aroused the distrust of the authorities and the mockery of the people. But we need, perhaps, to look beyond this and ask whether the violent reactions provoked are to be explained only by the scandal of the distortion of this Jesuit enterprise. It contained enough novelty with regard to the family and society, as well as in the manner of living one's religion, to disquiet the champions of tradition.

7. *Society*

However often the founders of the congregations said that they wanted to transform the world, it would be a mistake to see them as revolutionaries. Their words, it goes without saying, should not be understood in this mundane sense. This does not mean that their projects, though aimed at hearts and minds, did not have larger consequences. The charitable works undertaken in Naples and Paris alike are one demonstration of this. But there are consequences of greater importance to be explored. Initially established in harmony with social structures, would the congregations restrict themselves to reflecting these, or would they, on the contrary, little by little, affect them or influence their development? And in what direction? It was not, in practice, only a question of what was intended by the Jesuits. Princes, nobles, burgesses and craftsmen all had to be contended with; they constituted their own associations and had their own ambitions, which were by no means always, once the act of consecration had been spoken aloud, candle in hand, purely spiritual in character. It is this dialectical process between the original project, promoted better or worse according to place and persons, and the incessant interventions of history which we must now assess and examine.

FROM THE UNION OF PRINCES TO THE CHRISTIAN FATHERLAND

The desire to build a Christian State, widespread since the beginnings of Christianity, had been revived with stronger arguments and hopes since Erasmus and Christian humanism. The Jesuits made an important contribution to this line of thinking. In a way, and in the very muted form which was all that was compatible with the institutions and ways of thought of the kingdom of France, *La Cour sainte* belonged to this tradition. But, at the time when this work was published – and it immediately enjoyed a tremendous success – many people, both at court and throughout the country, thought that the moment had come to go further and contemplate the reconciliation and union of all the Catholic princes opposed to heresy, whether it be Louis XIII and the Huguenots of Béarn and soon of La Rochelle, or Ferdinand II in Bohemia.[1] There can be no doubt that this *parti dévot*, as it was called, enjoyed the sympathy and sometimes the active co-operation of many members of the Society of Jesus. The correspondence between Father Suffren, confessor to the King of France, and his colleague, Father de Lamormaini, responsible for the soul of the Emperor, is illuminating on this score.[2] And the activities of Father Suffren's successor, Father Caussin, in 1637, when France was fully committed to the Protestant princes in the Thirty Years' War, have to be seen in this context. 'I am doing everything in my power', he wrote to the General, 'for the peace and concord of the Christian world.'[3] What he really meant was, 'I must demonstrate [to the King] that it is an abominable crime, a crime advised by the Cardinal and by Father Joseph, to ally with the heretical princes and to bring the Turks into Germany to wage war on the Emperor of Austria.'[4]

This was a tough and uncompromising policy, in line, no doubt, with the ideas circulating in the devout world in 1625, but it was no longer appropriate a dozen years later, when war was raging only a few leagues from Paris, and Cardinal Richelieu was all-powerful. Nicolas Caussin paid for his blunders with exile to Quimper, which put a stop to his ambitious projects. Were they shared by the congregations and, in particular, by the Gentlemen of the Saint-Paul quarter? It seems highly unlikely. Its members, though very different in their careers and affiliations, were mostly too clever politicians not to see what was outdated and unrealistic in the schemes of an irresponsible churchman.[5] They were also, perhaps, too much 'good Frenchmen' to give them wholehearted approval. The idea of a 'devout international' aiming to restore the lost unity of the Catholic world, whatever its attractions, was totally unrealistic in the Europe of the 1630s.

On the other hand, it is perfectly consistent with the spirit and ways of the congregation to suppose that they would have greatly rejoiced

[1] See, on this subject, the excellent work of Victor-Lucien Tapié, *La France de Louis XIII et de Richelieu* (Paris, 1952).

[2] A. S. J. Rome, province of France, 33^{I}, fos. 22–3 (letter of 9 January 1630).

[3] Rochemonteix, *Nicolas Caussin*, p. 178. [4] *Ibid.*, p. 190.

[5] See chapter 6.

at the consecration of France to the Virgin by Louis XIII's famous vow in 1637, and even that they encouraged the monarch to accomplish this pious act (although no document, to our knowledge, provides proof of it).[6] It was, after all, Francis Coster himself who gave the congregation as its principal mission the restoration in all her glory of the Mother of God at the head of cities. To make her the protectress and mistress of states was to carry out the wishes of the man who had wanted to revive her cult throughout Christendom.[7] The act of the King of France was not unique in Europe. It was one of a cluster which included similar acts by at least the Emperor, the Duke of Bavaria and the magistrates of many towns, who all either belonged to or were strongly inspired by the congregation. The example was set in 1620 by the Emperor Ferdinand II, who, on the eve of joining battle against the rebellious Czechs, consecrated himself afresh to the Virgin (though long a congregation member) and publicly declared her to be the generalissimo of his armies.[8]

It was thus hardly by chance that Duke Maximilian I, wishing to demonstrate to the Mother of God the gratitude of the town of Munich and of a Bavaria which had emerged relatively unscathed from the Swedish assault, chose 8 November, the anniversary of the Battle of the White Mountain, for the solemn benediction of the Mariensäule (column to the Virgin) erected on what was to become the Marienplatz. It was the Duke himself, who was also the protector of the congregation throughout Germany, not to speak of prefect of the Munich Major, who presided over the ceremony in 1638. After the monument had been blessed by the Bishop of Freising, the Duke knelt piously at the foot of the column and, before the whole court, nobility and people of the town assembled in the square, humbly recited a prayer of gratitude; then, after making the sign of the blessing over himself, his family and all his people, he pronounced these words: 'Keep under your protection, O Holy Virgin, as its patron, your Bavaria, its property, its institutions, its lands and its religion!'[9]

Less spectacular, but equally significant, was the act of the young Emperor Ferdinand III, 'the very model of a congregation member',

[6] Louis Vaunois, *Le Vie de Louis XIII* (Paris, 1961), pp. 544–5 (on the King's vow).

[7] Coster, *Le Livre de la Compaignie*, introduction.

[8] Crasset, *Des congrégations de Notre-Dame*, pp. 109–11.

[9] Pichler, *Die Marianische deutsche Kongregation der Herren*, pp. 17–19.

who wrote in his own hand in the register of the Major of Louvain, under the date of 1640, a long entry which ended with these words:

> You will be the mistress of my States, my Kingdoms and my Empire; and also of my people and my armies. Protect them, render them victorious, reign over them, be their Empress, that is what I ardently desire. I who am yours by the duty of piety and justice.[10]

Following the example of these pious princes, magistrates placed their towns, too, under this lofty protection. After Antwerp, apparently the first, came Colmar, threatened by the Swedes, then Swiss Fribourg, threatened by Berne, and no doubt numerous others.[11]

This great European movement, which started in 1620 and culminated between 1630 and 1640, has to be considered in relation to the Marian congregations, which reached their peak from the point of view of numbers at just this period. Was this a dramatic manifestation of Catholic reform? Or was it a search for refuge and protection in the darkest hours of the Thirty Years' War? It was, no doubt, both. But it is difficult not to attach political significance to Ferdinand II's solemn act, imitated by other princes. In consecrating himself and his people to the Virgin, the Emperor was attempting to create a Catholic solidarity within Germany and to strengthen the often rather tenuous links which existed between him and the Catholics of the Germanic world. It was a community that he was trying to establish, and one which transcended the bounds of the Holy Empire. At Antwerp in 1620, public supplications were held in the church of the professed house on news of the imminent battle against the Calvinists. Preacher followed preacher, and their enthusiasm so fired the multitude that the latter thronged into the sanctuary and uttered fervent prayers. One of them, Father de Marca, preaching on the twenty-second Sunday after Pentecost on the text for the day, 'Render unto God the things which are God's and unto Caesar the things which are Caesar's', cried out three times, 'Palatine! Palatine! Render unto Caesar the things which are Caesar's.' At that very moment, hundreds of leagues away, the Imperial armies triumphed over the rebels – a supernatural sign which invested this feat of arms with a celestial, even miraculous,

[10] Crasset, *Des congrégations de Notre-Dame*, p. 119.
[11] B. H. Munich, Jesuits 104, fos. 141–4 (Colmar, 1632); N. P. Cologne, Hartmann MSS, vol. 3, fo. 26 (Fribourg, 1656).

aura. The explosion of joy which followed the news of the victory, accompanied by Te Deums in the churches, bonfires throughout the town and the firing of all the canons in the citadel, was on a scale appropriate to the event. It celebrated, in the words of the editor of the *Annals*, 'the glorious triumph of the Holy Emperor Ferdinand II, so devoted to the interests of the Society'.[12]

With such outbreaks of rejoicing so far from the battlefield, one can well imagine the enthusiasm in Austria and Bavaria. In Ingolstadt, Eichstätt and Munich supplications, processions and pilgrimages followed one another before the battle, and after it came demonstrations of gratitude. Statues of Our Lady of Victory appeared in every church belonging to the Society. The *sodales* of Ingolstadt placed themselves more particularly under her protection, and built a chapel in her honour in 1620.[13] Their resplendent Virgin drew all eyes with the inscription 'Sancta Maria de Victoria Urbis Tutela, Civium Patrona'.[14]

When, at the height of the Thirty Years' War, the victorious progress of Gustavus Adolphus threatened the Catholic territories of Southern Germany, unity was restored, stronger than ever, round the Virgin and the Emperor. This time, it was not only the bourgeoisie of Bavaria and Swabia who went on long pilgrimages and endured painful mortifications, but also the Neapolitans, who prayed and scourged themselves, united in intent with their brothers in Germany.[15] A chain of pro-Imperial solidarity was established across Europe; and it was composed primarily of the congregations, who made the Emperor's cause the Virgin's, and thus their own. They were not content with prayer and relaying news. They took up arms, joined battle and bullied the hesitant and the timorous. The fortress of Eichstätt was delivered in 1633 by an army composed to a large extent of student and bourgeois congregation members from Ingolstadt.[16] A certain noble member of the sodality who did not immediately spring to arms was held up to scorn until at last he did his duty.[17]

A play presented before the Duke of Bavaria and his court in 1636 had the significant title 'La vertu du *sodalis* n'obscurcit pas la gloire

[12] A. P. B. M. Namur, Droeshout deposit 24,1, pp. 424–6.
[13] B. H. Munich, Jesuits 103, fos. 11–18. [14] *Ibid.*, Jesuits 104, fo. 193v.
[15] A. S. J. Rome, province of Naples, 73, fo. 358.
[16] B. H. Munich, Jesuits 104, fo. 193v. [17] *Ibid.*, Jesuits 106, pp. 4–6.

militaire'.[18] It could hardly be made more plain that the virtue appropriate to a congregation member and military glory were perfectly compatible one with the other, and that the place of the true congregation member, in these tragic times when the future of religion was in doubt, was on the field of battle by his Emperor's side. It was a matter of religion, certainly, but also of the fatherland. The *sodales* of Munich were invited in 1632 to fight, through prayer, the 'enemies of the fatherland'.[19] A link was being forged between Catholicism, the Christian prince and the *Vaterland*, and the Marian congregations made a major contribution to its realisation. This was vividly demonstrated when, in 1639, Urban VIII decreed a national jubilee for the needs of Germany.[20]

At this point it becomes easier to understand why, from the beginning, the Dukes of Bavaria had put themselves at the head of the congregation of the town where they lived, and why the Archdukes of Austria, including, of course, the future Emperor Ferdinand II, had done the same. Piety and the desire to support the Roman religion in conformity with the directives of the Council of Trent were not the only reasons. Political preoccupations were equally important. In a divided Germany, where first the Reformation and its consequences and then the Thirty Years' War had multiplied the seeds of division, the congregation offered princes opportunities for consolidation. The Emperor could use the bases it provided to strengthen among all Catholics living within the Holy Empire the consciousness of belonging to a vast community. The Duke of Bavaria, by gathering round him all those who shared his devotion to the Virgin, perhaps saw the means to secure more firmly the loyalty of his nobility and his people, who, in consecrating themselves to the Virgin, in a sense also dedicated themselves to the person who was her first defender in the country. The missionary project of the Jesuits thus became in his hands the instrument which would enable him to consolidate his state and strengthen his power.

It also becomes easier to understand the attitude of Louis XIII in this regard. If the Most Christian King had everything to gain from a

18 *Ibid.*, Jesuits 105, fo. 99v. 19 *Ibid.*, Jesuits 104, fo. 89v.

20 N. P. Cologne, Aegidius Gelenius, *Supplex Colonia sive Admiranda prae Seculis anteactis S. S. Corporum, Cleri et Populi Agrippinensis in publicum Processio octo continuos dies celebrata* (Cologne, 1639), pp. 209–40; H. A. S. Cologne, Jesuits 9, fos. 367–72v (two very detailed descriptions of the octave of prayers decreed at Cologne).

solemn act of consecration of his kingdom to the Virgin, on the pattern of the act accomplished by the Emperor some years before, an act which could only consolidate the cohesion of Catholics around his person, he had nothing to gain, and perhaps much to lose, in going further. To assume, like Maximilian I, the headship of a Marian congregation would be for the King, in the France of the Edict of Nantes and the Grace of Alès, the France of the Gallicans and the partisans of Rome, to deepen divisions further and weaken his own power. Did this not, after all, come direct from God, not via the Pope or the Church? Would it not, in a way, be injurious to the plenitude of monarchical power, which ministers and lawyers had been attempting to extend and strengthen for a century, to become a full member of an association based in Rome?

The study of the Marian congregations makes it possible to distinguish two conceptions of the Christian State. In one, the French, the sovereign kept his distance with regard to this Roman institution, but was happy to see those close to him enter its ranks. In the other, the Bavarian, the prince joined enthusiastically, with the whole of his court and his principal officers, giving the Munich Major a quasi-official character. In the former, the congregation seemed external to the State, even if, in certain circumstances, it was able to influence a decision or its application. In the latter, it was intimately linked to it, even one of its constituent parts.

FROM CLASS DIVISIONS TO CLASS UNITY

It is quite clear that, in creating the congregations, the Jesuits had no intention of changing social structure, but rather, on the contrary, of adapting to it. But, in giving as yet ill-defined groups a distinct place in their churches, did they not help to activate a movement which was already well under way in the towns of the modern period? This was the opinion of some of their opponents as early as the end of the sixteenth century.[21] The study of the situation in Naples around 1640 can only strengthen this view.

With their prestigious sodalities, the nobility dominated the religious, like the civil, life of this city. The congregation of the Holy Sacrament was the oldest; it was the most pious, since its members called themselves the 'communicant brothers', and at the same time it

[21] See chapter 2, note 21.

maintained great secrecy. The *Zitti* (the 'Silent Ones') took care to avoid being talked about. In this regard, as in matters of piety, they ceded in nothing to their brothers of the Nativity. Both manifested themselves publicly through the intermediary of their Monti, which occupied an essential role in Neapolitan life. The imposing Casa di Santa Fede, soon housed in the great Olciatti Palace, managed and distributed the revenues for the activities of the brethren of the Holy Sacrament, which included a refuge for repentent women, the repurchase of Christian slaves, a 'converts' house' for Turkish slaves being prepared for baptism, assistance to the Jesuit missions, and, before long, the opening of a special house where, under the direction of the fathers, the Exercises of St Ignatius could be practised.

The nobles of the Nativity did not lag behind with their own Monte, which supported the Hospital for Incurables and assisted the 'shamefaced poor'.[22] These shared activities, frequent prayer meetings in their oratory, austere retreats first with the Jesuits and then at the special house for making the Exercises, and the secret deliberations in the offices of the Casa, all served to strengthen the ties between men who were already in contact through princely service and family relationships, or even simply business affairs. When in 1646 Father Vincent Carafa, formerly director of the Naples Nativity, was chosen as General of the Society of Jesus, the 126 members of the secret congregation sent him, as a gift to celebrate the happy event, a list of good works which they promised to perform for his sake. Conserved with pious care in the Roman archives, these little notes, written by the donors themselves, record the number of fasts, rosaries, hospital visits, strokes of the scourge, even of Communions and alms which they promised to offer on behalf of one of their number now raised to such a high position.[23] This act, perhaps not entirely disinterested, might encourage, or so, at least, it was hoped, the new Superior of the powerful order to remember each one of his brothers individually by name; it enables us to understand more clearly how the fellowship so carefully maintained within the congregations came to consolidate and perhaps even promote, within a social group, a feeling of unity which had more than once been lacking in the past.

What was true for the nobles was equally, or even more, true for the workers. The simple fact of the Society separating masters from

[22] A. S. J. Rome, province of Naples, 177, fos. 98–113; *ibid.*, 75, fos. 227–33v.
[23] *Ibid.*, 74, pieces 403–530.

journeymen, and founding for the benefit of the latter numerous congregations of young artisans in all the manufacturing towns of Europe, was pregnant with consequences at the beginning of the seventeenth century. The workers met together, by themselves, separate from their masters. This was a novel situation if one bears in mind that for more than a century State and Church had waged war on anything which might appear, even under the cloak of religion, as a disguised form of *compagnonnage*.[24] It is true that the Jesuits can hardly have given the impression of encouraging such combinations; on the contrary, the care which they lavished on these young people and the supervision to which they were subjected may have seemed the best guarantee against any future corruption by their colleagues. But these workers continued to travel, and they might well bring back from their stays in various foreign towns ideas which were hardly compatible with those inculcated into them on the oratory benches.

Furthermore, it is by no means irrelevant to draw attention to the cultural role of the associations, which, in addition to religious instruction, provided those capable of benefiting from it with an intellectual and even, in some measure, a political training, which could be utilised in other circumstances. Apostleship through books, with the establishment of public libraries, was a practice which spread rapidly amongst the artisans, both young and married, of Cologne and Antwerp. It was from amongst them, we must remember, that Father de Pretere chose his instructors for the 'Legion of the Brave', despatched to teach reading and arithmetic to the little shepherd-boys of Flanders.

The congregation, too, with its own institutions and way of operating, was a school of life. In his eulogy of Father de Pretere, the Antwerp annalist depicted him, in 1626, in the process of creating a sodality of young lads of between twelve and sixteen years old, most of whom must have been apprentices. The most urgent task was to provide them with a magistrate, as was the case with the adults, and it was with him that Father de Pretere dealt in all the affairs of the association. 'It was the government of a well-organised state', wrote the author of the account, 'rather than an assembly of children.'[25] Accustomed, therefore, to manage the affairs of the community from

[24] Emile Coornaert, *Les Compagnonnages en France du Moyen Age à nos jours* (Paris, 1966); Bessières, *Deux grands méconnus*, p. 225; Des Marez, 'Les origines historiques du mouvement syndical en Belgique', in *Extension de l'université libre de Bruxelles* (1913), pp. 16–23.

[25] A. P. B. M. Namur, Droeshout deposit 24,2, p. 245.

an early age, many journeymen quickly acquired a sense of responsibility and a consciousness of the common good.

They were introduced, at the same time, to the subtleties of politics. At Antwerp, we are told, the dignitaries were initially elected by the whole congregation, on a majority vote. But, as if by chance, when the sodalities of Flemish married men and of Walloons were established, it was suddenly discovered that there were 'difficulties' in continuing the old system. The electoral body was accordingly reduced. Henceforward, only present and former officers had the right to vote. And not even they were all equal, since the former used black balls which counted as one and a half votes, the latter white, which counted as only one. The father director and the prefect, however, each disposed of six black balls! Such contempt for the full association must have provoked serious discontent since, in the end, a compromise was reached. The new and former officers were to propose three names to the whole sodality, whose members subsequently each placed one penny in a named box to register their choice. It was then only necessary to count the contents of the three boxes to reveal who was the prefect, and who were the first and the second assistants.[26] One can easily imagine the discussions, and the sometimes heated proposals and counter-proposals, during meetings which have echoes of the meetings in the *Stuben* of the guilds, at the time when the latter still wielded some power in town administrations. When some insurrectionary movement erupted in a city, as so often happened during the seventeenth century, not only had the journeymen in the congregations no reason to remain detached, they were possibly better prepared than others to speak and intervene effectively.

In any case, the best efforts of the Jesuits in Naples, Cologne and Antwerp from the end of the sixteenth century, and the congregations rapidly established amongst all categories of their populations, with branches in every craft and district, did not prevent these same towns from experiencing particularly violent revolts. The most famous, without doubt, was that of 1647 in Naples, led by Masaniello. It was principally directed against the nobility, for having been in league with the Spanish. The threatened gentlemen began by making a vow to St Francis Xavier and proclaiming him protector of the town, and they sent Father Carafa, who was one of them, a picture of the saint.

[26] *Ibid.*, 24,1, pp. 287–91; 24,2, p. 360.

They then contributed a thousand men to the reconquest of the town, which was described as follows in an account drawn up for the greater glory of Don John of Austria:

Order was all the better observed, in that the Commanders, Officers and Soldiers had communicated the day before, Palm Sunday, and they seemed rather to march in procession than in battle ranks, having all earned the Holy Jubilee which was gained on that day, to which the prayers of the Holy Father have marvellously contributed. Thus his Holiness has borne witness to the joy which such a notable advantage wins for the benefit of all Christianity.[27]

The crusading character given to the repression of the insurrection (not without its echoes of accounts of the White Mountain twenty years earlier), the reference to the jubilee and, above all, the vow to St Francis Xavier, all show the full and effective participation in the operation by the nobles of the Nativity.

Where, meanwhile, were the artisans of the congregations, and what were they doing? It is less easy to say. It is certainly the case that the college, though seriously threatened – since, on the Jesuits' own admission, 'our people were thought to be linked to the Spanish monarchy' – was spared, whilst the palace of the Duke of Andria, only thirty paces away, was sacked. Was this a miracle produced by the great protector of the Society? Perhaps, but it is also not impossible that the saint had several zealous followers amongst the rebellious mob.[28] When calm was restored, the nobles began thinking about carrying out their vow and preparing splendid festivities in honour of the Apostle of the Indies.[29] The artisans, for their part, concentrated on setting up a mutual fund and assisting the poor wretches who had been thrown in prison.[30] For many years they could be seen, at regular intervals, going from house to house carrying containers to collect offerings for these prisoners.[31] The Jesuits, however, kept mum. Though they had been so threatened, they took great care to refrain from handing out either praise or criticism.

A similar policy was adopted in Antwerp a dozen years later, in the report of the very violent disturbances which shook the town.[32] And

[27] A. S. J. Rome, province of Naples, 74, fos. 387v–388v.
[28] *Ibid.*, fo. 219v. [29] *Ibid.*, 75, fos. 189–94.
[30] *Ibid.*, 74, fos. 246–58. [31] *Ibid.*, 75, fos. 241–57.
[32] A. P. B. M. Namur, Droeshout deposit 24,3, pp. 428–33 (1659).

discretion was even greater in Cologne, at the end of the century, with regard to the Gülich uprising (1680–6).[33] Nevertheless, in both cases, the participation of members of the congregations in the insurrections is almost certain. It seems likely that the sharp decline in numbers in the sodality of young craftsmen in Antwerp after 1660 is to be explained, in part, by the abrupt departure of some of them, forced to lie low for a while after the events of 1659. The consequences were even more marked in Cologne, where the famous congregation of the Three Kings seems to have been in a state of near-collapse for many years, whilst the lists of young artisans were suspended.[34]

The conclusion that the fathers' silence is to be explained by prudence or shrewdness must be treated with caution. 'As for the Antwerp fathers,' wrote Father Droeshout, 'our *Annual Letters* reveal that, by taking neither one side nor the other, they enjoyed universal approbation. In holding to this middle course, which gave each his due, they did not alienate the people and they retained the esteem of the leading families.'[35] In fact, they had little choice. With their troops to be found in both camps, they could not choose without risking the ruin of much of their good work. For them to make a choice would have meant losing all credit in one part of the town. But, however advantageous in the short run, this policy was in the long run untenable. It seems likely that the recorded departures from the sodality of the Three Kings in Cologne, were, at least in some cases, occasioned by disillusion with the excessively cautious attitude of the directors. On the other hand, the authorities were likely to feel some disquiet in the face of the fathers' ambivalent behaviour, and in view of the fact that many suspects were members of congregations. There are signs, in the last years of the seventeenth century, of a marked cooling off in relations between the college and the municipality.[36] In wishing to preserve the congregations as they were, the Society was doomed to please no one and lose prestige.

The great urban revolts of the mid-seventeenth century, therefore, justified a system and, above all, without it ever being said, a state of mind. From then on, the congregations of artisans were under

[33] Müller, *Die Kölner Bürger-Sodalität*, p. 27; for the Gülich uprising, which shook Cologne from 1680 to 1686, and which profoundly marked the town, see *Revolutionen in Köln 1074–1918*, catalogue of the exhibition from the Cologne municipal archives (25 April–13 July 1973) (Cologne, 1973), pp. 58–68.

[34] *Ibid.*, p. 27; H. A. S. Cologne, Jesuits 56, fos. 50, 55 (lists interrupted in the 1680s).

[35] A. P. B. M. Namur, Droeshout deposit 24,3, p. 433.

[36] H. A. S. Cologne, Jesuits A 642, fo. 127v.

surveillance. This started round about 1640, when a major campaign against *compagnonnage* was embarked on throughout France. The inspiration and directives came from the Society of the Holy Sacrament and, in particular, from its Superior, Gaston de Renty.[37] Action on the ground was entrusted to a simple shoemaker from Arlon in Luxembourg, Henry Buche, commonly called 'le bon Henry'.[38] His methods were straightforward, consisting of seeking out journeymen in their regular haunts – at town gates, and in taverns and gaming-houses. 'If there were any in a bad way', wrote his biographer, 'he did not leave them alone until they had promised to make a general confession.' To make absolutely sure, he took them to a confessor himself. Then he gave them instruction, exhorting them first of all to flee bad company, attend Mass and sermons assiduously, and, above all, never fail:

> on their knees to say a few prayers and examine their consciences night and morning. But as he feared above all Sundays and festivals, he accompanied them to the exercises and Christian duties of the parish on those days and then to other Churches, Hospitals and places where they could exercise their zeal and nourish their devotion, and he assigned them a place where he could speak to them in a more leisurely fashion.

He did not talk to them only about God and their religious duties. He also laid down principles of conduct in their daily lives and, in particular, he emphasised the 'great loyalty' they owed to their masters.[39]

With the most devout amongst them, he soon formed the Association of Servant Shoemakers, followed by the Society of Brother Tailors, foundations of a new type, which brought together bachelors who lived communally and in poverty, chastity and obedience to the parish curé, for whom they acted as auxiliaries whilst continuing to exercise their trade. They soon formed, at the heart of their respective crafts, nuclei of Christian workers who were joined by 'external' married servants and masters who shared, as far as was

[37] Allier, *La Compagnie du Trés Saint Sacrement*, p. 59; Bessières, *Deux grands méconnus*, pp. 225ff.

[38] J. Antoine Vachet, *L'Artisan chrestien ou la vie du bon Henry maistre cordonnier à Paris, instituteur et supérieur des frères cordonniers et tailleurs* (Paris, 1670); Bessières, *Deux grands méconnus*, pp. 225ff.; Marc Vénard, 'Christianiser les ouvriers, en France au XVIIe siècle', in *Transmettre la foi: XVI–XXe siècle: 1 Pastorale et prédication en France, Actes du 109e congrès national des sociétés savantes* (Paris, 1984), pp. 19–30.

[39] Vachet, *L'Artisan chrestien*, pp. 8–10.

practicable, their life of prayer and their ideals.[40] It is hardly surprising that this society was very close in spirit and practices to the congregations of artisans. Its first protectors were fervent congregation members as well as Superiors of the Society of the Holy Sacrament: Monsieur de Renty and *président* de Mesmes. The first prelate to approve the institution was Monseigneur de Montchal, Archbishop of Toulouse, a good friend of the Jesuits and half-brother of another important member of the Parisian sodality of the Gentlemen.[41] There is, nevertheless, a difference between this new society and the old congregation, which explains the interest of such men in the activities of Henry Buche: his clearly expressed intention of combating *compagnonnage* and of discrediting it in the minds of workers.

The Jesuits were too shrewd not to learn from experience. The rules intended for the congregations of artisans were modified after 1650 and certain clarifications spelled out. It was restated in the *Heures à l'usage de la Congrégation des Artisans du Grand Collège de Lyon* that a father of the Society of Jesus governed the association together with a prefect and two assistants. But it was also specified that: 'The father nevertheless, in certain circumstances and in matters of importance, has always full power to do that which he judges to be Godly.'[42] And to make quite certain that there could be no doubt on this score, it was clearly stated in the case of the prefect that 'even though he is the Leader, and like the Superior of the Congregation, he is nevertheless subordinate to the father'. That is why he could change nothing and receive no one without the father's consent and 'if someone requests entry, he should send him to the Father'.[43] It could hardly be made more plain that the elected officers, however carefully chosen, were subordinate.

The morals and the daily life of the brethren were even more carefully controlled. 'They should keep away from taverns', they were taught in Toulouse:

> especially on Communion days. They should carefully abstain from oaths, disputes, forbidden games, masquerades and all other such acts. If it so happens that they transgress in this way, they will be given a penance; if they refuse to perform it, or if they do not improve, they will be expelled from the

[40] Bessières, *Deux grands méconnus*, p. 279. [41] *Ibid.*, p. 233.

[42] A. D. Rhône, Galle deposit, *Heures à l'usage de la congrégation des Artisans du Grand Collège de Lyon*, p. 21 (general rules, article 2). [43] *Ibid.*, p. 30.

Congregation as scandalous and unworthy to be of the number of the Servants of the Holy Virgin. Those who bathe immodestly, especially in busy places, will be punished with the same severity; and if they drown, the Congregation will not attend their burial.[44]

In Lyons, brothers who spent more time at tavern tables than on chapel benches were to be deprived of the same honour ('who as a result of frequently getting drunk, end up dying drunk'). In the Beaujolais, it is true, some latitude was allowed to occasional sinners: 'But if someone falls by accident into this error, and dies, he will not be deprived of Funeral honours or of prayers.'[45]

The quarrelsome, blasphemers and thieves were subjected to the same penalties and exclusion. 'If someone plays some dishonest trick on an associate, or on his master, or if he is convicted of robbery, he will be expelled in disgrace from the Congregation.'[46] One method above all was used to control the behaviour of the journeymen who travelled widely, that is, the prospect of the refusal of the *testimonium* or patent. This, accorded or refused when a congregation member left town, increasingly assumed the character of a certificate of good conduct. Presented by a young worker to the officers of the sodality immediately he arrived in a town, it served as a passport enabling him to seek alms, or as a recommendation to an employer or a landlord. To be deprived of it was a serious disadvantage.

It should be said, nevertheless, that unlike the situation with the Servant Shoemakers, great discretion was observed in the Jesuit handbooks on the subject of relationships between masters and workers. *Compagnonnage* was never, to our knowledge, mentioned and cannot therefore be regarded as formally prohibited. From time to time, certainly, such and such a *sodalis* was held up as an example in the *Annual Letters* for having been able to resist temptation successfully during the course of his travels. The chronicler of Fribourg (Switzerland) includes in his roll of honour a group of workers who avoided towns which posed too great a threat to their innocence even though they might have been profitable from the point of view of work.[47] Might this panic at the prospect of 'vice'

[44] *Les Saints Exercices de l'artisan chrétien et Congréganiste avec les règles, les prières, les instructions et les cantiques spirituels des Congrégations d'Artisans établies dans les collèges de la Compagnie de Jesus* (Lyons, 1709), p. 187.

[45] A. D. Rhône, Galle deposit, *Heures à l'usage de la congrégation des Artisans du Grand Collège de Lyon*, p. 56. [46] *Ibid.*, p. 59.

[47] B. C. U. Fribourg, MSS, L 107 (1), p. 288.

conceal, in reality, fear of being excluded from certain towns by the will of a powerful workers' union? It is hard to tell, especially as in the Germanic world similar exclusions applied rather to the Protestant territories. In practice, it seems likely that the Jesuits, though exhibiting greater strictness after the crises of the mid-seventeenth century, were careful not to go too far. The policy adopted by the fathers seems in general to have been to exclude 'bad lots', and involve those under their direction in a way of life which was to a large extent incompatible with the habits and customs of *compagnonnage*. What purpose would be served by rejecting men who wanted to be good Christians and who could in addition, by their very presence, have a salutary effect on their milieu?[48] If in other regions, on the contrary, as in the Low Countries, the Rhineland and Southern Germany, the congregation was strong enough to occupy the place occupied elsewhere by *compagnonnage*, why deprive themselves of it?

It was prudent, in this case, so as to avoid any recurrence of incidents such as those of the 1650s, to take certain precautions. Apart from those already mentioned, one in particular seems to have enjoyed favour with the Society, that is to open wider the doors of the congregation. Thus in Lille and Antwerp, non-masters were admitted to the *grands artisans* and soon outnumbered them. In Munich, and even in Naples, simple burgesses were enrolled alongside nobles and top persons at court. In the French towns, merchants took their places by the side of counsellors and *présidents* of Parlement.[49] This practice was not entirely new,[50] but it became more common at the end of the seventeenth century. 'There is great benefit', wrote, in 1693, a correspondent of the Toulouse association, 'in the establishment of the Aas, because they unite persons of all Conditions and all countries, they stimulate them by various pious and charitable practices to work for their sanctification and the salvation of their families.'[51] In imitation of the Aas, the congregations seemed, at the dawn of the Age of Enlightenment, to turn in the direction of unity amongst men. But was this always a deliberate policy? Or was it the

[48] Bessières, *Deux grands méconnus*, p. 401. In Grenoble, as in Lyons, the creation of the worker brothers was due to the Society of the Holy Sacrament within the context of apostleship among workers, and not to the fight against *compagnonnage*, which was not regarded as reprehensible in these towns.

[49] As in Rouen; see Féron, *Sociétes secrètes*, pp. 74–114 (published list).

[50] See chapter 2.

[51] A. P. Toulouse, CA 101, vol. 1, fos. 157v–159.

evolution of urban society which was tending, as has been demonstrated in Lille and Antwerp, towards this openness, this drawing together of the various classes within the same pious associations?

FROM RELIEVING THE POOR TO CONFINING THEM

Care of the poor had, from the beginning, assumed a major role in many congregations, to the extent, even, of becoming their principal function. This was the case, in particular, with the Neapolitan nobility and the Monti discussed above. After the Casa di Santa Fede and the Monte of the brethren of the Nativity 'for the shamefaced poor' came the Monte of the Blessed Virgin for the poor and sick at the Hospital of the Incurables founded by the brethren of the Most Holy Conception of the Immaculate Virgin. Then there was the Monte of Mercy for the aid of prisoners, and that of the Holy Name of God to combat the usury which was rife in the city's prisons.[52] The operation of this institution, perfected at the end of the sixteenth century, was highly satisfactory, and was copied in the foundations of the early seventeenth century. It was the practice to acquire, with correct and proper authorisation from the Viceroy, an establishment in the town which was well away from the college. Its facade carried the arms of its distinguished protectors. Benefactors were numerous and came from all social classes, and governors and officers were both members of and elected by the congregation, which ensured that, despite appearances, strict control was retained over the Monte's policies.[53] Thus constituted, the Monte could receive gifts, legacies and endowments and make profitable investments and sales, all operations strictly forbidden to the congregations. One example of their wealth is that the Monte of Mercy, though only recently established, was able, in 1620, to assume responsibility for the construction of the church of the Jesuit college, without detriment to the work it had undertaken with prisoners.[54]

This useful formula was widely copied throughout Europe during the course of the century. When, by the wish of a *procureur* in the Senate, a hospital for the sick was founded at Chambéry, it was four

[52] A. S. J. Rome, province of Naples, 177, fos. 98–112, 185–91, 230–5, 247–8; *ibid.*, 73, fos. 100–1. [53] *Ibid.*, 177, fos. 247–8. [54] *Ibid.*, 73, fos. 143–4.

congregation members accompanied by the father director who were responsible for its administration according to the wishes of the testator (1647).[55] In Paris, most of the activities initiated and directed by the Gentlemen of the Saint-Paul quarter and the Society of the Holy Sacrament operated according to the same principles. This was the case with, for example, the Montreal Society and the seminary for foreign missions. It was probably the same with the great hospital foundations which sprang up in Paris and the provinces round about 1650. The general hospital, in particular, which, in Paris and other large towns, mobilised the energies of all pious men in the 1650s, appears to have been an institution of this type. It found, in any case, like the other great charitable works, its first and most generous benefactors amongst the congregations,[56] as well as its first administrators and directors: the seemingly ubiquitous bookseller Sébastien Cramoisy, the *avocat* Jean-Marie Lhoste, who also sat on the council which administered the Hôtel-Dieu and the Hospital for Incurables, and Monsieur Lecomte, who was one of the directors of the Hôtel-Dieu.

A society like that of the 'Gentlemen working for the release of the poor imprisoned for debt', said by Raoul Allier to have emanated from the Society of the Holy Sacrament, was reminiscent in organisation and aims of the Mercy of Naples.[57] It is almost as if the Society of the Holy Sacrament, intermediary between the congregations and the various charitable enterprises, the latter generally directed by members of the former, functioned as a supreme administrative council for all the great Parisian institutions, thus assuming the characteristics – at a higher level of centralisation and efficiency – of the Neapolitan Monte.[58] This explains the desire expressed right from the start to place a layman at its head. According to its memorialist, Monsieur Voyer d'Argenson:

> Whatever desire the Society had to honour the status of the priests and render them every respect with regard to the Holy Sacrament of which they are the ministers, it could not refrain, from the start, from almost always putting laymen in the position of Superior, since they generally have better knowledge of temporal affairs than have ecclesiastics.[59]

[55] Girod, *Notice sur la grande congrégation de Notre-Dame*, pp. 316–17.

[56] Very many legacies in wills of this period: A. N. Paris, series Y. Also, on this question, see the fundamental work by Jean-Pierre Gutton, *La Société et les pauvres: l'exemple de la généralité de Lyon, 1534–1789* (Paris, 1971), pp. 326–49, 377–93.

[57] Allier, *La Compagnie du très Saint Sacrement*, p. 70.

[58] See chapter 6, table 2.

[59] Beauchet-Filleau, *Annales*, p. 59.

This model continued to flourish throughout the seventeenth century and beyond. When, in 1699, the Gentlemen of Caen decided to create a benevolent fund for the relief of the poor artisans of the suburbs, they adopted a similar procedure. The money came from gifts made for this purpose by the *sodales* and also by non-members who wanted 'to participate in these good works alongside the congregation'. A receiver and a deputy-receiver from the congregation, specially appointed for the purpose, managed and invested the funds. It is true that, in this particular case, the separation between the fund and the sodality was not completely achieved. But when difficulties occurred, everything was in place for appearances to be maintained.[60] Thus the model of the Monte, as frequently employed in Italy in the sixteenth century for the relief of the poor, was the inspiration for the organisation of many French charitable activities in the seventeenth.

The advantage of the system lay in its efficiency and the speed with which it was capable of solving a problem or coping with a new, and often tragic, situation. In 1612 an epidemic struck the prisons of Naples. The mortality was high. Visiting congregation members observed the terrible state of the unfortunate victims. They slept, in effect, on the bare, damp ground of their dungeons. The Monte of Mercy was originally established to provide beds for prisoners. Later it extended its operations. Its officers, who visited once a week, gradually discovered certain realities of prison life: the ill-treatment suffered by inmates, the periods of punishment improperly prolonged by the warders, the large numbers imprisoned for debt, and the usury which was rife. They soon came to realise that an even more wretched group existed, the galley-slaves. A new institution was established on their behalf, the Holy Mercy, whose officers took on the task of rescuing from this hell those who had been unjustly condemned and alleviating the cruelty experienced by the rest. A hospital was founded, where men brought in chains from every region of the kingdom were cleansed, put to bed and fed.[61] Regular prison visiting soon became the rule in many congregations, especially those of the Gentlemen, and it often assumed the character of actual legal assistance to the most deprived.[62]

[60] Henri Fouqueray, *Les Oeuvres sociales de la congrégation des Messieurs de Caen au XVIIIe siècle* (undated), pp. 14–15.

[61] A. S. J. Rome, province of Naples, 73, fos. 100–1.

[62] Fouqueray, *Les Oeuvres sociales*, p. 10; Pra, *Les Jésuites à Grenoble*, p. 312.

It was probably a comparable misery, perhaps even more affecting, which stimulated initiatives with regard to hospitals. In 1605, the nobles of the Nativity, whose principal activity was the relief of 'the shamefaced poor', decided that once they had 1,500 ducats in their money chest priority should be given to putting new beds in the Hospital for Incurables. Care of the sick was the special concern of the brethren of the Holy Conception of the Immaculate Virgin, who undertook to provide them with a meal once a week.[63]

The 'shamefaced poor', that is, those who dared not beg, were the principal reason for the Monte founded by the nobles of the Nativity. A relief organisation was established to encourage the best possible distribution of the money in the fund. The four governors collected together all the cases which had been brought to their attention. They put them to the society, who discussed them and then responded to each case proposed by means of a secret vote on three questions. Should help be given? Should the case be deferred? Should it be postponed until the petitioner had been visited by representatives of the governors?[64] The Gentlemen of Caen adopted a similar procedure at the end of the century when a petition was received from a needy artisan.

> The Father nominates three commissioners to make enquiries; their names are written at the foot of the petition; these three commissioners, who normally consist of one ecclesiastic, one married man and one young man, between them collect information with great accuracy and in great secrecy, so as not to cause pain to those it is wished to help; after which they write their opinions at the bottom of the request and sign it, and then the Father, in the light of this advice, having himself carefully considered the matter, tells the secretary what is to be done.[65]

Other sufferings also claimed the attention of the congregations, such as the plight of prostitutes. This concern lay behind the Casa di Santa Fede in Naples, whose officers claimed in 1640 to support and instruct over six hundred women for whom they subsequently found positions or provided dowries if they found husbands.[66] And when, in 1631, a particularly violent eruption of Vesuvius caused thousands of refugees to flood into Naples, the Monte of Mercy and that 'for the shamefaced poor' took on the task of providing food and shelter.[67] In

[63] A. S. J. Rome, province of Naples, 177, fos. 187v, 247–8. [64] *Ibid.*, fo. 186v.
[65] Fouqueray, *Les Oeuvres sociales*, p. 5.
[66] A. S. J. Rome, province of Naples, 177, fo. 113. [67] *Ibid.*, 73, fos. 322–39.

1636, the peasants of the Nancy region, reduced to famine by the Thirty Years' War, were relieved by the Society of the Holy Sacrament and the intervention of the Fouquet brothers.[68]

The activity of the *sodales* was thus considerable, but also selective. In the catalogue of sufferings relieved, the 'shamefaced poor', the sick and prisoners occupied by far the most important place and excited the greatest charitable urge. Was it a question of assisting those who suffered most in those difficult times, or of accomplishing the most meritorious actions? 'I, Luigi Leone, offer for the good government of Father Vincent Carafa, our [!] General, five crowns, four Communions, ten offices, four hospitals in Naples, 20 January 1646', wrote one of the compilors of the little goodwill notes sent to Rome at the time of the election of the new general.[69] It should not be forgotten that care of the sick, the deliverance of prisoners and alms for the poor and for pilgrims were all 'charitable works', as we are reminded by the iconography of numerous baroque altar-pieces. A significant example is that the brethren of the Toulouse Aa had to continue their hospital visiting even in summer, when they were no longer needed to make beds. It was not the poor person himself who counted, but the act accomplished in the sight of God or for the good of the Church. This explains the Neapolitan marquis who undertook to make the beds of ten sick people during the year whilst reciting prayers on behalf of Father Carafa![70] Other motives explain the choices made, including the desire to convert sinners and to save those whose souls were in danger. Hence the confinement of Neapolitan prostitutes and the interest in the sick and in prisoners. Every visit to the latter was the occasion for instruction, lessons in the catechism and advice on how to confess and communicate. At the Hôtel-Dieu in Paris, Monsieur de Renty's preference was for attending to those most gravely ill, whom he taught how to die. Monsieur Barillon, shocked at the sight of the poor of his parish receiving, as if by right, alms after burials, arranged for the distribution to be made only after they had received instruction 'in our holy religion' and been urged 'to make good use of their condition and their distress'.[71] The Gentlemen of Caen, when they visited the most wretched families of the six suburban parishes, distributed bread and linen; after which 'they consoled the poor,

[68] Beauchet-Filleau, *Annales*, p. 67.
[69] A. S. J. Rome, province of Naples, 74, fo. 405. [70] *Ibid.*, 74, fo. 404.
[71] Beauchet-Filleau, *Annales*, p. 41.

exhorted them to have patience and to attend the sacraments frequently; they instructed the children in the presence of their parents; they sometimes discovered secret or scandalous irregularities which they remedied in association with their Pastors'.[72]

The desire to reform morals through charity was what, to a large extent, determined the choices made. The ideal was to succeed, as with the Monte of Mercy in Naples, in persuading the prisoners to lead quasi-monastic lives. They were to rise promptly in the morning at the first ring of the bell, pray in their cell for half an hour, attend Mass, then work in silence. After the meal came an hour of catechism, then instruction in how to scourge oneself and how to wear a hair shirt. This was followed by more work performed in silence, then a meeting before bed for the reading of a passage from a spiritual book. After which, safely in bed, they recited together the litanies of the Virgin, then examined their consciences before observing absolute silence till the bell rang.[73] There was nothing like prison for the successful conversion of sinners! They were always there, and they welcomed visitors with open arms.

Beggars, on the contrary, were a real plague, a major evil which had to be got rid of at all costs. There could be no question of giving alms to the likes of them as long as they remained in such a condition. 'Ordinary charity condones evil', concluded one member of the Society of the Holy Sacrament of Toulouse. Beggars lived in libertinage outside the Church, scoffed at the sacrament of marriage and drove their daughters into prostitution. It would not have been so bad if they had been content to damn only themselves, but they corrupted good Christians by their example and their very existence. 'The poor, who by order of their birth ought to serve the rich, are almost useless for work and service,' wrote the author of a report to the Society of the Holy Sacrament, 'having spent their early days in idleness, beggary and libertinage, and if for some reason they sometimes undertake something, they are generally the cause of innumerable fits of anger, blasphemies and imprecations on the part of their masters and mistresses.' Not to speak of the fact that these wretches had the deplorable habit of eating unripe fruit, which caused dysentery, and, in consequence, 'infection in every street in Toulouse'. In a nutshell, 'the disorder of the poor brings dishonour

[72] Fouqueray, *Les Oeuvres sociales*, pp. 6–7.
[73] A. S. J. Rome, province of Naples, 73, fos. 100–1.

on the whole town'.[74] Religion and the police were in total agreement that beggars should be condemned without appeal and locked up without delay. They had no place in a well-ordered Christian society where everything, from morning to night and from night to morning, should be accomplished for the greater glory of God. Or, more precisely, their place was in the general hospital, where they would learn to labour as Christian workers, or in the Hôtel-Dieu, where they would be taught to redeem a life of sin by an edifying death.

It would, of course, be an exaggeration to see the congregations as primarily responsible for the vast movement in the 1650s which aimed to achieve the large-scale confinement of the poor in general hospitals.[75] If they actively participated, it was in the company of many others, coming from other spiritual families and formed by different masters. But the men of the congregations knew about the great Neapolitan institutions established by their brothers over half a century earlier. And they had, above all, perfected a model of the Christian life which they tried to instil into all categories of society. The very success of their enterprise could only highlight the scandal of the life led by beggars, who existed quite outside those norms which had just been more precisely delineated and widely diffused.

Forces for order, supporting the Christian prince and urging the workers and the poor to accept their lot, the congregations of the seventeenth century appear, in some ways, to be at the origins of the bourgeois spirit in Europe. But at the same time, by their constant adaptation to social transformations, and by the concern of their leaders to reach all social classes and involve themselves with every type of suffering, they offered those who participated in their activities the opportunity for an exercise of conscience. The worker with other workers, or the treasurer of France and the Neapolitan marquis confronting the destitution of the suburbs, were all alike in a position to discover another reality. With the passage of time, it was the spirit and the purpose of the institution which might, as a result, be modified.

[74] Alphonse Auguste, *La Compagnie du Saint-Sacrement à Toulouse* (Paris–Toulouse, 1913), pp. 47–8.

[75] For this project and its realisation, see Gutton, *La Société et les pauvres en Europe (XVIe–XVIIIe siècle)* (Paris, 1974), pp. 122–57.

8. *The religious life*

Primarily created to defend the Catholic religion wherever it was threatened, the Marian congregations remained true to their vocation throughout the seventeenth, and even in the eighteenth, century. The artisans of Augsburg were moulded by controversy, and the magnificent procession through the town which they organised on Corpus Christi Day was intended to make a dramatic demonstration of the Catholic presence and to edify the Protestants.[1] The Revocation of the Edict of Nantes was greeted with enthusiasm in the Toulouse Aa, and prayers were ordered to 'seek a blessing for the efforts the King was making to subdue the heretics'.[2] The congregation of burgesses and artisans founded in Pau in 1693 was created for the purpose of strengthening the attachment of the newly converted to Catholicism.[3] And the sodality of the German burgesses of Strasbourg included in its rules in 1717 the defence of the Mass against the Lutherans.[4]

Nevertheless, as early as the first years of the seventeenth century, Pope Clement VIII had to defend these 'holy associations' against the faithful of the Roman Church and the clergy who opposed their establishment and their growth.[5] Father Crasset, in the work frequently quoted here, in comparing the *sodales* to the early Christians, referred to the 'atrocious calumnies' of which they were the victims, and the 'false suspicions of the *Politiques* who maliciously accused their Meetings of being faction and cabal'.[6] How is this opposition, widespread in certain circles, and destined only to increase in the second half of the seventeenth century, to be explained?

[1] B. H. Munich, Jesuits 106, p. 29 (1645), Jesuits 108, fo. 102 (1651), fo. 345v (1645).

[2] A. P. Toulouse, CA 113, pp. 324ff. (21 July 1685).

[3] Abbé J. B. Laborde, *La Congrégation des Bourgeois et Artisans de la ville de Pau* (Pau, 1911).

[4] *Regeln und geistliche übungen, deren Hrn Teutschen Bürgeren der Stadt Strassburg* (Strasbourg, 1747), pp. 121–33.

[5] Crasset, *Des congrégations de Notre-Dame*, p.14. [6] *Ibid.*, pp. 18–19.

CHAPEL BEFORE PARISH

The chapel of the burgesses of Ingolstadt, under the name of Our Lady of Victory, became the centre of the religious life of this little town at the end of the Thirty Years' War[7] – and a source of immense pride to the Jesuits. But such success bred discontent. The priest of the largest parish church saw his services deserted, and protested. The warden of the Recollect friars had to look on, powerless and outraged, when every Sunday, just as he embarked on the peroration of his sermon, the *sodales* made a precipitate departure, anxious to get to their meeting.[8] Curé and warden set off to petition the Bishop of Eichstätt, and put to him the basic question: was it not the case that the faithful should, according to the Council of Trent, perform their duties as parishioners before those, however estimable, of the pious associations?

In this case, it was only a matter of the Sunday sermon and unspecified 'offices'. But in Antwerp, Cologne and many other towns, the congregations had long adopted the habit of attending Mass on Sundays and holidays in the church of the Jesuits, and even in their own chapel. The fathers, indeed, did everything in their power to encourage them. In Poitiers, at the beginning of the century, they declared 'that it was not a mortal sin if the parishioners failed, one Sunday in three, to attend Mass in their parish church'.[9] In Antwerp, they went much further. They celebrated a special Mass every Sunday in the oratory immediately before their meeting, 'in order to obtain a better and more consistent attendance of the brethren'.[10] In Cologne, this was so large that on festivals the Jesuits had to start their offices and meetings at five o'clock in the morning.[11] We may assume that wherever possible the congregations behaved like those of Antwerp and Cologne. For them, it was a convenient solution. What is more, it gave the directors the opportunity to assess the constancy and the quality of the devotion of their troops. In many dioceses, it is true, particularly in France, the bishops were quick to react, often vigorously. But, quite apart from the fact that in large towns like Paris and Cologne, control was in practice more or less impossible,

[7] B. H. Munich, Jesuits 107, pp. 7–8 (1646).
[8] B. S. Munich, MSS, Clm. 26479a.
[9] Villaret, *Les Congrégations mariales*, p. 570.
[10] A. P. B. M. Namur. Droeshout deposit 24,4, p. 24 (1665).
[11] H. A. S. Cologne, A 642, p. 17 (1680).

the bishops could not demand of their parishioners more than was compulsory. Beyond this, the latter were free to hear sermons and practice their devotions wherever they chose.

There was no shortage of feast days, or of ordinary or extraordinary meetings, especially during Lent. Above all there was what the burgesses of Eichstätt called the 'law' of monthly Communion which, as a result of the plenary indulgence granted by the Pope, became the general Communion which all congregation members took together. On the first or the third Sunday of the month, they did their duty in the company of their families.[12] This was still a minimum, since frequent Communion was a constant concern of the Jesuits. It was even one of the underlying reasons for the congregations. 'We will soon be Saints', it says in *Les Saints Exercices de l'artisan chrétien*:

> if we approach the holy Table with the preparations of which I have spoken; and the blessed times of the early Church will soon be seen to be reborn among us, when Christians showed themselves worthy by their fervour to participate every day in the divine mysteries: why do we not imitate them? Is Jesus Christ less lovely? Is he less worthy than in the past of our zeal, our respect and our love?[13]

The author emphasised, of course, the preparations necessary to receive the Eucharist frequently. And to assist the devout on this difficult path, he was not averse to providing a means to make confession easier. The daily examination of conscience could be made by using the simple methods of artisan accounting. You had to begin by determining, in agreement with your confessor, a ruling vice you wanted to conquer. Then every day, at midday, you drew up a preliminary balance-sheet, by means of strokes of the pen on a line, and repeated this in the evening. You then compared one day with another, and one week with another. Don't worry, added the good father, 'it will seem that your faults increase to begin with', but 'this is because you are paying more attention'.[14] So you should not be discouraged. The more strokes there were on the line, and thus the more sins committed, the more surely was the penitent on the right path, clearsightedness being the first stage on the way to repentance.

[12] A. P. B. M. Namur, Droeshout deposit 24,2, pp. 463–4 (1636).
[13] *Les Saints Exercices de l'artisan chrétien*, p. 63. [14] *Ibid.*, pp. 20–9.

The Christian artisan's sin-reckoner

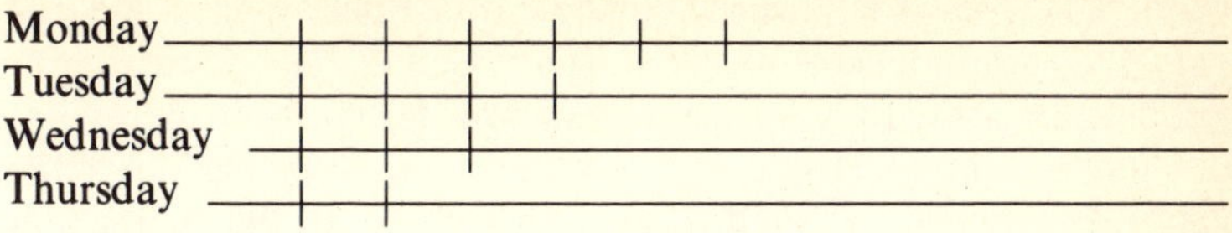

Monday ——|——|——|——|——|——|————————
Tuesday ——|——|——|——|————————
Wednesday ——|——|——|————————
Thursday ——|——|————————

This meticulous accounting was designed to lead the artisan to the confessional more frequently, and confident of having something to say to his director. Every effort, in fact, was made in the seventeenth century to enable the simple and the illiterate to perform this act. Instructions in the form of questions and answers, in the manner of the little catechism of Peter Canisius, were provided for their use. They had to read them or learn them by heart with the help of their instructors in the weeks preceding their final entry into the congregation.

Q. What must you do to confess properly? A. Five things: 1 ask the Holy Spirit for grace to know your sins and detest them; 2 examine your conscience; 3 conceive a firm desire to repent of your faults and make the act of Contrition; 4 declare your sins to the Priest; 5 perform the penance he imposes.

The simple workman should, of course, be aware that there were two sorts of contrition, one, perfect, 'by which you detest sin from the motive of pure love of God', the other attrition, 'by which you detest sin for a less noble motive, such as fear of Hell, or hope of Paradise'. He was also warned against sacrilegious confessions.

Q. How do you come to make a sacrilegious Confession? A. By confessing: 1 without real sorrow; 2 without an effective plan to satisfy your obligations; 3 by not declaring all your mortal sins, either by concealing them, or by not revealing them fully, out of shame; or, lastly, by forgetting them through culpable negligence in self-examination.

If you were guilty of such sacrilege, it was necessary, in order to make reparation:

to declare afresh the sins already confessed in all the previous sacrilegious confessions: because they had not been remitted by the absolution; 2 to say how often you had communicated and abused the Sacraments during this period: because there were so many sacrileges.[15]

[15] *Ibid.*, pp. 269–73.

This is why, when entering the congregation, the new servant of Mary made a general confession intended to cleanse him of all the sacrilegious confessions made in his past life. He repeated this important act each year, preparing himself for it in advance.

The laxity of which the Jesuits were so often accused after the forthright accusation levelled against them by Pascal in the *Les Provinciales* is thus not obvious. But their fervent desire to make frequent Communion a part of Christian habits led them, if not to tolerate incomplete confessions, at least to provide a formula for compensating, which boiled down to admitting that such acts of sacrilege were common. In practice, was not every curé or missionary who had, day after day, to strive for the conversion of large numbers of people, driven to make similar accommodations? Doubtless, but they omitted to write the fact down in booklets or works intended for a large, sometimes extremely large, public.

Another reflection which inevitably springs to mind when reading these texts intended for craftsmen is the very simple, it is tempting to say simplistic, manner in which these very delicate theological problems were dealt with – or evaded. When the reply on the difference between contrition and attrition had been given, the interrogator followed immediately with this simple demand: 'Make an act of contrition.' We are a long way here from Pascal's interrogation of his erudite Jesuit!

The more recruitment to the congregations widened, and, for many of them, assumed a more markedly popular character, the more the grip of the fathers tightened. More than ever, they controlled in the most minute detail, from the liturgical day to the liturgical year, the religious life of their *sodales*. In so doing, they inculcated specific Christian habits which were not always compatible with those current in the parishes.

THE FAMILY BEFORE THE INDIVIDUAL

Increasingly, during the course of the seventeenth century, the Society of Jesus aimed to go beyond craftsmen and gentlemen and reach the family. As early as the 1610s, the men of the Civica of Cologne were assembled every evening to learn the litanies of the Holy Virgin, prior to having their households recite them.[16] At the

[16] H. A. S. Cologne, Jesuits 9, fo. 240v (1612).

same period, 'pious colloquies' employing the methods of Jacques Rem were organised for the bourgeois of Munich in order to educate them in the wise and Christian direction of their families.[17] It was probably similar motives which impelled the Jesuits, despite the prohibitions of successive generals, to take an interest in activities involving women.[18] In Switzerland, in fact, this had been the case from the beginning, whether in Lucerne, Soleure or Fribourg. In this last town, in particular, the congregation of Ladies flourished, seeming to be even more active, and to enjoy greater prestige, than that of the men. With more than nine hundred members in 1670, it trained the town's mothers in an orderly religious life, and both imposed strict moral rules and encouraged them to involve themselves with the poor and the sick of the canton.[19]

In other places, such as Porrentruy, on the edge of the Jura, and Ensisheim in Alsace, confraternities of the Rosary were established specially for women.[20] The confraternities of Our Lady of the Seven Sorrows and of the Good Death which were founded in numerous colleges from the middle of the century, though open to both sexes, were more particularly intended for them. And in the kingdom of Naples, Bavaria and Alsace alike, the success of these confraternities was soon considerable.[21] In any case, with the passage of time, wives were invited to join their husbands at festivals or in certain of the pious exercises of the sodality.[22] In Ingolstadt, the Civica was, in practice, almost mixed by mid-century. In 1656, in the celebrated chapel of Our Lady of Victory, more than seven hundred women, kneeling before the altar, made their act of consecration to the Virgin according to the ritual formula.[23]

This desire of the fathers at local level to go against the original rule restricting their apostolic activity to the male faithful alone cannot be explained solely by their desire to spread ever wider the beneficial effects of the congregations. It was also the consequence of a shift of

[17] B. H. Munich, Jesuits 102, fo. 18 (1615).

[18] Mullan, *La Congregazione Mariana*, pp. 67–68.

[19] B. C. U. Fribourg, MSS, L 107 (1), p. 288.

[20] B. H. Munich, Jesuits 102, fo. 10v (Porrentruy, 1614); *ibid.*, fo. 26 (Ensisheim, 1615).

[21] A. S. J. Rome, province of Naples, 75, fo. 6 (Nola, 1653); B. H. Munich, Jesuits 108, fo. 212 (Neuburg, 1652), Jesuits 110, fo. 42 (1660); Châtellier, *Tradition chrétienne et renouveau Catholique*, pp. 187–8 (Sélestat, 1654–80).

[22] A. P. B. M. Namur, Droeshout deposit 24,5, p. 224 (Antwerp, 1713).

[23] B. H. Munich, Jesuits 109, fo. 66v.

interest: from the individual in isolation to the family. Was it not essential to proceed via the family if one wished to establish a Christian society? In its present state, based solely on money, and maintained by material interests, it was very far from the model presented by Father Cordier in his work entitled *La Famille saincte*. 'Everyone pretends to be rich', wrote this author:

when he has a son or a daughter to marry; he values his belongings beyond their real worth, he minimises his debts if he cannot conceal them. Some people send their children away, so that their house appears less crowded. I have known a man of quality so anxious to conceal the number of his children, whom he had despatched hither and thither, that those who lived at home had no idea how many brothers they had.[24]

Father Caussin was even more severe on the subject of noble marriages.

The first thing wrong is that such alliances are hardly ever contracted except out of avarice . . . And as a result, marriage is no longer truly marriage; but a mercenary traffic, a fair, a market, where rational creatures are sold like animals . . . And if, in such cases, the girls are what they ought to be, seeing the avarice of the men, they resolve rather to choose God in a state of virginity than give their bodies and their riches to a husband who has no interest in them. St Jerome tells the beautiful story of Martia, daughter of the great Cato, who said that, amongst so many Lords who sought her, there was no husband. Say the same, girls, away with these mercenary husbands, who are in love with money; they should marry the mines of Peru, not honourable girls.[25]

'And if they only knew', he wrote:

into whose hands this precious treasure was to be consigned . . . But you, poor girl, who have been so gently cherished and reared . . . they are going to put you into the hands of a husband, as if into the claws of a sparrowhawk . . . And what is worse, this poor girl buys her servitude at great price . . . see how they have done her hair, ornamented her, decorated her like a temple, and they lead her to the galleys to the sound of violins.[26]

Was it surprising that after such beginnings households were usually unhappy? 'Marriage', declared Father Caussin, warming to his theme:

[24] Jean Cordier, *La Famille saincte ou il est traité des Devoirs de toutes les personnes qui composent une famille* (Paris, 1643), p. 30.
[25] Caussin, *La Cour sainte*, vol. 1, pp. 156–7. [26] *Ibid.*, p. 152.

is a long pilgrimage which has only three stopping places: the first is called false pleasure, the second, repentance, and the third, calamity; and if you go further, you will find despair.[27]

Mutual distrust, quarrelling and adultery were the normal concomitants of such unions. And if only that were all! But the corruption fatally influenced the children brought up according to such principles by such parents. It even affected the Church, to which were consigned, out of motives of self-interest, canons and nuns who had no wish to serve her. Listen to Father Cordier on the subject of how girls sacrificed in this way by their families entered religion.

They go to someone who makes nuns' habits, who has been tipped off to respond to the wishes of her parents, but not to hers; they dress her up like a little goddess, or rather they gild her head, like a victim they are going to slaughter on the altar of the good fortune of her brothers and sisters. She has to put on a good face, otherwise they will ill-treat her. They assemble the relatives, and they ask her, 'Daughter, do you want to be a Nun?' Her conscience tells her no, but her mouth, which betrays her heart, says yes. They throw her into Religion, as they would into the arms of an Idol; to live a life of weeping, and to pine gradually away, consumed by fierce regrets, which never leave her till death, which she perhaps tries to anticipate, either by means of a rope, like the girl in Paris, or by a precipice, as many have done. The whole gathering nevertheless rejoices with her, they tell her she is very fortunate, that in the world there is only suffering, that she has chosen the better part, that she is leaving earth for Heaven. These congratulations prevent her from bursting out and giving way to the internal upheavals which she is experiencing; she weeps, but it is in the depths of her soul and what is saddest of all, it is for the rest of her life. Whereupon, the father and mother congratulate themselves on having given their daughter to God; they think they have done something clever. But God already has the thunderbolt in his hand to destroy them.[28]

It was to prevent just such results, painted here in the blackest colours, that the congregations were also conceived as schools for good and holy marriage. Father de Pretere was preparing his young Antwerp artisans for this sacrament as early as 1610.[29] His colleague in Cologne did the same, and the Eichstätt annalist states that this was the principal reason for the creation of a congregation of unmarried workmen, 'so that they would learn to be good and pious fathers of families'.[30] The concept of a 'noviciate of marriage', to use

[27] *Ibid.* [28] Cordier, *La Famille saincte*, pp. 395–6.
[29] A. P. B. M. Namur, Droeshout deposit 24,1, p. 85.
[30] B. H. Munich, Jesuits 104, fo. 55 (1631).

the expression of the Abbé de Portmorand, one of the Gentlemen of the professed house in Paris, and a member of the Society of the Holy Sacrament, began to spread. This powerful society even, at one time, supported this project, intended, it is true, exclusively for poor young men from 'respectable families'.[31] Concern for the fathers of families was, as we have already seen, no less great. It was why many bourgeois and artisan sodalities were popularly called 'of the married men', or, as in Lyons, 'of the "Gentlemen" of Holy Marriage'.[32]

Behind these activities and this constant preoccupation lay a very elevated and altogether Tridentine conception of the sacrament of marriage. It was one of the greatest, wrote Father Cordier.

> O Holy Marriage! O mysterious sacrament! How little you are respected by men, how precious you are in the eyes of God! How ignorant we are of your merits! How those who approach you fail to consider your dignity! They omit to purify their minds! They fail to cast off their shoes, like Moses, so as never to approach you without reverence! They never think of the nuptial bed as holy ground, which cannot be profaned without wronging those three adorable unions, of God with us, of Jesus Christ with his Church, and of our humanity with the Second Person of the Most Holy and Most High Trinity.[33]

This quotation contains a veritable theology of marriage, which did not lack courage at a time when condescension towards it was common in the writings of clerics.[34] The text also reveals in this regard a state of mind diametrically opposed to that of Port-Royal as expressed in the letter written by Mother Agnes to her nephew, Antoine Le Maître, when he was on the point of getting engaged. 'You want to become a slave', she wrote:

> and still remain king in my heart, that is impossible . . . You will say that I blaspheme against the venerable sacrament to which you are so devoted, but do not trouble yourself about my conscience, which knows how to separate the sacred from the profane, the precious from the contemptible, and which finally pardons you with St Paul, and be content with this, if you please, without seeking approval or praise from me.[35]

The apology for Christian marriage undertaken by the Jesuits, at

[31] Alfred Rebelliau, 'La Compagnie du Saint-Sacrament', *Revue des Deux Mondes* (15 August 1908), pp. 853–60. [32] A. D. Rhône, B. P. 3991.
[33] Cordier, *La Famille saincte*, p. 14.
[34] Clearly visible, in particular, in the work of Father Caussin.
[35] Quoted by René Taveneaux, *La Vie quotidienne des jansénistes* (Paris, 1973), pp. 157–8.

least by those responsible for the congregations, appears at first sight to be the consequence of a theological reflection which was original, even advanced for its time. But it was primarily the fruit of their pastoral experience, as well as of their desire for reform. Families were left to fend for themselves, wrote Father Cordier in his introduction, whilst publications intended for the religious abounded. 'But of the four Parts which compose the Christian world, at least three are involved in Families.'[36] An immense field was open to apostleship, but one which lay fallow, since people behaved as if the Christian principles in which the faithful were deemed to be educated had no role within the home. It was this interior world which had now to be changed, and above all the inherited behaviour of spouses towards one another.

First of all, a climate of confidence and an equitable distribution of duties must be established within the household. 'I find two sorts of occupation in a family', wrote Father Cordier, 'the one requires the husband, the other the wife. External matters are more proper for the husband; internal matters are the business of women.' This was hardly very original, but he went on to say:

> I like not at all those miserly and mistrustful husbands, who forget to be men outside, but play the master of the women within the family; who give everything on account and want to be so fully informed about everything which is spent in their homes that it is a crime to heat the water without obtaining their permission. If you were to ask them if they had married a woman or a slave, what would they say? Is it not to reduce a wife to the condition of a servant to leave her nothing in hand, except what one wishes to lose?[37]

That said:

> it is intolerable for a woman with a husband who is not a fool to get involved in business affairs. It is enough that she looks after the inside; that if the condition of her husband obliges her to take some cognisance of his affairs, she should go no further than the shop. Women should be like the soldiers of a garrison, who are never permitted to go beyond the walls to do battle.[38]

Though limited, their sphere of action was nevertheless essential. It was on mothers, in practice, that fell responsibility for the education and instruction of children in their infancy. 'A woman', he wrote:

[36] Cordier, *La famille saincte*, introduction, not paginated.
[37] *Ibid.*, p. 110. [38] *Ibid.*, p. 111.

is capable of saying the same thing a hundred times. Few men could do this, and nevertheless these repetitions are absolutely necessary to little children who only ever give you half their attention. Let us give this praise to women, for it cannot be denied them, that they can do more to nurture children than can men.[39]

As an experienced pedagogue, the Jesuit was capable of appreciating the immense labour accomplished every day, in obscurity, by mothers of families. Father Caussin's praise was even warmer. 'Men', wrote the author of *La Cour sainte*:

who want to turn everything to their own advantage, speaking of this subject, throw everything on to women, and frequently say that we need not ask whence come the ills of marriage, that it is enough to say that you cannot be married without a wife, and that women are the source and the seminary of all the disgraces and ills which are found in this arrangement. This is a very delicate area; what shall we say in reply? It seems that to blame women in general is to show more evidence of passion than of judgement. They are mothers of men by nature, nurses from charity, and almost servants out of patience. They are the devout, the compassionate and the charitable sex. They perform every day an infinity of good deeds, they see to the needs of the poor, they visit hospitals, prisons and the sick, they fill Churches and they edify homes with examples of piety, and then to speak ill of them?[40]

Nevertheless, he admitted that 'those who are once given over to wrongdoing and abandoned to sin are the cause of great evil'.

A timid enough defence of women, but a defence all the same, and Caussin did the same for children, where he perhaps exhibited greater boldness. He propounded a rule. 'Parents are in a sense more obligated to their children than are children to their Parents.'[41] Cordier went into the most minute detail and emphasised throughout his work the love which ought to be shown in the daily behaviour of parents towards their children. This should start as soon as they are born.

Do those women who are so desirous to be mothers never consider that in failing to give the breast to their children, they lose the better half of the quality of mother! . . . If she is a mother, she is only half a mother, because she gives only half a life. No, no, she is not a mother to her offspring, she is only a mother for her own pleasure.[42]

[39] *Ibid.*, p. 337. [40] Caussin, *La Cour sainte*, vol. 1, pp. 153–4.
[41] *Ibid.*, p. 172. [42] Cordier, *La Famille saincte*, p. 371.

The same love and concern for the well-being of the child should dictate the behaviour of the parents in the matter of education. They should avoid imposing their will on their sons when it comes to their choice of occupation.

If parents do not wish to go wrong, let them yield much in order to follow the inclination of their children. If children want to choose wisely, let them heed the advice of their parents. Reason will prove faulty, if it is not supported by inclination; inclination will prove unwise, if it is not guided by reason.[43]

And if a young man has talents which his father lacks, the latter should have the good grace to recognise them and help his son to rise, instead of confining him to the family business.

Certain restless spirits, who always want what they have not got, and despise what they have, hanker after an old custom of certain peoples, amongst whom a son was not permitted to take another trade than that of his father . . . Can they not see that this law which they wish to revive was made only for the advantage of certain powerful persons . . . Can they not see that it means leaving the best spirits in the dust, forbidding them to aspire higher.[44]

The same was true, naturally, with marriage. 'How I wish that the inclination of the children should take account of the reason and judgement of the parents', insisted Father Cordier, who made no distinction in this regard between sons and daughters. He sprang even more strongly to the defence of the latter, because he had observed 'the former have as a rule more opportunity to show their displeasure; but the latter, who are trained in acquiescence, agree to anything'.[45]

This criticism of abuses and this defence of women and children may still be found rather timid. The fact remains that a new conception of the family, characterised by a revaluation of the sacrament of marriage, a sharing of responsibilities between the couple and a dilution of the despotic power of the father, was in the process of emerging. The patriarchal family was not the 'holy family'. This last would continue to appear a pious hope, destined to remain buried in books, unless the congregations of young men, grown men and women amongst whom these principles were diffused constituted fertile ground for their implementation, and effective relay stations for their diffusion throughout society.

[43] *Ibid.*, p. 382. [44] *Ibid.*, p. 378. [45] *Ibid.*, pp. 409–10.

PUBLIC DEVOTIONS BEFORE THE INNER MAN

Of still greater consequence, indeed most important of all, in some eyes, was the effect that all this had on piety. Congregation members prayed and practised their religion differently. Little by little, they influenced those close to them, those who observed them, and even the inhabitants of whole towns, to follow their example. This applied not only to confession and Communion on set dates and in groups, but, more generally, to all the pious acts of the Catholic faithful. Daily attendance at Mass was no longer practised as in the days of Father Coster, who wrote primarily for students. 'If you wish, you can say your Chaplet during Mass', advised Father Le Blanc in a book intended for craftsman brethren and lay brothers in monasteries.[46] This was still something for an élite advanced in the religious life. For the rest, the great mass of journeymen and workers, the author of the *Saints Exercices* proposed canticles sung in chorus at key moments such as the Confiteor, the Creed, the Elevation, the Lord's Prayer and Communion.[47] This explains the new importance in the great urban congregations of the choristers, who taught these songs to newcomers and sang them at the right moment during the offices. This soon became a habit, and the faithful, whether congregation members or not, knew that when *O Dieu, qui voyez mon crime* began, they were at the confession of sins.

The prayers and the devotions required or recommended by the Church at the different moments of the liturgical year were performed in the same way. The meditations themselves were increasingly directed. This is what Father Le Blanc suggested for Christmas:

> It was in winter, and in cold weather, the path was muddy and difficult; they [Mary and Joseph] set off nevertheless, very joyful at having this opportunity for suffering. They entered the Town . . . They found an empty stable, near the hill. It was full of rubbish, it stank . . . The Queen of Heaven and Earth went inside . . . She at once busied herself with St Joseph in cleaning the stable . . .

The account continues in this fashion, with the same wealth of detail. One can almost hear the preacher, who, in any case, had no hesitation in revealing his method.

[46] Thomas Le Blanc, *Le Saint Travail des mains ou la manière de gagner le ciel, avec la pratique des actions manuelles: ouvrage autant utile que nécessaire aux Religieux et Religieuses qui sont occupez aux Offices, et Exercices corporels, et à toutes sortes d'Artisans pour faire leur travail avec esprit* (Lyons, 1669, 2nd edn), p. 140.

[47] *Les Saints Exercices de l'artisan chrétien*, pp. 80–101.

While Memory tells us this Story, the imagination forms an idea and a picture of it, and contemplates it, as if we were actually present, and as if it were happening before our eyes; this holds and concentrates the mind, and prevents it from being distracted.[48]

In Lent, to ensure such concentration, the meditations took place in church. At Antwerp, the choir of the sanctuary was transformed for the occasion into a veritable theatre whose décor and characters evoked the subject on which the preacher wished to speak. He described, in the style of Father Le Blanc, the scene of the Passion which was portrayed. He paused, and, while the musicians performed an appropriate short piece, the congregation immersed itself in what was before its eyes. The father began to speak once more, relating to the life of the sinner the sad images described. There was another musical interlude which allowed each person to withdraw into himself. Then came the third stage of the sermon, also followed by music, which was designed to accentuate the effect of the instruction by encouraging pious reflections and firm resolutions in the listener.[49]

All these acts of Christian piety, including the most internal (such as the prayers of the Mass and the meditations during Holy Week), were performed communally, according to strict rules and, for the most part, aloud. The same was true, with more reason, of those which were restricted to the congregation. The custom of a solemn 'renewal' of the act of consecration to the Virgin on her feast day spread amongst the *sodales* from the mid-seventeenth century. The Fribourg annalist described the ceremony in detail: the prefect, mounting with dignity the steps of the altar, knelt before the tabernacle and solemnly pronounced the words of the formula, while the congregation members, behind him, repeated each word distinctly, like an echo.[50] In Cologne, where the practice seems to have been established very early, the *sacramentum*, as it was called, was the occasion for a particularly impressive spectacle.[51] In 1708, it constituted the high point of the festivals arranged on the occasion of the centenary of the famous Three Kings congregation. This 'renewal' of a thousand *sodales* in the Jesuit church impressed the chronicler even more than the splendid procession of the *Römerfahrt* which preceded it and the highly acclaimed theatrical piece which followed. Repeated aloud and in unison by all the brethren together,

48 Le Blanc, *Le Saint Travail*, p. 73.
49 A. P. B. M. Namur, Droeshout deposit 24,5, pp. 165, 186–7.
50 B. C. U. Fribourg, MSS, L 107 (1), p. 328 (1682).
51 H. A. S. Cologne, Jesuits 52, fo. 14.

the formal phrases filled the nave with such a burst of sound and gave an impression of such conviction and such unity that those present at the ceremony were moved to tears.[52]

Here we have a perfect expression of the fact that, within the congregation, everything took on the character of a collective rite. The religion that its members practised, and whose triumph they wished to assure, was, before all else, a communal religion. But where did the community stop? The walls of the Church of the Assumption in Cologne shook when a thousand brothers spoke aloud their oath of allegiance to Mary. The streets of Antwerp and Cologne were not large enough when all the sodalities thronged into them. And when a town made a certain saint (Francis Xavier at Naples in 1657, or Joseph at Antwerp in 1625 and Fribourg in 1648) its second patron, imposing on all its inhabitants the obligation to stop work and attend Mass on the feast day, one can say that the community, in this regard at least, extended to the whole city.

We must remember, nevertheless, that the establishment of collective attitudes in religious life and the promotion of group, not to say mass, piety, were not unique to the Jesuits, but characteristic of the baroque world as a whole. The congregations were a part of a much wider movement. But, by their number, their activity and their organisation, they did much to spread and implant the new, or renewed, devotions and practices. Take, for example, the stations of the Cross, which can be seen gradually assuming definitive form amongst the congregations of Austria, Southern Germany and the Rhineland during the seventeenth century. The first Good Friday processions were organised at Augsburg in 1605, and at Cologne in 1610.[53] In 1619, in the little town of Neuburg, the funereal procession assumed a quite exceptional scale and spectacular character. It took place at night, in torchlight. On the first float was the Infant Jesus carrying the instruments of his Passion in a basket, while one of seven angels presented him with a cross, the others with the symbols of his Agony; they were followed by a dozen men on horseback representing Pontius Pilate and the centurions; then came nine Jews of the order of priests, demonstrating the reason for the Crucifixion. On a second float was Christ carrying his Cross, bound, and dragged by the soldiers; this was followed by the statue of the sorrowful Virgin, her heart pierced by seven swords, and accompanied by John and

[52] H. A. S. Cologne, A 643, fos. 2–3.

[53] Villaret, *Les Congrégations mariales*, pp. 385–6; H. A. S. Cologne, Jesuits 9, fo. 223v.

various holy women singing laments; twelve armed men surrounding the robbers walked behind. On a third float was the Cross, accompanied by the Virgin, her heart pierced with a sword. Then came the choristers, the musicians, the clergy, the prince himself, and the prefect of the congregation accompanied by the members.[54] In the course of time, this procession developed to such an extent that it finished by taking up every day of Holy Week. Flagellants followed the cortège or, very often, formed another on Holy Saturday, accompanied by men bearing crosses, sometimes in large numbers (several dozen, even seventy or eighty, as in Straubing in 1660).[55]

The scenes portrayed on the floats were often repeated, with greater attention to sequence, detail, décor and action, in theatrical performances. Thus the representations of the Passion on Holy Thursday or Good Friday became institutionalised not only in Straubing, but in Amberg in Bavaria, Porrentruy in Switzerland and Molsheim in Alsace, by the middle of the seventeenth century. The edifying spectacle attracted crowds from the town and its environs; the notables, the governors and even the princes themselves deigned to grace these performances with their presence. The theatrical performance did not exclude the procession, which usually progressed in the direction of the Holy Sepulchre and started from the 'Mount of Olives', as it was called in Alsace, and which was restored and decorated for the occasion.[56] A penitential route began to be inscribed into the countryside, extending beyond the town and annexing the nearby hill or mountain, now surmounted by a Calvary reached by a stony path along which were placed carved scenes from the Passion, which it had become an act of piety to build or erect with one's own hands. A chapel was often built alongside the Calvary, near to the summit. These stone constructions, visible from afar and visited all year round, are a clear testimony to the important place in religious life occupied by the ceremonies of the Passion. They were the high peak of the liturgical year at Reichenhall, Landsberg in Bavaria, Feldkirch in Vorarlberg, Molsheim in Alsace and in many little towns and villages of Southern Germany, Austria, Switzerland and the Rhineland. They were the most striking manifestation of the activities of the congregations, and even, in many cases, their *raison d'être*. The celebrated Passion Play still performed every ten years at Oberammergau in Bavaria is an example of this type of piety.

[54] B. H. Munich, Jesuits 102, fos. 205v–206.
[55] *Ibid.*, Jesuits 110, fo. 57.
[56] *Ibid.*, Jesuits 107, p. 107 (Landsberg, 1647).

The same is true of those devotions which were new or revived by the Counter-Reformation. The congregations were not responsible for the cult of Our Lady of Loreto, but they made an important contribution to its success in the seventeenth century. In the middle of the Thirty Years' War, the Civica of Constance decided to erect a 'Loreto House' to bring about the departure of the Swedes.[57] It was quickly built and inaugurated with great pomp by the Prince-Bishop before a large crowd; and the congregation adopted the habit of processing to it twice a year in thanksgiving.[58] The Holy House reproduced as exactly as possible in a quiet spot some distance from the town became a feature of the countryside in Catholic areas, as, for example, in Augsburg and Fribourg. In the latter, the construction of the chapel was decided on in 1647 by the Senate itself, under pressure from the congregations and from the powerful Father William Gumppenberg; the latter succeeded, the following year, in having the feast day of St Joseph celebrated and made into a public holiday throughout the canton. Built on high ground near the Porte de Bourguillon, the Holy House could be seen from all around, and seemed to protect the citizens of Fribourg in all their activities. A splendid procession was held in its honour, and took place on the second Sunday in October ('Loreto Sunday') for two centuries without a break. A knight in full armour, bearing in his hand an unfurled banner, and surrounded by archers, rode at its head. The children of the schools and the college followed, then the congregations, the members of the various religious orders, the clergy, the Senate and the armed burgesses. Four councillors carried the dais which bore the statue of the Virgin and the Bishop. Martial music accompanied the procession. Between two pieces, the burgesses raised their guns and fired a volley of shots. Having reached its destination, the crowd piled into the chapel, spilling over on to the terrace. They heard vespers, sang the litanies of the Virgin with fervour, then recited the rosary, whose every Ave Maria was saluted by canon-fire, while the Paternoster and the Gloria were signalled by fireworks. After which, the Guard of State and the town *carabineers*, each stationed in their own entrenchments, embarked on a mock battle.[59]

Such popular success can only be explained by the continued

[57] *Ibid.*, Jesuits 105, fo. 106v (1636).

[58] *Ibid.*, fo. 179 (1637); Jesuits 106, p. 28 (1644); Jesuits 108, fo. 202v (1652).

[59] N. P. Cologne, Hartmann MSS, vol. 4, fos. 16v–17.

existence of ancient traditions. It was by using old rites (*les bravades*), and by frequently constructing their chapels on old holy sites, that the congregations were able to make the festival of Our Lady of Loreto into a popular custom. In the case of St Januarius of Naples, the tradition was already alive and well. When, on the saint's festival in 1710, the archpriest of the cathedral arrived to take the famous ampulla and present it to the people of Naples, he was astonished to see the blood of the martyr bubbling in the reliquary before congealing into a solid block of murky and repugnant appearance! The crowd, expecting dire calamities to ensue, was terrified. Public penances, processions and flagellations were immediately decreed to ward off imminent catastrophe, and the *sodales* accepted their share of the common burden by promising an annual novena in honour of the great protector of Naples.[60]

At Eichstätt in Bavaria, in 1619, the burgesses went to ask St Willibald, whose chapel had been deserted since the Reformation, to put a stop to the bad weather. The prince in person came from Neuburg, accompanied by his principal officers. Their success was complete; a book was published; and the faithful began once again to throng to this holy place.[61] It was the same with St Beatus, restored to grace thanks to the activities of the congregations of Fribourg, whilst the congregations of Freiburg-im-Breisgau regularly processed to the fountain of St Landelin at Ettenheimmünster.[62] The congregations thus embarked on a major campaign, frequently successful, to restore ancient cults.

One aspect of the religious life was particularly dear to their hearts: pilgrimages, especially those of the Virgin. From their earliest days the sodalities had enjoyed close relations with those holy places frequented by pilgrims. This was so in both Naples and Cologne by the end of the sixteenth century, while members of the Antwerp congregations were amongst the first to seek the protection of the Virgin of Montaigu;[63] they carved a statue in precious oak, and it was this which was solemnly carried through the streets of the town on the festival of the patronal saint of the sodality of young men.[64] The great

[60] A. S. J. Rome, province of Naples, 76^{II}, fo. 370.
[61] B. H. Munich, Jesuits 102, fo. 187.
[62] N. P. Cologne, Hartmann MSS, vol. 4, fo. 27 (Fribourg-en-Suisse, 1657); B. H. Munich, Jesuits 109, fo. 166 (Freiburg-im-Breisgau, 1657).
[63] A. P. B. M. Namur, Droeshout deposit 24,1, p. 36 (1609).
[64] *Ibid.*, Droeshout deposit 24,4, p. 202 (1672).

Marian pilgrimage to Altötting in Bavaria became, in the seventeenth century, the favourite of all the congregations in the country. Ever since the Prince-Elector Maximilian I had placed his act of consecration to the Virgin, written in his own blood, in a casket near the altar, and since, after his death, his heart had been placed there in an urn, the chapel at Altötting had assumed the character of a national sanctuary.[65] But the vows made during the Thirty Years' War, and the miracles performed, were enough in themselves to explain the flood of pilgrim *sodales* who, on set dates, town by town, came every year to beseech the protectress of Bavaria. In Alsace, the Jesuits had been involved from the beginning in the restoration of the pilgrimages to the Virgin. Marienthal, Altbronn, Wiwersheim and Neunkirch were to a large extent their creations. Several miracles a year were said to be taking place at Marienthal soon after the Thirty Years' War ended, and the faithful flocked there in their thousands.

The congregations played an important role in this revival. They processed regularly, with banners and statues, from Molsheim to Altbronn, and from Haguenau to Marienthal, and erected carved stone stations along the route.[66] Those linking Lille to the Chapel of Our Lady of the Reconciliation at Esquermes, served by the Jesuits, are known to us today. Distributed the whole length of the route, they represented 'the seven Journeys that the Glorious Mother of God made on earth and the eighth that she made from earth to Heaven'. They were favoured by indulgences for 'all those men and women who visited them in a state of grace and prayed devoutly there, either by reciting the prayer indicated for this purpose, or the Paternoster, the Ave Maria or the Creed, praying for the needs of the country and the ordinary aims of the Church'.[67]

A similar path marked out by stones to remind the pilgrim of the prayers to be said during his pious journey must have existed between Munich and the Chapel of the Holy Cross at Forstenried, which the *sodales* adopted the custom of visiting in the 1640s.[68] One must also have existed between Lucerne and Our Lady of Werdenstein, between Neuburg and the Chapel of the Holy Cross, between Trent and the Chapel of the Holy Virgin, about a mile away, and between

[65] Pichler, *Diè Marianische deutsche Kongregation der Herren*, pp. 21–2.
[66] Châtellier, *Tradition chrétienne et renouveau Catholique*, pp. 192–205.
[67] A. D. Nord, D 630/3; Alain Lottin, *Lille citadelle de la Contre-Réforme? (1598–1668)* (Dunkirk, 1984), pp. 265–6.
[68] B. H. Munich, Jesuits 106, pp. 8–9 (1644).

Strasbourg and the shrine of the Three Crosses at Lingolsheim. Almost everywhere, the congregations were associated with a place of pilgrimage situated not too far distant, which they visited regularly and endeavoured to make widely known, and which sometimes became almost a second oratory for them. The chapels dedicated to Our Lady of Loreto discussed above often fulfilled this role from the 1630s onwards. Even Paris was no exception, with its two much-frequented popular sanctuaries on the periphery, at Montmartre and Mont Valérien.[69]

Processions, pilgrimages and devotion to the saints and, above all, to the Virgin Mary are all characteristic features of baroque piety. Not only did the congregations participate fully in the movement as a whole, but by their dynamism, and by their active role in the revival of many religious practices, they constituted one of its agents of transmission and can be considered as partly responsible for its rapid diffusion amongst Christians.

THE ANTI-BAROQUE REACTIONS: THE FRENCH SCHOOL AND PORT-ROYAL

This way of practising Christianity was not universally accepted. In France, in particular, the representatives of what has been called, since Henri Brémond, the French School, offered a quite different teaching to the faithful.[70] It was the inner life which concerned Pierre de Bérulle when he advised the Christian to concentrate his attention on the most elevated 'states' of the life of Jesus, and asked him to strive for a complete 'adherence' to Christ.[71] This mystical tension by no means excluded activity in the world, good works or participation in collective devotions, but it gave them secondary importance. A disciple of Pierre de Bérulle, Father Bourgoing, of the Oratory, wrote, 'Our religion should be a life of elevation and inner society.'[72]

The Curé of Saint-Sulpice, Jean-Jacques Olier, composed a *Catéchisme chrétien pour la vie intérieure* followed by a *Journée chrétienne* to help beginners in the spiritual life to make of every instant a moment of ever more intense union with Jesus Christ. 'When the Christian', wrote Olier:

[69] A. P. Toulouse, CA 101, vol. 1 (letters written to the Toulouse Aa).

[70] Henri Brémond, *Histoire littéraire du sentiment religieux en France depuis la fin des guerres de Religion jusqu'à nos jours*, 12 vols. (Paris, 1916–32), vol. 3.

[71] René Taveneaux, *Le Catholicisme dans la France classique*, 2 vols. (Paris, 1980), vol. 2, pp. 406–7.

[72] Brémond, *Histoire littéraire*, vol. 3, p. 117.

feels himself perpetually failing in his being, with the passage of time, by which his body and life waste away, he should let himself be raised to God the Father by Jesus Christ, above all when the clock strikes, marking another portion of life expired, saying, 'God, I adore you, I adore your eternal being, I rejoice that my being perishes with every moment, so that with every moment it pays homage to your eternity.'[73]

What is here no more than a difference of emphasis in the main points of Christianity was to become, at Port-Royal, firm opposition.

The great books of Antoine Arnauld (*De la fréquente Communion*, 1643) and Pascal (*Les Provinciales*, 1656) seem to announce the start of a war. Neither author, certainly, was concerned with the Marian congregations. Nor was Jansen in the *Augustinus*, even though, as a former professor at Louvain and a bishop in the southern Low Countries, he must have known them well. But how are we to explain the violence of this counter-attack, which erupted precisely in those mid-century years when the Society of Jesus was greatly expanding its missionary activities in the towns of Europe, if not by the success of the sodalities? Because, at bottom, what importance could the moral theology of the Jesuits have, if it was not practised and spread throughout the entire Catholic world by hundreds of groups of active and respected men? This was the real danger, denounced in Lyons, before Pascal, by the author of a pamphlet entitled *Le Théophile paroissial*. In it, he showed how the Jesuits, by separating the faithful from their legitimate pastors, by regrouping them and by providing an instruction which did not conform to the traditions of the Church, were, in fact, preparing a schism.[74]

It was the threat of schism which led Pascal to put his pen to the service of the curés of Paris. In his *Cinquième Ecrit des Curés de Paris*, he showed clearly why the Jesuits constituted, in his eyes, a far greater danger to the Catholic faith than even the Calvinists. 'One sees, for all these reasons', said his letter to the curés:

how one should keep one's distance from the Calvinists, and we are persuaded that our people will defend themselves easily from this danger; because they are accustomed to flee them from infancy, and brought up to abhor their schism. But it is not the same with the lax opinions of the casuists; and that is why we have more to fear on their behalf from that direction. Because though it may be a far lesser evil than schism, it is nevertheless more

[73] *Ibid.*, p. 470.

[74] Justin Godart, *Le Jansénisme à Lyon: Benoît Fourgon (1687–1773)* (Paris, 1934), pp. 54–63.

dangerous, in that it is more in conformity with natural feelings, and in that men are already that way inclined, so that constant vigilance is needed to protect them. And it is this which has impelled us to warn those under our guidance not to extend the charitable sentiments which they should have for the Jesuits so far as to follow them in their errors, because they should remember that even though they are members of our body, they are sick members whose contagion we must avoid; and we must be observant at the same time, both to avoid cutting them off from us because that would be to wound ourselves, and to take no part in their corruption, because that would be to render our members corrupt and useless.[75]

The reason for such severity towards these 'sick members whose contagion we must avoid' was entirely a matter of the 'lax opinions' taught by the Society of Jesus. But what exactly did this mean? One calls to mind the famous passage in the *Neuvième Provinciale* where the good Father reveals to his interlocutor some of the easiest devotions to the Mother of God, which constitute a sure way to heaven:

Salute the Holy Virgin when you see her statue; say the Little Chaplet of the Ten Pleasures of the Virgin; say the name of Mary frequently; ask the Angels to revere her on our behalf; desire to build her more churches than have all the monarchs together; bid her good day every morning and good night at the end of the day; say the Ave Maria every day in honour of the heart of Mary.[76]

We should remember that these, including the earnest tone, are exactly the daily devotions recommended to the congregations since the time of Father Coster. What does Pascal take exception to in this collection of pious practices? This is what he says:

In truth, Father, I know that devotions to the Virgin are a powerful means to salvation, and that the least of them are of great merit when they arise from an impulse of faith and charity, as with the saints who have practised them; but to make those who employ them without changing their evil lives believe that they will be converted at death, or that God will raise them from the dead, seems to me much more likely to maintain sinners in their errors by the false peace which this rash confidence brings, than to draw them away by a true conversion which only grace can produce.

The Jesuit's reply is hardly less characteristic. 'What does it matter

[75] Blaise Pascal, *Cinquième Ecrit des Curés de Paris* (Paris, 1965) ed, Louis Cognet, p. 442.

[76] Blaise Pascal, *Les Provinciales* (Paris, 1965), ed. Louis Cognet, p. 154.

which way we enter Paradise, as long as we enter.'[77] No clearer expression of the two conflicting positions could be found.

At bottom, what the author of the *Pensées* held against the Society of Jesus was not only the laxity of its teaching, or even the errors of its theology, but a conception of religion which held individual conscience cheap. On the one hand, there was a Christianity lived primarily communally, where confession, the Mass, and even eventually the Lenten meditations, took on the character of collective rites, and where prayer was transformed into canticles or rosaries recited in common; on the other, Christianity was understood as an internal experience which involved men in what was most profound. Was it still the same religion? It is this which makes *Les Provinciales*, beyond its mordant irony, a work permeated with anguish. The reader is drawn, like the author of the *Divine Comedy*, into a pilgrimage to hell. Each letter, like each infernal circle, reveals a new evil, and, at the end of the Odyssey, sad and alone on the banks of the Styx, he contemplates with terror the extent of evil. Was this still anguish? Was it not already despair? The Catholicism preached by the Jesuits, which was not that of a few, but what was taught by a 'body of the most numerous of the Church', which every day won over new towns, regions, and even whole countries, was no longer Christianity and was becoming ever more remote from it. Was Jansenism, perhaps, in the name of Christian tradition, but also of humanism and reason, an anti-baroque reaction directed against the Roman Catholicism which was practised by thousands of congregation members, and which appeared, in the 1640s, to be ever more pervasive?

[77] *Ibid.*, p. 156.

9. *Tartuffe and the* dévots *in the classical period*

It would, no doubt, be mistaken to look for an accurate portrait of the *dévot* of the classical period in Molière's *Tartuffe*. Dramatic requirements, simple prudence, the desire to create a character of universal validity, not to speak of his genius, all precluded the dramatist from offering a simple copy of reality. It is, nevertheless, the case that the play would not have been written but for the importance acquired, both at court and in town, by the *dévots*. For this phenomenon, *Tartuffe* is valuable evidence. In fact, even if Molière did not, as has sometimes been argued, aim to portray such and such an actual person, he took from life enough suggestive traits to capture the distinctive characteristics of the pious members of the congregation and of the Society of the Holy Sacrament as they appeared to a notably perceptive observer.[1] In other words, Molière does not give us a complete portrait but a number of characteristics drawn from various sources, which, when compared with others, may provide an approach to reality.

For us, the play has another interest. Revealing the ascendancy of the *dévots*, it also reveals how they were viewed by public opinion – part of it, at least – and what criticisms they aroused. It may thus help us to understand the failure of the great project to reform French society embarked on in the reign of Louis XIII, and explain more clearly the unique position occupied by France within devout Europe.

HOLY FROM HABIT

> Laurent, serrez ma haire avec ma discipline
> Et priez que toujours le Ciel vous illumine.

[1] Was Louis Pocquelin, brother-in-law of Philippe Lempereur and member of the congregation of the Gentlemen of the Rue Saint-Antoine, a relative of Molière? A. N. Paris, Y 187, fo. 192.

Si l'on vient pour me voir, je vais aux prisonniers
Des aumônes que j'ai partager les deniers. *(act III, scene 2)*[2]

In these four lines, everything which, to the external observer, seemed to characterise the *dévot* is encapsulated in masterly fashion. A carefully regulated employment of time was from the beginning an essential element of the *dévot*'s life style. So were rigorous mortifications, ever since the Neapolitan congregations, followed by the Aas, for which it was one of the justifications, had included them in their normal practices. Visiting the poor, and, more particularly, prisoners, was not only recommended from the beginning, but, as has been demonstrated, actually practised by the majority of congregations of Gentlemen in the seventeenth century. In the rules for Grenoble, it was clearly spelled out that such visits should take place on Sundays and feast days:

after dinner, and that to this end, the Father of the Congregation should be sure to indicate every meeting day two persons with whom he will himself go to visit the prisoners, to acquaint himself with their needs, to take note of the good offices which he could render them, for which the Gentlemen visiting with the Father would be responsible, and to give some holy instruction to the prisoners on the principal mysteries of the faith and the most important duties of a Christian, of which they are usually quite ignorant. To this end, the Father, after a short and moving exhortation of a quarter of an hour, should question them, and the better to encourage them to remember what he teaches, he should reward with some little dole those who answer best, for which the money found in the congregation chest may be used. The Gentlemen of the Congregation who visit the prisoners should, for their part, also dispense charity, in the way that is customary, and according as the devotion aroused by the sight of the misery of the poor suggests.[3]

Molière not only showed precisely what acts a *dévot* should accomplish, but also the manner in which this was done. Take, for example, Monsieur Gautier Duclos, one of the 'illustrious men' of the congregation of Gentlemen of the professed house of the Rue Saint-Antoine. Striking, indeed ostentatious, demonstrations of his piety held no fears for him. Not content with taking only bread and water on Saturdays and the vigils of the festivals of the Virgin, he further edified his brethren by turning up first every day for the earliest Mass.

[2] Laurent, put away my hair shirt and my scourge, and pray that Heaven will always enlighten you. If anyone comes to see me, I am going to the prisoners to distribute alms. [3] Pra, *Les Jésuites à Grenoble*, p. 312.

Just like the young man of Fribourg whose edifying traits have been described, 'he was often discovered on his knees at the door, waiting for it to be opened'. An ardent defender of the cult of Mary, 'he seemed to have neither enemies nor friends, except those he regarded as either enemies or friends of his Queen, patron and mother'.[4] Like those brethren whose zeal is revealed by a letter from the Aa of Paris, he exerted himself to defend at all times and to propagate everywhere the feast of the Immaculate Conception.[5]

In the case of Monsieur Le Vacher, it was the cult of the Holy Sacrament of the Altar which he wished to spread. Every year on Corpus Christi Day he arranged for a preacher to come to the parish of Charonne, where he had a house.

> There he established perpetual adoration throughout the octave, notifying each of the inhabitants of the hour and the time they should pass before the Holy Sacrament, animating and sustaining all by his example, his piety, his vigilance and his charity.[6]

Here, proselytism and 'vigilance' with regard to the practice of others was added to the ostentatious demonstration of piety. Monsieur Courtois, another member of the renowned sodality of the professed house, who 'had served the Most Holy Virgin for fifty-six years', 'was not one of those timid souls, fickle and craven, who blush at their own devotion, and who are almost ashamed of the name and status of servant of Mary and of Congregation Member'. He, too, was amongst the first to arrive at meetings. Not content with these pious practices, he supplemented them with charity.

> The Prisoners above all were the sad objects of His Compassionate Charity, he visited, consoled and solaced them, and he was amongst the most assiduous at the meetings of a Society Instituted to work every Monday for the relief of prisoners . . .[7]

It was written of another servant of fifty years' standing, Nicolas Prèches, merchant and burgess of Paris, that he loved to visit the poor. He was often despatched to families which the congregation assisted. On Sundays and feast days, like so many other *sodales* in France, Switzerland and Germany, he spent all day following the

[4] B. Maz. Paris, MSS, 3335, 'Hommes illustres de la Congrégation de la Vierge. Maison professe des Pères de la Compagnie de Jésus', pp. 31–58.

[5] A. P. Toulouse, CA 101, vol. 1, fos. 191–2v.

[6] B. Maz. Paris, MSS, 3335, p. 134. [7] *Ibid.*, pp. 1–29.

offices of his parish and of the congregation. Twice a week, he went to the 'great office for the poor' of which he was one of the administrators. His days were filled with devotion and charity, which did not prevent him being of 'a sweet temper, without violence, or fits of anger, ready to oblige everyone and solace the wretched'.[8]

This even, 'sweet temper', which made men sensible of their own least faults but prompt to pardon those of others, was another characteristic of the *dévot* observed by Molière.

> Ah! laissez-le parler; vous l'accusez à tort,
> Et vous ferez bien mieux de croire à son rapport.
> Pourquoi sur un tel fait m'être si favorable?
> Savez-vous, après tout, de quoi je suis capable?
> . . .
> [addressing Damis]
> Oui, mon cher fils, parlez; traitez-moi de perfide,
> D'infâme, de perdu, de voleur, d'homicide;
> Accablez-moi de noms encor plus détestés:
> Je n'y contredis point, je les ai mérités,
> Et j'en veux à genoux souffrir l'ignominie,
> Comme une honte due aux crimes de ma vie. *(act III, scene 6)*[9]

These words could have been spoken by Monsieur de Serres, who never ceased to heap on himself 'bitter reproaches . . . for the little faults which escaped him and which he confessed to daily with much humility and sorrow'.[10] Humility was a cardinal virtue for congregation members and, even more, for those who belonged to the Aa. It demonstrated a profound sentiment of respect for the majesty of God and a dread of any possible irreverence. It was shown 'by a humble and respectful posture of the whole body, by a very correct restraint of every sense', these being 'a tangible sign of his inner sentiment of the grandeur of God, of the presence of Jesus and Mary who watched over him, and of his good angel who was at his side'.[11] A congregation member's whole bearing expressed his inner disposition. Father Cordier, addressing mothers as educators of their

[8] A. P. Toulouse, CA 101, vol. 1, fos. 173–4.

[9] Ah, let him speak; you accuse him wrongly, and you would do much better to believe his story. Why, in such a case, be so favourable to me? Do you, after all, know what I am capable of? . . . [addressing Damis] Yes, my dear boy, speak; call me perfidious, infamous, lost, a thief, a murderer; heap even worse names on me; I deny nothing, I have deserved them, and I am ready, on my knees, to suffer the ignominy as a disgrace merited by the crimes of my life.

[10] B. Maz, Paris, MSS, 3335, p. 120.

[11] *Pratique de Devotion*, p. 12.

young children, wrote: 'Teach them that they should keep their eyes down, their head erect, their face serene and cheerful; that their speech should be mild and respectful; that their gait should not be hurried nor their gestures extravagant.'[12]

It was even more important for the congregation member to control his every gesture during Lent. He ought, therefore, to walk with 'his eyes down and his body bent towards the ground, as if unworthy of appearing before such a high Majesty justly incensed. From time to time during the day he should despatch sighs to Heaven, as if he were David, or the wretched Publican . . .' When he entered a church, he should 'proceed . . . with shame, to examine himself, as if he were a criminal before his judge, from whom he expects a death sentence'.[13] It was not only gestures and body which were so carefully controlled, but also conversation, and even language. The 'password' which the brethren of the Aa were supposed to exchange when they met in the street served the purpose of averting vain talk, lacking in spiritual content. 'What time is it?', they asked each other in Toulouse during Lent, 1678; the answer was 'The mystery.'[14]

Language had to be meticulously purged and cleansed of anything which might recall the material world.

Above all, one should always keep in mind rule 6, which tells us to express our thoughts with great simplicity and in a language redolent of the Gospel, without affecting certain thoughts which are only curious, and without choosing words which might distract or detain the spirit; this is so important that if anyone fails in it, the *Commis* is obliged so to act that he is charitably warned of it.[15]

This extended even to the most common rhetorical formulas, which were strictly forbidden. 'There are those who fail in this when they explain their reasons; they say words like "as Monsieur has just said", or "as Monsieur has remarked"; they should remember that such ways of talking belong only to *Monsieur le commis*.'[16]

Couvrez ce sein que je ne saurais voir;
Par de pareils objets les âmes sont blessées,
Et cela fait venir de coupables pensées. *(act III, scene 2)*[17]

[12] Cordier, *La Famille saincte*, p. 363.
[13] *Pratique des vertus chrestiennes*, p. 46. [14] B. M. Toulouse, MSS, 277, fo. 5.
[15] *Pratique de Devotion*, pp. 40–1. [16] A. P. Toulouse, CA 113, p. 44.
[17] Cover this breast which I should not see; such objects offend the spirit, and cause sinful thoughts.

A true *sodalis* considered chastity as the first virtue. It was no coincidence that the little manual intended for the Aas and entitled *Pratique des vertus chrestiennes* began with it.[18] Jacques Rem established the Colloquium Marianum at Ingolstadt in order to form 'a group of true Children of Mary, amongst whom there would be not one soiled soul'. Entry came only after a test lasting several weeks and a commitment to lead not only an edifying life in the eyes of the world, but a life of perpetual purity.[19] Aloysius of Gonzaga, and later Stanislaus Kostka, much venerated in Italy and in the Germanic countries well before their canonisation at the beginning of the eighteenth century, represented the models to be imitated. They had disciples almost everywhere, who, after the example of St Aloysius, who dared not raise his eyes to his mother, fled the very sight of women. This was common practice from the beginning of the seventeenth century at Dillingen, Trent, Augsburg, Lucerne and, as we have seen, at Fribourg.[20] It was not, of course, unusual in the period of Catholic reform, or confined only to the *sodales*. To preserve in the child and the adolescent the grace of baptism was a constant concern of all the spiritual schools. The Jesuit congregations of the Angels were matched by the 'Little Schools' of Port-Royal, whose initial aim was identical to theirs.[21] What was less common was the encouragement and glorification of such perseverance in adults. The members of the Regensburg Civica scourged each other every week in an attempt to become more resolute in their chastity.[22] A certain burgess of Cologne was held up as an example because, in thirty years in the town, he had not had a single conversation with a woman.[23] In the funeral eulogies of the 'illustrious men' of the professed house the words 'candour' and 'innocence' recur repeatedly to describe their most eminent qualities. 'When you want to talk to your children about chastity,' Father Cordier advised mothers:

> which is the most beautiful ornament of youth, it is better to tell them about the glory of this virtue which they should practise, than about the vices which are its opposite and which they are exhorted to flee. To be ignorant of evil is

[18] *Pratique des vertus chrestiennes*, pp. 7–13.

[19] Delplace, *Histoire des congrégations de la Sainte Vierge*, p. 93.

[20] B. H. Munich, Jesuits 104, fo. 256 (Trent, 1633); Jesuits 105, fo. 11 (Dillingen, 1634); Jesuits 106, p. 11 (Augsburg, 1644); S. A. Lucerne, KK 25/2, p. 64 (Lucerne, 1698).

[21] Taveneaux, *Le Catholicisme dans la France classique*, pp. 65–8.

[22] B. H. Munich, Jesuits 106, p. 26 (1644).

[23] H. A. S. Cologne, Jesuits 9, fo. 357v (1637).

to be wise in virtue. There are many who would have died in innocence, if an indiscreet zeal had not taught them about vice, under the pretext of turning them away from it.[24]

This was the condition described in some detail by Father Claude Bernier in the account sent to Rome by his brethren, doubtless with the intention of turning him into a French Aloysius of Gonzaga. This is how he began his 'story':

I thank you, O Blessed Virgin, and you, My Angel. And You, above all, O Good Jesus, that in my infancy and all the rest of my life, it has pleased you to prevent me from knowing what is carnal pleasure, and that your Goodness has so successfully kept all evil away from me that no one has ever talked to me of it, nor I to anyone. And this by a *natural insensibility*, a great shame which has always kept me away, but even more, O God, it is your grace which has achieved this, for which I thank you and pray to all the saints.

This was extremely effective, since he added:

I thank you, O my God, that having had so little desire for any great sin against Chastity, I did not know what it was, by a *holy ignorance* which your Goodness has operated in me. I also thank you that hearing that some great sins were committed against the same virtue I did not enquire what they were, having a horror of them. I further thank you that when a certain companion of mine threw himself on me, your goodness gave me the grace to resist without my knowing that if I had let myself be conquered *I would have been lost . . . for ever*.[25]

This text has the merit of spelling out the virtue of chastity. It was Father Bernier's 'natural insensibility' and 'holy ignorance' which permitted him to be ignorant of evil, and thus protected against it. It was in no way the result of human effort. This, indeed, counted for very little, since, if the young Claude Bernier had let himself be conquered by his enterprising companion, he would have been 'lost for ever'.

This, then, is the portrait of the *dévot* of the classical period. A man of good works and devotion, he did not count the time when it came to caring for the poor or for prisoners. Humble and gentle, he wished to be open to all, while being closed to the outside world. Fleeing temptation, he made purity, on the pattern of St Aloysius of Gonzaga, the model for all congregation members, the principal

[24] Cordier, *La Famille saincte*, p. 361.
[25] A. S. J. Rome, province of France, 33^{I}, fos. 84–107 (1632). Author's italics.

virtue. These practices and this behaviour, instilled into him from an early age, became, with the passage of time, spontaneous, almost natural. Thus it is hardly surprising to read, in the 'eulogies' bestowed on dead brethren, references to the same qualities of 'gentleness', 'even temper' and 'patience' endlessly repeated. More than a matter of style, it was a question of stating facts: these men had been formed in the same school, they bore the same indelible mark. But it was the result of education – almost of drilling. The prayers repeated morning and night had all been learned, the words spoken on life's various occasions had all been laid down. Where was the real man? The response of Molière, revealing a lubricious Tartuffe beneath the paragon of virtue, was doubtless a caricature. It went, nevertheless, to the heart of the problem: could the lived religion be achieved solely by education, by the repetition of acquired gestures? The masters of the French School, in their own language, said that the *dévots* who immersed themselves in good works did not 'pray' enough and were not 'inner Christians'. Furthermore, did this fear of impurity carried to the point of anguish, especially in the case of grown men like Claude Bernier, not contain an element of infantilism?

REVOLUTIONARIES, WITHOUT REALISING IT

> Chaque jour à l'église, il venait, d'un air doux,
> Tout vis-à-vis de moi se mettre à deux genoux.
> Il attirait les yeux de l'assemblée entière
> Par l'ardeur dont au Ciel il poussait sa prière;
> Il faisait des soupirs, de grands élancements,
> Et baisait humblement la terre à tous moments;
> Et, lorsque je sortais, il me devançait vite
> Pour m'aller à la porte offrir de l'eau bénite. *(act I, scene 5)*[26]

Apart from the hurried departure to rejoin Orgon at the exit, all the actions described here could be those of a congregation member piously and intently following the various parts of the Mass. Participation in the office was such that one wonders if they were not celebrating it along with the priest, as, indeed, was advised by Father

[26] Every day, in church, with a mild manner, he came right up to me and knelt down. He attracted the attention of the entire gathering by the ardour with which he despatched his prayers to heaven; he sighed deeply, he was in transports, and he constantly, humbly, kissed the ground; and when I left, he quickly preceded me, so he could offer me holy water at the door.

Coster, who invited his pupils to serve at Mass as often as they could. The ceremonial in use amongst the Gentlemen of the Paris professed house is preserved in the library of the Arsenal. From it, we learn that at the congregation's own offices, it was the prefect, a layman, who led the prayers and canticles and who was the real master of ceremonies. The annual solemn ceremonies of the Immaculate Conception, the festival from which the sodality took its name, were opened the day before by him with these words: 'Beloved brothers, we will sing the Veni Creator, to implore the assistance of the Holy Spirit in obtaining the grace to celebrate our great festival in a worthy manner', after which he was to intone it slowly, and on his knees. The next day, the day of the festival, it was the prefect who, at seven o'clock, led the brethren in prayer, announced the nocturns to be sung during the octave, and intoned the psalm *Domine Labia mea aperies*, then the lessons, alternating with his assistants. 'When Lauds was over, they should begin the Holy Mass and while the Father enrobes, the Prefect will say, "Beloved brothers, we will sing the Veni Creator for the probationers who are about to be received." When Mass is over, the Prefect, accompanied by two assistants and standing in the middle of the Rail, recites, candle in hand, the formula of consecration.' Communion followed and when it was finished, 'the act of Grace will be read after which the Prefect, with the two assistants at the foot of the altar, will intone the Te Deum but in Psalmody. When the Te Deum is completed, the Prefect will say *Benedicamus Patrem et Filium cum sancto spiritu.*'

After the brief reception of those admitted to the probationary stage, 'the Prefect will say, "Beloved brothers, we will now sing Prime and Terce."' In the afternoon, at quarter-to-two, they told their beads, after which they began Nones, always under the same direction. Then they said seven Paters and seven Aves to earn the indulgence. At the evening service, they sang the Rorate and the litanies of the Holy Virgin. After the father had said prayers, it was once again the chief officer who assumed responsibility for drawing the day to a close with prayers for the dead, past and future.[27] This almost conventual office reveals even more clearly the quasi-ecclesiastical functions of the prefect and the senior officials. When one remembers that these were performed not only on the festival of the Immaculate Conception, but every Sunday and every feast day,

[27] B. Ars. Paris, MSS, 2042.

one can understand how they came to give those who assumed them a quasi-ecclesiastical comportment: modest bearing and a dignified expression, a voice full of unction, and an exterior austere and devoid of elegance. Which meant that on observing a *dévot* leaving the oratory, walking modestly, eyes down, enveloped in his black cloak, a passer-by might be forgiven for wondering if he was not a man of the church.

> Et tout ce qu'il contrôle est fort bien contrôlé.
> C'est au chemin du Ciel qu'il prétend vous conduire. *(act I, scene 1)*[28]

Priests, or almost, in the churches, the *dévots* also ruled at home. The pious pupils of the Cologne college prided themselves, as early as the sixteenth century, on turning the houses of their landlords into semblances of boarding schools, banishing indecent pictures and regulating home life according to a strict timetable.[29] At the beginning of the seventeenth century, a special congregation, that of Saint-Isidore, widespread in the towns and countryside of Austria, Southern Germany and the countries of the Mediterranean, had as its aim the suppression of blasphemy.[30] It also took an interest in morality in the home and in the family. Its members had to promise not to make male and female servants sleep in the same room.[31] The same rule applied, even more stringently, to children, who had to be rigorously separated according to sex. The Gentlemen of Caen, for their part, could conceive of nothing more urgent, when a needy family was drawn to their attention, than to provide 'beds to separate people' and to 'prevent by this means serious irregularities'.[32]

Food and drink were also the subject of great vigilance. In 1610, the brethren of the Cologne Civica distributed tracts against drunkenness about the streets.[33] Violations of fasts were denounced with especial vigour. Abstinence from meat on Fridays and during Lent was, after all, a tangible sign, above all in countries where there was contact between confessions, of belonging to the Roman Church. Anyone who broke the rules was soon deemed to be half-Lutheran and publicly denounced as such. One demonstration of this was the unhappy fate which befell a burgess of a little town on the lower

[28] And all that he controls is very well controlled. He claims he is leading you on the path to heaven. [29] See above, pp. 12 and 20.
[30] B. H. Munich, Jesuits 89, piece 7. [31] *Ibid.*
[32] Fouqueray, *Les Oeuvres sociales*, p. 6.
[33] H. A. S. Cologne, Jesuits 9, fo. 222.

Rhine, sitting peacefully at table surrounded by his family, eating meat on a fast day; all of a sudden, a commando of congregation members burst into the room, sending food and plates flying; 'You are a Lutheran in Lent and a Catholic at Easter', one of them shouted at the culprit, who, assailed by the gibes of the mob, did not know where to put himself.[34]

The houses of declared Protestants were kept under surveillance, especially when Catholic domestic servants were employed there. It was a work of piety to rescue the latter from these places of perdition.[35] In exclusively Catholic countries, a whole town might end up living according to the rules decreed by the fathers. This was the case in Swiss Fribourg in the seventeenth century. After remonstrations by the Jesuit preacher of Saint-Nicolas, the Senate in 1665 forbad secular meetings and, with greater vigour, evening dances.[36] In fact, anyone seen in the streets of this small town at night was suspected of being up to no good. A *sodalis* discovered in such circumstances, especially if he carried no light, was urged to confess without delay.[37]

This preacher, who enjoyed considerable power, won further concessions from the town council. The latter came, in effect, to regulate the length of female dress. Women should be covered to their wrists; there were to be no bare arms, much less bare breasts. At this point, by a happy chance, a comet was seen in the skies of Fribourg, which spread terror amongst the inhabitants. Further measures ensued in an attempt to appease heaven: there were to be no more masques, no more balls, and an end to Carnival.[38] A few years later, in response to a request from the same father, the magistrates had the bell of the principal church rung every Thursday afternoon at five o'clock to remind everyone of Christ's Agony on the Mount of Olives. The inhabitants, immediately they heard the bell, wherever they were, interrupted their activities to say five Paters and five Aves.[39] The culmination of the dozens of years of understanding between the two powers, religious and secular, came in 1699, when it was decided that any pupil expelled from the college should

[34] N. P. Cologne, Reiffenberg MSS, vol. 1, p. 209 (1632).
[35] H. A. S. Cologne, Jesuits 9, fo. 358v (1637).
[36] N. P. Cologne, Hartmann MSS, vol. 4, fo. 36.
[37] B. C. U. Fribourg, MSS, L 107 (1), p. 292 (1669).
[38] N. P. Cologne, Hartmann MSS, vol. 4, fo. 36 (1665).
[39] *Ibid.*, fos. 42v–43 (1673).

immediately be banned from the town too.[40] Fribourg, like Molsheim and Ingolstadt at the same period, and like the 'reductions' of Paraguay, seemed to be ruled by the Jesuits.

In Paris, certainly, things were very different. But this did not prevent the brethren of the Aa from feeling free to remove from the hands of men of quality books which they reckoned to be 'full of obscenities'.[41] Others, having, like Molière's Tartuffe, gained entry into good houses, did not forbear from chiding masters they thought too indolent in their concern for things of the spirit, too free in their conversation with their children, or too frivolous in their reading. They resolutely took things in hand, gathered the family together in the evening for communal prayers, despatched the servants to confession, and made a point of checking whether they went.[42]

Taking the place of priests in the churches, of magistrates in the towns, and of fathers in their own homes, were the *dévots* not in the process of overturning the social order and installing new powers? Naturally, they acted for the greater glory of God, with no other aim in mind. According to Monsieur de Renty:

> It is a fine humility to see in oneself only nothingness, and he who sees there only nothingness sees nothing; thus the soul which sees nothing in itself finds in itself nothing to distract it, and by this means is always directed towards God; it is like a needle drawn by a magnet, which having been enveloped in all sorts of clutter, is freed; for it at once turns towards its North, and remains fixed there, even though the tempestuous sea and the winds overturn the vessel. This is the disposition and the vision of the truly humble soul, seeing nothing in itself, and a vision of God in his grandeur.[43]

Only, this humble man was everywhere. In church, at the hospital, in the prisons and in the hovels of the poor he assisted, he ruled and was master. And he did so with all the more authority in that he was supported by a powerful organisation with ramifications everywhere, extending throughout the kingdom and flourishing outside royal authority.

REJECTED IN PARIS, RESPECTED IN MUNICH

> C'est à vous d'en sortir, vous qui parlez en maître:
> La maison m'appartient, je le ferai connaître. *(act IV, scene 7)*[44]

[40] *Ibid.*, fo. 67. [41] A. P. Toulouse, CA 101, vol. 1, fos. 134v–137v (1691).
[42] *Ibid.*, fos. 137v–141v (1692).
[43] Saint-Jure, *La Vie de Monsieur de Renty*, pp. 67–8.
[44] It is for you, who speak as master, to leave: the house belongs to me, I will make this clear.

The strong words which struck fear into Orgon and his family had perhaps the value of a warning. They were addressed first of all to the King. The danger was at the heart of the kingdom. At court, in the royal entourage, among the great officers, in the great bodies of state, the congregation and the Society of the Holy Sacrament were present. They risked influencing the policies of the sovereign, and, above all, of interposing themselves like a screen between the latter and his subjects. But families were even more threatened. Paternal omnipotence, already criticised in the writings of certain Jesuits such as Father Cordier, might well be reduced to insignificance if the *dévots* had their way. The latter were in effect in the process of establishing a new power, their own, a real intermediary power between the superior authorities, which they did not contest, but on which they did not depend (king and bishop), and the basic structures of daily life (parish, family and craft).

Nor was it only society which was at issue. The dominant culture, that of the majority of cultivated French people of the period, was equally threatened. Cléant reproaches Orgon for his tendency to:

> Confondre l'apparence avec la vérité. *(act I, scene 5)*[45]

Could this accusation not be levelled against the *dévots*, preoccupied more with demonstrating their piety to the outside world than testing it within themselves, more concerned with imitating models than with examining their underlying principles? The Cartesian method enunciated at the beginning of the *Traité de la lumière* ('The first thing that I want to tell you is that there may be a difference between the feeling that we have, that is to say the idea which forms in our imagination through the medium of our eyes, and what is in the objects which produce this feeling in us') had no credit in the congregations.[46] Nor did they have much regard for rules of honesty and propriety. Their 'sighs' and 'transports', their kissing of the ground and lengthy kneeling before church doors must have appeared somewhat affected.

Nevertheless, the fear and even rejection of the *dévots* which is revealed in Molière's play, and which must have been shared by many who saw it, bourgeoisie and men of the court, was found neither in Germany nor in Italy. The Munich Major and the noble sodalities of Naples enjoyed great prestige amongst the general public. This was

[45] Confound appearance with reality.

[46] René Descartes, *Le Monde ou traité de la lumière*, ed. Geneviève Rodis-Lewis (Paris, 1966), p. 221.

visible on the occasion of the festivals they organised and in the catalogues of members which they published. To be inscribed alongside so many titled and illustrious men was an honour, and tantamount to certification as a man of quality. It was a manifest proof of belonging to the country's élite. Far from exciting suspicion, the academic congregations provoked envy. This situation was doubtless connected with the presence of the prince at the head of the congregation. Account must also be taken, at least in Germany, of the situation in towns such as Mayence and Munich, where the social structures had not yet acquired in the seventeenth century the rigidity which was visible in Paris at the time of Louis XIV. Rather than foreign bodies introduced into a society already formed, were the congregations of the Rhineland and the Germanic countries not, on the contrary, the constituent elements of a social body in formation?[47]

Last, and perhaps not least, the French *dévots* were not quite the same as those of other countries. Nowhere more than in France, not even in the kingdom of Naples, whose congregations and Monti had served as models, had an organisation both so solid and so discreet been established, country-wide, and affecting the principal charitable works as well as the centres for the training of the clergy (see figure 11, p. 106). The devout system was unique. When it was revealed, it was a source of unease; when it was known to have connections with the Society of Jesus, and to be partly inspired by it, it caused fear. In a country where the Jesuits had never been accepted by the majority of Catholics, where they had always aroused the distrust of one section of public opinion, including amongst the entourage of the king, it was inevitable that the discovery of this organisation would provoke a violent reaction. This was all the greater in that the secrecy, or at least the discretion, which embraced the whole system, made the danger obscure and therefore worse. *Tartuffe* was one sign of this shift of opinion. The King had already let it be known that he wanted the Society of the Holy Sacrament to cease meeting. From the period 1665–70, the *dévots*, at least those from the ruling class, were under surveillance, and their organisation in the country, without disappearing completely, lost its cohesion. In Munich, on the contrary, this period saw the start of the great forward surge of the Major and its immense success throughout Bavaria. A divergent evolution was

[47] See below, chapter 12.

beginning, one sign among others of the distance separating the two cultures.[48]

The portrait of the *dévot* of the classical period as it has appeared in the course of this analysis is full of contrasts and presents many apparently contradictory features. Conservative in some ways, the *dévot* was an innovator – even a highly disquieting one – in others. The religion he practised was very simple, even naive. Traditional devotions such as the cult of the Virgin, great manifestations of piety such as pilgrimages, charitable works such as the care of the poor and of prisoners, concern with purity and a special reverence for saints who had retained a 'holy innocence', were its main features. But at the same time, its desire to 'reform the world' had never been expressed so forcefully nor employed such effective methods. The danger of the movement perhaps lay, for its opponents, in this dual character: the *dévots* practised the religion of the people, and could influence them through the congregations, whilst, on the other hand, they risked, though certainly without any subversive intent, toppling the social order. They constituted a threat to both state and society. But the threat was perhaps even greater for classical civilisation. For, by their religious sentiment and by their behaviour, the *dévots* showed that they did not share the same culture as that which was beginning to be dominant in France, the culture of Bérulle, Pascal and Descartes. *Tartuffe* can be seen as a form of reaction against a phenomenon which had also its cultural implications. The specificity of the kingdom of France was thus confirmed at the heart of the Europe of the devout.

The effects of the Marian congregations are thus visible in domains as different as the political conduct of princes, the behaviour of craftsmen during the great crises of the seventeenth century, the changes taking place within the structure of the family, and assistance to the poor, the sick and prisoners. They left their mark on the evolution of lived religion. The great pilgrimages, the various features of baroque devotion and, above all, the communal piety developed within the congregations are elements which still mark the religious life of numerous populations, from Belgium to Bavaria. Jansenism can, in a way, be understood as a reaction against practices which, thanks to the Jesuits and their congregations, overran the whole of

[48] See Tapié *La France de Louis XIII*, especially pp. 154–263.

Europe. And, lastly, men, too, were changed. A type, the *dévot*, visible only in colleges and some chapters at the end of the sixteenth century, had spread, half a century later, to the town and the court. A play like *Tartuffe* is in its own way evidence of this.

Nevertheless, with the passage of time, the differences between the various countries increased. Whilst in some, like Bavaria, the congregations were utilised by the prince to strengthen the state, in others, like France, they were suspected of injuring it. While the sodalities created to promote religion were accepted as such in most Catholic countries, in France, on the other hand, there were people who accused them of seeking the ruin of Christendom. While in Munich and Mayence the *sodalis* was highly regarded, in the state of the Most Christian King he was often viewed with distrust, when he was not the object of mockery. A geography of the devout movement for the high point of the period 1660–70 shows that the kingdom of France was characterised by a reserve found nowhere else. Such reticence was perhaps due, as Molière's comedy reveals, to the fact that the consequences of the sodalities were sometimes very far removed from those anticipated by their founders. Devotion concealing turpitude, charity serving as a pretext for confining the poor, apostleship in workshops favouring professional associations, even *compagnonnage*, the active participation of Christian princes and their nobilities in sodalities as a means of strengthening the cohesion of states – these were all deviations which contemporaries observed and criticised. Was this just the imperfection inseparable from any work of man or was the institution vitiated from the start by an order, the Society of Jesus, which was accused of having only 'faction' and 'cabal' in mind? Whatever the answer, the direct and indirect consequences for the society and mentality of modern Europe were not negligible.

PART IV *Towards the birth of a Catholic society*

For the Marian congregations, as for other manifestations of religious life, the eighteenth century was a time of great paradox. After considerable progress in the seventeenth century, decline seemed to set in as early as the 1680s. In Antwerp, Rouen and Paris alike, recruitment dried up and membership slumped. The attacks directed against the Society of Jesus soon extended to include the congregations themselves. The suppression of the Jesuit order in several countries, then, in 1773, by the Pope himself, entailed the disappearance of the institutions with which it was linked.

However, it was at this very period that these old associations demonstrated their greatest vitality, spreading to the countryside, opening up to women, children and the whole family, and adapting to social change. Condemned along with the Jesuits, they found fertile ground in the parishes, where they developed in new ways, and survived the French Revolution, often unharmed.

It was in the eighteenth century – especially towards the end, which appeared least propitious for religious institutions – that the long-term effects of the congregations began to make themselves felt. The primary objective of the founders was on the point of entering the realms of reality. A Catholic society emerged, and new ways of thinking appeared amongst the Gentlemen and the artisans. The *dévots* gave way to men of action and Christian workers. Elites of a new type were formed as the nineteenth century dawned, ready to regroup Catholic forces in powerful associations with social and political ends, and adapted to the needs of contemporary Europe.

10. *Crisis*

Appearances were hardly propitious, either in France or in the great northern towns such as Antwerp and Cologne, which had for so long seemed models for the success of the congregations. Everywhere, there were signs of decline. Reasons are not hard to find. After more than a century and a half of varied initiatives and often intense activity, the Marian congregations were perhaps simply running out of steam. The effects of Jansenism, or, more particularly, of a certain distrust, increasingly widespread, of the Society of Jesus, help to explain the withdrawal of, in the first place, the élites and then a loss of enthusiasm on the part of the masses. Besides, fiercely criticised by the royal lawyers in their charges against the Jesuits, the congregations were, like them, condemned and suppressed after 1760.

THE SYMPTOMS

The crisis was suddenly apparent round about 1720. 'See, Holy Virgin, the sad state to which we are reduced', exclaimed the author of the obituaries devoted to the 'illustrious men' of the professed house in Paris.[1] This was not just the ritual lamentation of a man of the Church regretting the past. The acts of consecration to the Virgin preserved in the Archives Nationales show that whereas there had been an average of over ten registrations per year in the celebrated congregation between 1670 and 1700, there were only five between 1711 and 1720, and fewer than three between 1721 and 1730.[2] The same was true of the Gentlemen of Rouen: there were ten entries a year at the end of the seventeenth century, but only three between 1726 and 1735, and only one between 1756 and 1761. This congregation presented a sorry picture in 1740, when it consisted of only a handful of elderly gentlemen who were reluctant to climb the thirty-three steps leading to their chapel! So much so that out of the twenty-

[1] B. Maz. Paris, MSS, 3335, p. 10. [2] A. N. Paris, MM 649, 650.

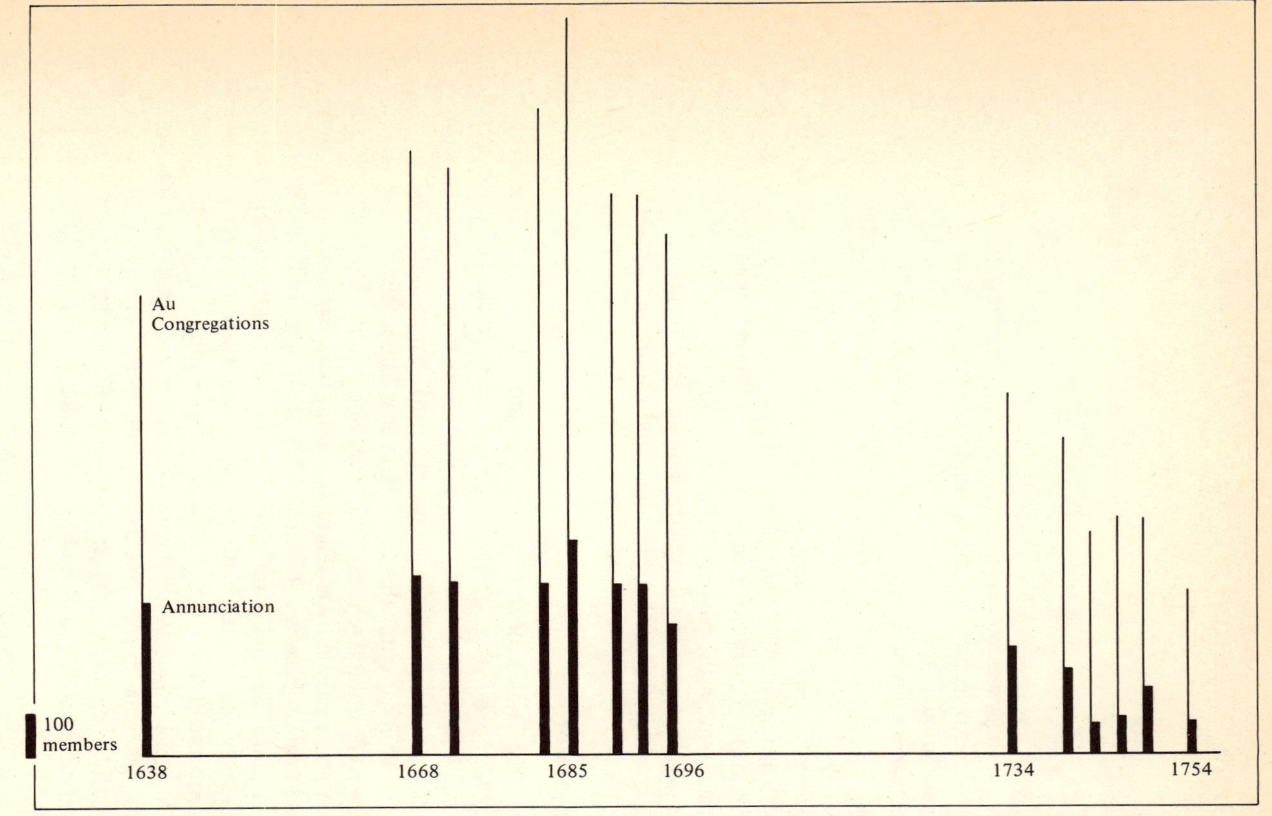

12. The congregations in Antwerp in the seventeenth and eighteenth centuries (evolution of membership)

five to thirty members registered, no more than eight or ten, at most, were still regular attenders at the offices or the ordinary meetings.[3] It was the same in Dijon, Rheims and Rennes.[4] In Cologne in 1726, 229 young artisans suddenly left their congregation.[5] In Antwerp, four years later, 150 members of the famous sodality of the Nativity, the sodality of the artists and specialised workers, suddenly disappeared from the registers. Ten years later, it was the sodality itself which showed no sign of life.[6]

Even more spectacular was the collapse, in the same town, of the very important congregation of Flemish married men, that of the Annunciation. In 1685, at the height of its glory, at the time of its jubilee, it figured in the statistics with a thousand members. Sixty years later, it had fewer than a hundred. The great register of enrolments preserved in the Bibliothèque Royale in Brussels confirms these figures, and paints an even gloomier picture of the situation:[7] 442 entries only for the eighteenth century, as compared with 3,663 for the century before (see figure 12 opposite). Further, most of these eighteenth-century registrations were made between 1700 and 1730. After that, only thirty-four names were recorded, that is 7.7% of the total for the century. Even allowing for negligence (in itself significant), it is clear that the congregation was moribund. As early as the beginning of the century, the annalist was saying that charity was not what it had been.[8] In 1720, it was the processions which were hard to keep going, even for the main festivals, due to the small number of participants.[9] In 1740, it was the offices, including the most solemn, which were deserted. It had been the custom to display the Holy Sacrament on the occasion of the re-election of the magistrates. The custom had been abolished some years back, it was explained, 'as a result of the small number of brethren who then communicated'.[10] A few years later, it was the foundations which were in danger.

Our sodality found itself in the same unhappy state [as that of the Walloons], to the point where, as a result of the small sums collected, we would have been unable to continue our services, if in the year 1722 the magistrates and the

[3] Féron, *Sociétés secrètes*, pp. 66–7.
[4] A. S. J. Rome, province of Champagne, 13, 14, 15, 16, 17; Delattre, *Les Etablissements des jésuites*, vol. 4.
[5] H. A. E. Cologne, parish of Saint-Alban, A II/42, fos. 35–7v.
[6] A. P. B. M. Namur, Droeshout deposit 24,6, p. 54.
[7] B. R. Brussels, MSS, 20088.
[8] A. P. B. M. Namur, Droeshout deposit 24,5, pp. 134–5.
[9] *Ibid.*, p. 362. [10] *Ibid.*, 24,6, p. 54.

former prefects had not imposed an annual tax of two florins, by means of which we can now meet all the expenses of our service.[11]

In 1753, according to the father director, Mass was very rarely said in the oratory during the week.[12] Fifteen years later, the principal function of the congregation had become the organisation of a great annual banquet. The decorated floats of the processions, the carved scenes on trestles in the churches, the open-air theatres on the feast days of the canonisation of the Society's saints were replaced by elaborate confectionery! Thanks to the skill of the *pâtissier*, on the occasion of his jubilee, the father *praeses* could admire three impressive constructions depicting stages in his career, the Church triumphing over heresy and the unity of the *sodales* – in marzipan, nougat and crystallised fruit.[13] One of the last decisions taken by the magistrates is particularly indicative of what this great congregation had become by the end of the eighteenth century. Fines were no longer to be levied on brethren who failed to attend meetings on Sundays and the principal festivals. On the other hand, 'it was resolved to demand a voluntary subscription of four sous a month from all those who wished to meet sociably once a year at a gathering where they would eat and drink according to how much money there was in the chest'.[14] After two centuries of existence, the celebrated congregation of the Annunciation, the congregation which had restored the statue of the Virgin to the pediment of the Hôtel de Ville, which had been founded by Father Coster and inspired by him to perform every exercise of piety and apostleship, had been reduced, not just to a simple confraternity, but to a bourgeois society of *bons vivants*.

Nevertheless, in this great Flemish town, the changes were effected in a spirit of harmony, which was not everywhere the case. In the early years of the eighteenth century, a certain ill temper was often visible, leading to actions which were hardly compatible with the spirit of the rules or with simple Christian charity. There were exclusions. The burgesses of Pau did not want a *cagot*, that is a leper, in their ranks;[15] the artisans of Grenoble did not accept persons 'of the lesser sort, such as archers, sergeants, butchers, tripemongers, porters, the lower sort of domestic servants'.[16] There were disputes. In 1729, the same Grenoble

[11] *Ibid.*, pp. 146–7. [12] *Ibid.*, p. 241. [13] *Ibid.*, pp. 417–18 (1767).
[14] *Ibid.*, p. 425 (1768). [15] Laborde, *Les Congrégations des Bourgeois.*
[16] Pra, *Les Jésuites à Grenoble*, p. 314.

congregation was split over the question of the composition of its council; some held to the custom by which ex-prefects and ecclesiastics were life members of the council by right with the title *conseillers-nés*; others, led by a certain Stephen M., master tailor, wanted no more *conseillers-nés*. The partisans of tradition thought they could put an end to the dispute by striking Stephen M. off the register. But Stephen, who was not without friends in high places, renewed his challenge. On the day of the council re-elections, each party elected its own. The scandal was immense, and needed all the diplomacy of the Provincial to impose a compromise.[17]

At Montpellier, those who were excluded from office protested and threatened to register with the White Penitents. In an attempt to appease them, the number of places on the council was increased; by 1725, it had fifty members.[18] At Rodez, thirty years later, the council had sixty-eight members.[19] A veritable congregation was constituted within the larger whole. This in itself must have been a source of further conflict. Incidents of this type were by no means exceptional; a systematic investigation would certainly reveal many more.

Absenteeism and discord, often both, were the manifestations of a malaise which seems to have affected many congregations during the course of the eighteenth century. The drying-up of recruitment was a logical consequence. In Antwerp, once an exemplary town, the collapse was such in less than half a century that the congregations had virtually disappeared well before the suppression of the Society of Jesus (see figure 12, p. 178).

THE CAUSES

Time, it may be thought, was perhaps the chief culprit. Was it not inevitable that, with its passing, men would drift from the enthusiasm of the early days into conformism, routine, and the pettinesses of everyday life? Even in the Aas, those schools for the heroic life, this loss of impetus soon made itself felt. The brethren of the Paris Aa, which, in the middle of the seventeenth century, had energetically inspired all the secret associations in France, recognised in 1699 that they had sunk very low and that they were no longer in a position to

[17] *Ibid.*, pp. 324–40.
[18] Delattre, *Les Etablissements des jésuites*, vol. 3, cols. 526–35.
[19] *Ibid.*, vol. 4, cols. 481–4.

perform those practices which they had formerly imposed on their 'daughters', such as a regular correspondence. They wrote to the brethren of Toulouse:

For it must be admitted, Gentlemen and dear brethren, that we should be covered with shame for not having earlier performed a practice as ancient as it is useful for preserving unity between the children of the divine Mary, but we have had the sorrow of seeing our congregation, which you recognise as the source of your own, almost destroyed and dissipated by the activities of some, the apathy of others, and, to speak frankly, by the laxity of almost all its members – only three or four brothers, still retaining their respect for the association, have been unable to bring themselves to follow the torrent of bad example, and have not ceased to meet from time to time for the discussions, and have tried to restore it to the proper practice of its rules without which it can never survive.[20]

Four years later, the situation was no better. It had even deteriorated.

It is not without real pain that we have so delayed writing . . . but it must be admitted that the few things we have to tell you have been in part the cause of our delay.[21]

This was followed by total silence: the Paris Aa had ceased to exist.

In towns where the Aa continued, like Toulouse, it seemed to be afflicted by a certain suspicion towards intellectual labour and those who practised it to effect. 'The persons whose opinions we should most respect', wrote the author of the *Histoire abrégée de l'Aa*, 'tell us on all sides that there is not enough study within the Aa.'[22] This judgement, made by someone who knew the association well, is doubly significant when it is compared with a rule from the mid-eighteenth century which says:

Nor will someone with distinguished and surpassing abilities be judged appropriate for the Association, unless his piety equals them. As for what has been said about the less gifted, we observe that we may receive someone who, being only a little below average, nevertheless exhibits an exceptional piety, known and respected as such within the community.[23]

It is clear that in the century of Enlightenment, men of ability were not only not sought after in what should have been the gathering of

[20] A. P. Toulouse, CA 101,1, fos. 189v–191.
[21] *Ibid.*, fo. 208v (20 March 1703). [22] A. P. Toulouse, CA 167, p. 178.
[23] Quoted by Comte Bégouen, *Une société secrète émule de la Compagnie du Saint-Sacrement: l'Aa de Toulouse aux XVIIe et XVIIIe siècles d'après des documents inédits* (Paris–Toulouse, 1913), p. 83.

the élite of the congregations, but were even kept at a distance. In which case, it is hardly surprising that an institution made to adapt to all circumstances and intended to attract men of all conditions seemed on the road to ruin. The original intention of Fathers Leunis and Coster, as of Fathers Bagot and Vincent de Meur, was surely to reach the best elements amongst the clergy, the students and men of influence, though without neglecting the simple urban craftsmen. This contraction was a disturbing sign for an institution conceived with the intention of transforming the world.

The Society of Jesus, it is true, was probably no longer what it had been. At the very least, it no longer seemed to accord to the direction of the congregations the same great importance as formerly. The second Aa founded in Toulouse with the intention of meeting the needs of the clergy and the pious laity was soon faced with a serious problem, that of its direction. There was no father to see to it. For 5 January 1687, the deputy noted in the register: 'The meetings [have been] discontinued for some months, in default of finding a father who found it convenient to attend.'[24] A year and a half later, the matter had still not been settled, since:

> it was agreed that to effect an improvement, it was necessary to have some Jesuit father who wished to take the trouble to direct the meeting. That is why it was resolved to offer extraordinary prayers to God and our patron saints for nine days, each priest having volunteered to say a Mass for this purpose so that we can find someone who is in a position to revive and maintain our spirit.[25]

The absence of a director was a frequent cause of the decline, even the actual disappearance, of a congregation. Similar consequences ensued when the person designated by the rector lacked the requisite qualities or necessary health to carry out his duties. This was the explanation given by the Antwerp annalist for the rapid decline of the membership of the sodality of the Flemish married men in the eighteenth century – the father was impotent. He retired in 1743 and was replaced by an excellent preacher who attracted large crowds.[26] Too talented, doubtless, in the eyes of his superiors for the function entrusted to him, he was soon replaced. His successors did not put the same care into performing their duties.

[24] B. M. Toulouse, MSS, 277, fo. 51. [25] *Ibid.*, fo. 61v.
[26] A. P. B. M. Namur, Droeshout deposit 24,6, p. 97.

This year [1752], on Christmas Eve, there was no meeting of the sodality nor catechism, because of the rush of people to the confessionals; for the same reason, the discussion that day at the church of the professed house did not take place.[27]

If meetings were held less frequently, and sermons became rare or boring, it is hardly surprising that attendance was smaller and less regular, and that, little by little, it ceased.

The opposite might also happen. As well as fathers too little present, there were those who wanted to run everything. 'They want to be masters in everything', they began to say in Fribourg at the beginning of the eighteenth century, having put up with this for decades without complaint.[28] The perpetual minor frictions between Jesuits and curés over burials or the times of the offices assumed, after 1700, major proportions, and became prolonged and bitter conflicts. This happened in Grenoble and even in small towns like Molsheim (Alsace), where the Jesuits had initially been particularly well received.[29]

Is it still necessary, therefore, to invoke the Jansenist sympathies of the clergy, as did the editors of the *Annual Letters*, to explain the difficulties of the congregations in the eighteenth century? It was certainly the case that the antipathy of a bishop towards the Jesuits might have serious consequences for the activities of the congregations. The three sodalities of Auxerre appeared in the Roman lists during the episcopate of Monseigneur de Caylus with the note: 'Not active by the wish of the Jansenist Bishop.'[30] In Rheims and Châlons-sur-Marne, their limited success in the second half of the seventeenth century may be largely attributable to the same cause.[31] The crisis at Antwerp was heralded in the 1690s by reports addressed to the Bishop on the subject of the processions organised by the fathers on the feast days of the Virgin. They were accused of encouraging practices which reeked of 'a sort of idolatry'. Their opponents grew increasingly virulent and it was not long before their doctrine and their practice of confession was attacked from the cathedral pulpit itself.[32]

27 *Ibid.*, p. 226. 28 N. P. Cologne, Hartmann MSS, vol. 4, fo. 85.

29 Pra, *Les Jésuites à Grenoble*, pp. 318–20 (Grenoble); A. B. R., G 1945, letter of 17 November 1768; G 1946, letters of 16 and 17 November 1748 (Molsheim, correspondence of the Bishop of Strasbourg).

30 A. S. J. Rome, province of Champagne, 17, fos. 77–8.

31 *Ibid.*, 13, 14, 15, 16, 17.

32 A. P. B. M. Namur, Droeshout deposit 24,4, pp. 259–60, 548, 645.

But, in many cases, a simple abatement of the apostolic zeal of the sons of St Ignatius in a sector which had formerly been regarded as privileged, together with the desire expressed by some of them to rule everything, paradoxical in such circumstances, explains the decline of their activities. Added to which, the Society no longer, in the Age of Enlightenment, enjoyed those external supports from which it had once benefited. The Kings of France, who, with the exception of Louis XIII, had never demonstrated a marked affection for the congregations, showed themselves distant, if not openly hostile, in the eighteenth century. In 1716, the Regent went so far as to prohibit soldiers from joining.[33] This repudiation from on high damaged the congregations as a whole, and above all that of the Gentlemen. Meetings in the professed house of the Saint-Paul quarter of Paris were interrupted for a period. When they resumed, the number of members and their fervour had greatly diminished.[34].

For their part, the bishops, even those – the majority – who were entirely faithful to Rome, and whose doctrine in no way differed from that taught by the Jesuits, no longer showed for their works the same solicitude as previously. The reason is simple: they had at their disposal a diocesan clergy very markedly superior to that directed by their distant predecessors in the early years of the seventeenth century. Why encourage in the churches of the regulars devotions which might now just as well be practised, and, what is more, under episcopal control, in the parish?

A CRISIS OF THE CONGREGATIONS OR A CHANGING SOCIETY?

This was not, however, the most serious problem. The congregations established at the end of the sixteenth century, in close symbiosis with specific economic, social and political structures, found themselves, two centuries later, in a wholly changed environment. Did their difficulties perhaps spring from the problems of adapting to a new external situation?

The Antwerp annalist, recording the crisis which afflicted the congregations, particularly that of the young craftsmen, around 1730, offered the following explanations:

As for our seven sodalities of the Blessed Virgin, we have to say, sadly, that they have lost a certain number of brethren; this diminution cannot be

[33] Villaret, *Les Congrègations mariales*, p. 575.
[34] B. Maz. Paris, MSS; 3335, fly-leaf.

attributed to the negligence of the father directors, but principally to the ever-increasing depopulation of the town of Antwerp, occasioned by the exodus of many citizens, who are either guilty of false moneying, or suspected of being accessories to it, or forced by the harshness of the times and the meagreness of wages to leave their homes.[35]

Putting on one side the question of the fabrication of false money, on which we are in no position to pronounce, let us consider the 'harshness of the times' and the 'meagreness of wages'. If the congregations in Antwerp were in crisis in the eighteenth century, it was perhaps because the town itself was experiencing serious difficulties. The silk industry, one of the pillars of economic activity, which provided employment for between eight and nine thousand people in 1698, suffered a serious crisis from the beginning of the eighteenth century as a result of the massive import of cheaper products from China. The protectionist policies of the United Provinces, too, had unfortunate consequences for the activity of the other branches of the cloth industry, such as hemp, linen and lace. It was this malaise, which spread rapidly and led to the unemployment of thousands of journeymen and the failure of numerous masters, which explains the often violent disturbances of the year 1718.[36]

China and Holland were not entirely to blame. The increasingly fierce competition which the towns faced from the rural industries was another major development of this century. The considerable progress of the industries of the regions of Verviers and Limbourg threatened the position acquired by the great Flemish towns.[37] They maintained their control over the manufacture and marketing of the products, it is true, but at the price of a complete transformation of their industrial structures. The independent masters disappeared, and were replaced by entrepreneurs and workers. When, in 1775, the government lifted the prohibition on the employment of machines for making ribbons, the trade of the Antwerp ribbon-makers was transformed within the space of a few years. The hundred or so masters who had dominated it disappeared; in their place, seven merchants confronted eight hundred journeymen. One calculation from the end of the eighteenth century shows that 76 % of the weavers

[35] A. P. B. M. Namur, Droeshout deposit 24,5, p. 505.

[36] *Ibid.*, pp. 506–8 (numerous remarks about false moneying in Antwerp at the time when France was experiencing the repercussions of Law's System).

[37] Jan Van Acker, *Anvers d'escale romaine à port mondial* (Antwerp–Brussels, 1975), pp. 336–48; Van Cauwenberghs, 'L'industrie de la soie à Anvers', pp. 105–46.

of stuffs and 82% of the weavers of linen were already wage-earners.[38]

What was true of the cloth trade, the main industry, was found in other sectors. Goldsmiths and diamond workers were in crisis from 1715. It is hardly surprising that the population fell sharply, from 65,000 inhabitants in 1710, to 40,000 in 1765. There was an increase from that date (55,000 in 1795), but it was at the cost of a complete change in social structures. Affluent Antwerp became a town of workers, many of them living on the edge of poverty. It was calculated that 22% were needy in 1790, and the cloth workers, whose two or three sous a day barely enabled them to survive on coarse rye bread, were in an extremely precarious position.[39]

In Cologne, too, the situation of the artisans and journeymen was often desperate in the eighteenth century. There were, in brief, too many workers and not enough work; hence a fall in wages and an increase in begging. The picture painted by the fiscal archives is very bleak: half the population paid the minimum tax or none at all. Cologne was a town of poor people.[40] And they were without hope, since, even for those in employment, access to a mastership was now quite beyond their reach. In Cologne, as in Antwerp and Liège, journeymen who were unable to establish themselves still got married. In a proposal for a general hospital, it was said that:

> Young people find in these gatherings [evening encounters] the opportunity to form liaisons which they are always eager to realise too soon; as on either side there is often no dowry but love, the formalities are brief, the two interested parties soon achieve their end. The fecundity so desirable and so desired . . . often becomes in itself a source of unhappiness.[41]

Thus the journeyman and his family found themselves doomed to even blacker poverty. The conditions of work, extremely harsh in Cologne as everywhere, drove these poor wretches to extremes. Revolt was the natural outlet for so much accumulated misery. It is hardly surprising that, from 1731, the workers and sometimes even

[38] Alain Lottin and Hugo Soly, 'Aspects de l'histoire des villes des Pays-Bas méridionaux et de la principauté de Liège (du milieu du XVIIe siècle à la veille de la Révolution française)', in *Etudes sur les villes en Europe occidentale* (Paris, 1983), vol. 2, p. 231. [39] *Ibid.*, pp. 260–3.

[40] Ingrid Nicolini, *Die politische Führungsschicht in der Stadt Köln gegen Ende der reichsstädtischen Zeit*, Dissertationen zur neueren Geschichte, 7 (Cologne–Vienna, 1979), pp. 45–87.

[41] Lottin and Soly, 'Aspects de l'histoire des villes', p. 225.

their masters should appear in the large towns of the Rheno-Flemish world as the principal representatives of the 'dangerous classes'.[42]

The atmosphere of unrest was not only felt in the streets and workshops. The Marian congregations, too, were affected. This was sometimes the case even before the emergence of open discontent. At Gray in Franche-Comté, the artisans criticised the direction of the Jesuits and claimed their independence before attacking the merchants and the civil authorities.[43] At Grenoble at the same period, in the course of a fierce conflict which opposed one party in the congregation of the Assumption against the *conseillers-nés*, the director was accused of supporting the latter. When, on the revolutionary day of 26 June 1729, he tried to restore calm by reminding the rebels of the rules for the election of the council, they protested even more strongly and one of them made as if to snatch from his hands, with threatening gestures, the list of officers up for election.[44] In Lucerne in 1737, the young artisans took their director to court, accusing him of spreading calumnies about their piety, because he had reprimanded them rather sharply.[45]

A few years later, a veritable revolution broke out in Constance, in the course of which both the statutes of the association and the direction of the Jesuits were thrown out.[46] At Sélestat in Alsace, in the year of the suppression of the Society, a fierce dispute broke out between the brethren of the Agony of Christ and their former directors. The latter were accused of no more, no less than the theft of precious objects belonging to the confraternity. The Curé, during the pastoral visit of 1765, declared:

> It is strongly suspected that they have been removed to the other side of the Rhine, and that they are in some Jesuit house in the Province of Mayence, but it is not absolutely certain. In these circumstances, Sire Schaumas, as Superior, should be responsible.[47]

Disputes about the ownership of the objects of the cult or of the congregation chapel, which further embittered relations, were found in very many towns in the eighteenth century.[48] In Turin, they led to

42 Nicolini, *Die politische Führungsschicht in der Stadt Köln*, p. 125.
43 Delattre, *Les Etablissements des jésuites*, vol. 2, cols. 673–6.
44 Pra, *Les Jésuites à Grenoble*, p. 330.
45 S. A. Lucerne, KK 25/2, pp. 256–7.
46 Villaret, *Les Congrégations mariales*, p. 315.
47 A. B. R., C 343, fo. 43.
48 A. D. Rhône, D 1 (great artisans, Lyons); Féron, *Sociétés secrètes*, p. 67 (Gentlemen, Rouen); A. S. J. Rome, province of Naples, 76^{II}, fos. 640–3 (house of exercises, Naples).

the nobles declaring themselves independent of the Jesuits.[49] Without fuss or lengthy proceedings, many congregations distanced themselves from the Society. The brethren of the Visitation in Obernai in Alsace, for example, who had been directed by the fathers of Molsheim since the end of the sixteenth century, replaced them in the 1750s by Premonstratensians from the monastery of Mont Sainte-Odile.[50] The Gentlemen of Swiss Fribourg, on the other hand, asked to be transferred to a parish church.[51]

The example of the Aas is even more striking. Whereas in 1670 attachment to the Society was regarded as a characteristic feature of the secret associations, sixty years later this was no longer the case. In Paris, Bordeaux and Poitiers, the ties with the college were broken. Toulouse appears as an exception, though, at this period, several brothers, 'having an aversion for the Jesuits', 'founded another association to which they admitted ecclesiastics from all schools'.[52] In 1570, those who were trying to restore life to those Aas still in existence in France did so without reference to the fathers. The author of the *Histoire abrégée de l'Aa* reveals that a certain Monsieur Lacerre 'promised to try to bring together all the different Aas, but on the sensible and perfectly practicable condition that this business should be entirely concealed from the Jesuits'.[53] In Toulouse itself, they refused to attend a Te Deum which the latter had sung for the King's recovery (after the attempt on his life by Damiens) 'because they wanted the ecclesiastics to be mixed with the young fathers'.[54] They also refused – 'very wisely', wrote the chronicler – an invitation to a collation at the professed house.[55] At the same period, the brethren were occupied with re-editing their book of spiritual conduct, the old edition being considered to be inappropriate because it 'did not once speak of the religious state'. They did this on their own responsibility, and despite the opposition of their director.[56]

The same contentious spirit was everywhere apparent. At a period when this was on the increase, the congregations could not remain immune, all the more so since their structure, based on the structures of society, disposed them to be quickly affected by anything which

[49] Alessandro Monti, S. J., *La Compagnia di Gesú nel territorio della provincia Torinese: memorie storiche compilate in occasione del primo centenario della restaurazione di essa compagnia*, 5 vols. (Chieri, 1914–20), vol. 2, pp. 129–32.
[50] A. M. Obernai, GG 7a (accounts of the Visitation, 1747–93).
[51] N. P. Cologne, Hartmann MSS, vol. 4, fo. 145 (1771).
[52] A. P. Toulouse, CA 167, p. 51. [53] *Ibid.*, p. 88. [54] *Ibid.*, p. 80.
[55] *Ibid.* [56] *Ibid.*, pp. 91–3.

disturbed the latter. In taking root in these pious associations, the spirit of the century appeared in a specific form, that of a desire for independence with regard to the religious who had for decades imposed their tutelage on all the organisations they directed. For the artisans, it was a question of combating the authority of the father who governed their congregation; the events in Grenoble make this quite clear. For the congregations of burgesses and Gentlemen, it was a question of upholding (and if necessary extending) their rights in the face of ecclesiastical power. In the congregations of priests and theology students, it was the honour of the secular clergy which had to be defended against the age-old domination of the regulars. The dispute erupted, therefore, over emancipation. It may still be asked why this demand appeared in all the disputes which broke out in the eighteenth century between the Jesuits and those under their direction. Had the Jesuits accomplished their task so successfully that their role as tutors had become superfluous? Could the congregations, solidly constructed and instructed, perhaps now function without their guidance? Or, on the contrary, were they, too, their structures in upheaval as a result of social changes, and corrupted by the miasmas of the philosophical spirit, on the point of succumbing to anti-Jesuitism?

THE CONGREGATIONS AND THE SUPPRESSION OF THE SOCIETY OF JESUS

Decadent or not, the congregations were always singled out, and had the finger pointed at them, by the many people who, from the 1750s on, made accusations against the Society of Jesus. Monsieur de Caradeuc de La Chalotais, in his celebrated *Compte rendu des constitutions des jésuites*, set the tone by disclosing the true identity of those people who lived in the world as ordinary Christians, but who in reality acted in all things on the orders of the General in Rome. The idea of a Jesuit conspiracy took shape.

> There are still, following the Bull of Paul III, persons living in obedience to the General who enjoy exemptions, powers and rights which would seem to remove them from his authority, and of whom Pope Paul III declares that the General will conserve full and entire jurisdiction. Who are these people? Are they the anonymous Jesuits, living with their families, who do not wear a religious habit, but dress respectably, in conformity with the custom of the place where they live, and who are never loath, as the Constitutions provide,

to profess poverty? Are they the invisible Jesuits who have been talked about for two centuries? Grotius, who was bound by ties of friendship to several learned men of the Society, mentions them in his History of the Low Countries, *dant nomina conjuges*.

It is difficult to ascertain the truth of things in an Order as mysterious as that of the Jesuits. They have male and female affiliates, whose existence is not in doubt. These are aggregations and affiliations which the Generals of the Order are in a position to give to people favourable to their Institution.[57]

What was still given only vague, and thus all the more disquieting, expression in the Rennes report, became much more precise in that of Pau. The counsellors de Belloc and de Mosqueros declared to the court:

We find in a little book which has been sent to us in consequence of our last decree, a book entitled *Règles et Coûtume de la Congrégation des Habitans de Pau*, that all those who wish to be admitted into this Sodality have to spend three months on probation, to remain in a place apart from others, to learn the Rules, Customs and Practices, and when they are received, they make, at the foot of the Altars, torch in hand, Promises for which we do not see the formula; they renew them every third Sunday in January, when celebrating the Anniversary of the Establishment of the Congregation; they consecrate their promises by a Communion which they all make together; the Solemnity accorded to these promises bears a close resemblance to that employed at the making or renewal of Vows by the Jesuits.

It resembled most of all, according to Messieurs de Belloc and de Mosqueros, the ceremony of reception into some secret society or Masonic lodge. Did the congregations constitute a veritable Jesuit freemasonry in the eyes of the men of Parlement who spoke against them? The report continued:

That same spirit which runs through the Constitutions has determined the design of the Sodalities; it is remarkable that the General must know the name of every Congregation member; equally that they owe him obedience, also that they are not free to choose a Confessor, also that the Director alone has the right to expel them without any formalities, and, most of all, that the General, possessed of the right to dissolve them, becomes the Master of the Movables acquired by the body he had just abolished; it is remarkable, lastly, that a foreign Monk can give orders, on any matter whatsoever, to perhaps two hundred thousand French Subjects – we may assume this number, given

[57] Louis-René de Caradeuc de La Chalotais, *Comte rendu des constitutions des jésuites* (no place of publication, 1762), pp. 60–1.

the four hundred we can see in this little town [Pau], where the Vocation is not yet communicated to the Superior Classes of the Citizens.[58]

The various charges are clearly laid out here. The congregations were criticised for holding secret meetings dangerous to the state, for establishing within France 'the Empire of the General', in contempt of the laws of the kingdom and the rules of the Gallican Church.[59] They were also accused of evading the legitimate authority of bishops and curés, because the sodalities 'are parishes created on top of the other parishes', wrote Monsieur de La Chalotais, 'in whose favour Christians are given dispensation by Bulls from attending the offices of their church, as required by the canons'.[60]

Such accusations were not only made in the French courts. In Munich it was stated in an anonymous memorandum that the burgesses of the Annunciation constituted a veritable 'microcosm' within the town, with their oratory, their own administration and their own money chest, that they had secret formulas, that they met in the dark to engage in suspect rites, and that in consequence the interest of the state required the suppression of this association at the same time as that of the Society of Jesus.[61]

But an even worse accusation was made. By means of their congregations, the Jesuits were said to be preparing to subvert society. The royal *procureur* of Aix-en-Provence, Monsieur de Monclar, exclaimed, 'Who can withstand the shock of this phalanx whose ranks are so close and which marches always in column . . . scattering on all sides a light infantry of affiliates and congregations?'[62] Even more precisely, the members of the Brussels committee charged with the execution of the writ *Dominus ac Redemptor* (by which the Pope suppressed the Society of Jesus in 1773) in the southern Low Countries explained that the sodalities of the Jesuits 'were only the means devised by their policy to wield – under the cloak of religion – general influence over all classes of people'.[63] It was not only the authority of princes which was flouted, it was the social order too. They were preparing a revolution.

[58] Quoted by Laborde, *La Congrégation des Bourgeois*, pp. 36–7.

[59] *Apologie générale de l'institut et de la doctrine des Jésuites*, 2 vols. in one (Soleure, 1763), pp. 160–9.

[60] Caradeuc de La Chalotais, *Comte rendu des constitutions des jésuites*, p. 176.

[61] S. A. Munich, Cult, 967 (memorandum certainly of 1774).

[62] Quoted by Villaret, *Les Congrégations mariales*, p. 580.

[63] A. P. B. M. Namur, Droeshout deposit, dossiers on the suppression of the Society in the former Low Countries.

In fact, the adversaries of the Jesuits had realised that a transformation of society was brewing by means of the congregations and that this transformation was well under way. Indeed, this may even have been one of the main reasons for the violent campaign waged throughout Europe against the Society. In Paris, Parlement acted first against the sodalities, which had all to cease their activities throughout the extent of its jurisdiction in 1761.[64] In Naples, King Ferdinand IV was not content with decreeing the expulsion of the Jesuits in November 1767, but extended the measure to the laity linked to them.[65]

Nevertheless, despite the actions instituted, in spite of the writ of Clement XIV (1773) which seemed to put a stop to all the activities of the Society of Jesus, the associations of men continued to survive in Strasbourg, Cologne, Epinal, Munich and Fribourg. Elsewhere, as in Toulouse, Pau and Lyons, they re-formed once the storm had passed, established themselves in new places, followed the instructions of new directors and were well able to adapt to circumstances.

[64] Villaret, *Les Congrégations mariales*, p. 577. It was followed by the provincial Parlements. Last was the *conseil souverain* of Alsace.

[65] A. S. J. Rome, province of Naples. 76^{II}. The order was called a 'Bando'.

11. *Renewal*

Such tenacity poses a problem. Would it have been the same if the decadence of the sodalities – and this might well have been equally true for the Society of Jesus as a whole – had been a fact recognised everywhere? There were doubtless towns, perhaps even whole regions, where the signs of decline which we have tried to record did not exist. There were even places where a vitality and a prosperity which had not always been present a century earlier were manifested at the end of the eighteenth century. Activities with rules and a spirit which were entirely new were initiated and developed in mid-century.

Another geography, another public, and other functions appeared. The institution founded at the beginning of the Counter-Reformation to adapt to the society of its time was in the process of changing like the world which surrounded it.

EXPANSION, AFTER ALL

In baroque Munich, the Munich of the Church of the Theatines and the Church of the Holy Trinity, a town being transformed, covered with building works employing artists from Italy and the whole of Southern Germany, an artistic centre where architects, sculptors and painters from Bavaria and Swabia were trained, the congregation of burgesses wished to play its part, and, in building its meeting place, raise a magnificent temple to Mary. The decision was taken on 22 April 1709. The first meeting in the new room was held on 15 August 1710. In the following years, painters, sculptors and artists in stucco made their contribution. The result was the marvellous and immense Bürgersaal in the Neuhauser Strasse, obligatory stopping place for tourists starting their tour of the old town and for pilgrims come to reflect at the tomb of Father Rupert Mayer (director of the congregation in the Nazi period), which must have been even more beautiful before the destruction of April 1945. Rather than on the feast of the Assumption, when the town is invaded by outsiders, it should be visited at Christmas. It is when the light of the candlelit windows is reflected on snow falling silently in the street, when whole families crowd into the entrance and climb the narrow stairs to admire the famous crib before attending a service, that the Bürgersaal rediscovers its former glory, animated by the pious and faithful crowds which have filled it for nearly two and a half centuries. For when the Jesuit order was suppressed in 1773, the congregation of burgesses in Munich numbered over 3,000 members. It had more or less the same number a century and a half later, at the beginning of the twentieth century, and more than 7,000 when Father Rupert Mayer was its director in the 1930s. Rather than declining, therefore, the congregation expanded and developed new activities.[1]

In 1732, in Ingolstadt, the Major congregation decided to build a new meeting place. This, Our Lady of Victory, was one of the high points of Bavarian baroque. The greatest painter in Southern Germany, Cosmas Damian Asam, created, in the vast ceiling fresco and the paintings on the altar and elsewhere in the church, a hymn to the reign of Mary in heaven and on earth.[2] Similarly, in 1763, just when the Jesuits were being expelled from numerous countries in both Southern and Western Europe, the main preoccupation of the Major congregation in Augsburg was the embellishment of its buildings. The members of the Major chose, to decorate the hall where they met, the celebrated artist in stucco from Wessobrunn, Johan-Michael Feichtmayer.[3]

The festivals and great processions continued as in the past. In Augsburg in 1713, the young craftsmen and the bourgeois *sodales* organised, for the jubilee of their two congregations, splendid festivals which lasted throughout the octave of the Assumption. They were completed by a great procession with sumptuously decorated floats, which took over the town. The theme was the Virgin, city of refuge. Scene followed scene, charged with a symbolism which was sometimes abstruse but which was explained to the spectators by numerous legends. On each side walked the brothers, all in pilgrim's

[1] Lothar Altmann, 'Zur Geschichte des Bürgersaals', in *1778–1978: Der Bürgersaal: 200 Jahre Kirche in München: 30 Jahre Ruhestätte von P. Rupert Mayer S. J. Eine Festschrift* (Munich, 1978), pp. 7–24.

[2] Georg Lohmeier, 'Maria de Victoria in Ingolstadt', in *Bayern für Liebhaber: Barock und Aufklärung*, ed. Herberth Schindler (Munich, 1972), pp. 35–47.

[3] *Die Jesuiten und ihre Schule St. Salvator in Augsburg 1582*, ed. Wolfram Baer and Hans Joachim Hecker, catalogue of the exhibition for the fourth centenary of the Jesuit college of Saint-Salvator (Augsburg, 1982), pp. 49–54.

garb, with cloak, staff and rosary in hand. The different social groups were represented, from the Fuggers and magistrates, to artisans and peasants.[4] A splendid baroque procession, it was reminiscent of those held a century earlier during the festivals of the canonisation of St Ignatius and St Francis Xavier. But here, as in Cologne five years earlier, it was the virtues of the congregations which it was intended to extol, communicate to the inhabitants, and see triumph within the town, to make of it the holy Marian refuge. The population of Augsburg, however, was nearly half Lutheran at the beginning of the eighteenth century.[5] In a sense, therefore, the jubilee festivals assumed the character of an apotheosis of Catholicism, carrying into the streets and beneath the windows of the Protestants the anthem which filled the baroque churches and oratories in honour of the Virgin queen.

These manifestations were proof of a vitality which time had not dimmed. In eighteenth-century Bavaria, fraternity life seems to have experienced an extraordinary new surge of energy. A survey in 1768 revealed that the arch-confraternity of the Rosary founded under the Dominicans of Reichenhall counted 5,000 members; that of the Holy Scapular in the village of Nussdorf had more than 5,300, and the very recent confraternity of the Holy Trinity of Reit im Winkl, a mountain village of several hundred inhabitants, had enrolled 9,000 members, from all over the region, within ten years of its foundation![6]

The Marian congregations fitted into this movement perfectly. In the little town of Mindelheim, the Jesuit sodality brought together 2,904 men and women. In Munich in 1770, there were, in addition to the 3,000 burgesses, about 800 unmarried artisans, and also 2,082 academics in the Major.[7] Even taking into account that these last often came from all over Bavaria, between 5,000 and 6,000 male congregation members is still very considerable for a medium-sized town of 37,000 inhabitants. In other words, more than one in two

[4] O. P. Munich, D II 596, *Marianisches Erstes Jubel-Jahr von der Löblichen Kongregation Unser Lieben Frauen Himmelfahrt der Herren Burger zu Augsburg und von der Löblichen Congregation Mariae-Reingung der jungen und ledigen Gesellen allda Im Jahr 1713 den 13. Augusti Glücklich beschlossen und durch folgende Freuden: Octay in der Kirchen der Societet Jesu bey Sanct Salvator zu Augsburg . . . Predigen* (Augsburg, 1715).

[5] Etienne François, 'Das System der Parität' in *Geschichte der Stadt Augsburg von der Römerzeit bis zur Gegenwart* (Stuttgart, 1984), pp. 514–19.

[6] B. H. Munich, GR, fasc. 554/198.

[7] B. H. Munich, GL, fasc. 2708/559; O. P. Munich, C VI 46, *Album Marianum*, 1766; Altmann, 'Zur Geschichte des Bürgersaals', pp. 7–24.

Munich families were involved with the congregations at the end of the eighteenth century. The impact, it is true, was not the same everywhere, because Munich, like other German towns, grew very rapidly during the Age of Enlightenment, and many congregation members in the 1780s were probably new arrivals in the town.[8] But many of them, either they themselves or their fathers, may well already have been members in their villages. In any case, the congregations in Bavaria, two centuries after their creation, were so successful that, there at least, the intentions of their founders seemed close to realisation. Blue and white Bavaria lived increasingly in the manner taught by the Jesuits.

It was the same in Alsace. In this recent province of the kingdom of France, however, the Lutheran presence completely changed the nature of the problem. It did not stop the congregations. In Colmar, a small town of 8,000 inhabitants, the new bourgeois congregation established in 1730 had 250 members in 1748, and 400 fifteen years later. The suppression of the Society of Jesus made no difference. Affiliations continued at the rate of fourteen or fifteen a year, as before 1765, and meetings were held as always. Now, however, they were presided over by a secular priest, who might well often have been a former Jesuit. Hence this reference demonstrating the calm maintained in the midst of change:

> Today, the first day of January [1766], I, Frantz Joseph Pflug, burgess and butcher of Colmar, was elected prefect of the unmarried journeymen under the title of the Annunciation of the Virgin. Father Cury was the first *praeses* since [the departure of the Jesuits].[9]

It was not until 1794 that meetings were temporarily suspended. Temporarily only because the members soon took stock, re-established the council, and opened new registers, lovingly embellished with beautifully decorated letters, and even pretty watercolour paintings depicting the trades of the dignitaries against a background of the Alsatian countryside.[10] What would Voltaire, who, when he stayed there in 1753–4, considered Colmar to be a 'town of Hottentots, governed by German Jesuits', have said, had he been able

8 Jan de Vries, *European Urbanization: Fifteen Hundred to Eighteen Hundred* (Harvard, 1984).

9 A. P. Saint-Martin, Colmar, register of the congregation of the unmarried artisans, fo. 109. Monsieur H. Gruninger kindly alerted me to the existence of this record and helped me to consult it. I would like to thank him most warmly.

10 *Ibid.*

to witness this constancy?[11] The fact was that, once the fathers had left, the members' work continued to flourish more actively than ever.

Nearby, in the little town of Ensisheim, the first place in Upper Alsace where the Jesuits had established themselves, their success was even more striking. From 300 men in 1746, the congregation grew to 480 in 1754 and 800 in 1761. The most zealous formed themselves into a confederation which alone numbered more than 230 persons on the eve of the Revolution.[12] In Molsheim, in Lower Alsace, a similar association created within the Major enjoyed great prestige throughout the province, and even beyond. The reports of the meetings which have survived for the period 1765 to 1790 reveal their regularity and the care with which the routine activities were performed (prayers and Masses for the dead, the annual publication of a presentation book, and the celebration of the feast day of the title saint). They also show the constant influx of candidates. The pressure was such that it became impossible to adhere to the decision to hold the number of members at a maximum of four hundred.[13] A list which survives for 1790 shows that the old rule had in effect been broken.[14]

The distribution of members at the end of the eighteenth century is surprising (see figure 13). It was almost the inverse of the confessional geography. It was in the towns and regions which were strongly, even mainly, Lutheran, that most congregation members were found. This cannot be coincidental, as it is confirmed by two statistical surveys thirty years apart.[15] Was the trend towards associations amongst Catholics all the stronger where they were less numerous, even in a minority? Was this a defensive phenomenon, an act of consolidation, or did the Protestant presence in some way spur the young Catholic communities and their pastors into action?

The case of Strasbourg is, in this context, quite remarkable. This town, almost entirely Lutheran in 1681, was opened up, after its capitulation, to the religion of the King of France. Catholic immigration, particularly from those regions of Alsace which had

[11] Voltaire, *Correspondance* (Paris, 1978), ed. Théodore Besterman, vol. 4, pp. 79–81 (letter dated 5 March 1754 to M. d'Argental).

[12] A. S. J. Rome, province of Champagne, 17, fos. 244–55 (1761); B. G. S. Strasbourg, *Catalogus Dominorum confoederatorum Pact Mariani congregationis Ensisheimanae* (Colmar, 1782).

[13] A. B. R., Parish Archives deposit, Molsheim 7.

[14] B. M. Colmar, Chauffour collection, no. 1997 (year 1790).

[15] *Ibid.*; A. H. R., Parish Archives deposit, Saint-Hippolyte (year 1762).

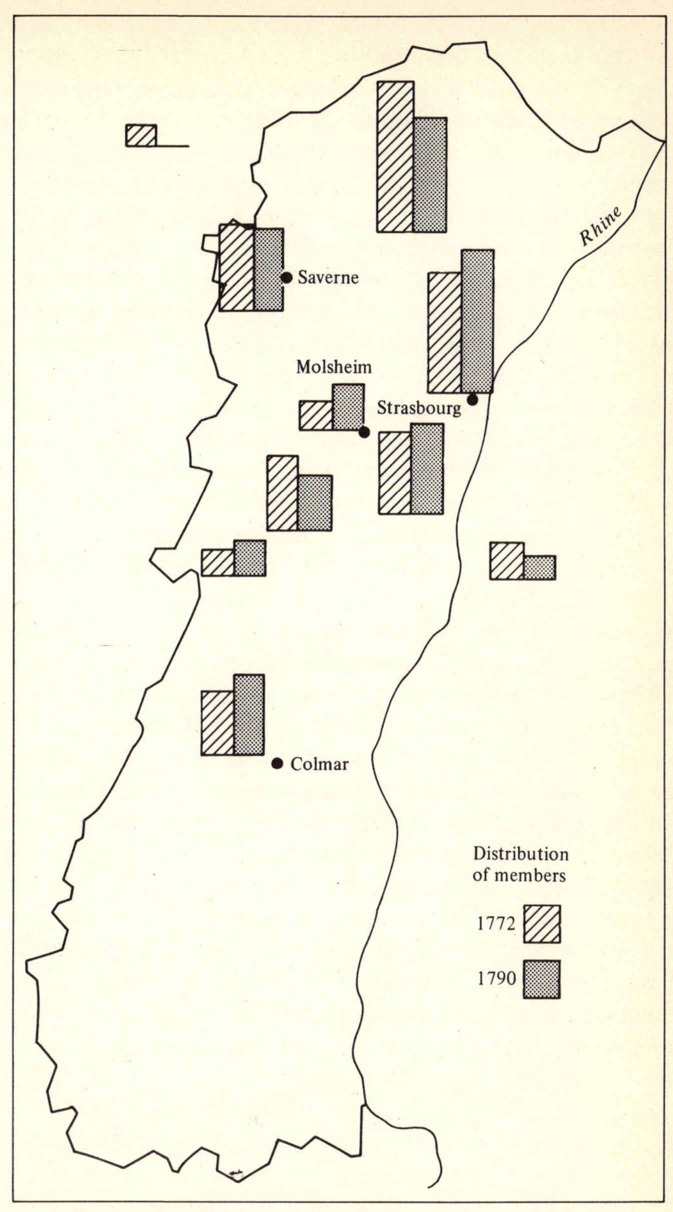

13. The academic congregation of Molsheim (Alsace): distribution of members at the end of the eighteenth century

remained attached to the Roman religion, increased in the eighteenth century. In mid-century, Catholics and Protestants were more or less evenly balanced. Twenty years later, Catholics were easily in a majority.[16] The congregations, for long discreet and small, rapidly expanded. In 1700, there was only one sodality for non-collegians, for craftsmen from the 'interior' (as they said in Alsace) and merchants from Savoy. In 1705 a separate association was founded for journeymen, where, already, the Alsatian dialect was predominant. In 1717, the congregation of men split into, on the one hand, the 'French burgesses', and on the other, the 'German burgesses', that is, Alsatians, who were soon a large majority. This evolution was symptomatic, reflecting the influx of migrants from Catholic areas. In 1746, there were already 500 'German burgesses'. Less than twenty years later, they numbered over 1,000. The unmarried craftsmen numbered 400, whilst there were only 100 'French burgesses'.[17]

These 1,500 congregation members, grouped by district and by guild, as in Antwerp and Cologne, constituted a force within a Catholic population of between 22,000 and 23,000 persons, still disparate and lacking roots in the Strasbourg of the 1760s. As in Antwerp and Lyons a century and a half earlier, the Marian congregations acted as an element of consolidation in a Catholic society which was still young and vulnerable. They brought to it their rules for the Christian life, and they shaped its behaviour. Swept along by their activity at the end of the eighteenth century, they remained undisturbed by the suppression of the Society of Jesus. Both before and after 1765 (the date of the expulsion of the Jesuits from Alsace), congregation members were to be seen, candle in hand, following the priest carrying the Host to one of their brothers, or, garbed in flowing red cloaks and bearing torches and banners, accompanying their dead brethren through the narrow streets of the town to their final resting place.[18]

Alsace was no exception. Lorraine, particularly fertile ground for the Counter-Reformation in the immediate aftermath of the Council of Trent, experienced a similar situation in the eighteenth century. In Nancy, the congregation of men, which numbered 600 members at the end of the seventeenth century, had 1,500 at the time of King

[16] 23,900 Catholics and 18,550 Lutherans in 1770; cf. Châtellier, *Tradition chrétienne et renouveau catholique*, p. 347.

[17] A. S. J. Rome, province of Champagne, 16, 17.

[18] Châtellier, *Tradition chrétienne et renouveau catholique*, p. 425.

Stanislas. This is a considerable number, bearing in mind that the total population of the town did not at that time exceed 23,000 inhabitants. In other words, in 1750 more or less one head of family in three was a congregation member. In Metz at this period the artisans alone numbered 1,200. In Pont-à-Mousson there were 450, and a similar number at Epinal.[19] Here, not only were numbers maintained after the departure of the Jesuits, they actually increased. There were over 500 members in 1770, from a population of about 6,000. A note preserved in the municipal archives reveals the method adopted by the brethren to keep their association in existence. Hardly had the Jesuits left than the burgesses of Epinal presented the Bishop of Toul with a petition that their foundation should be 'established with the title of a parish association' and that they should be 'authorised to continue their meetings and exercises . . . in the college church . . . all under the direction of the Curé of the parish'.[20] Thus, nothing changed but the director.

There was an identical procedure at Pau, where 'the burgesses and artisans' quickly had their congregation re-established in the old college with the Benedictines of Saint-Maur as directors.[21] In Switzerland, in the towns of the Rhine valley, the congregations were as a rule content, when danger threatened, to seek asylum in the nearest parish church. And life went on as before. Thus the sodality of the Three Kings in Cologne, which seems to have gone through a difficult period at the beginning of the eighteenth century, was by 1775 installed in the Church of Saint-Martin, and directed by the Benedictines. A printed list dating from 1801 reveals that it had never ceased to function. The division by district had remained unchanged; so had its organisation with local officers and deputies. At that date it had 750 members, which, given the period and the crises it had undergone, was a sign of health.[22] The same was true of the unmarried artisans, whose difficulties during the period 1720–30 have already been discussed. Five hundred New Year pictures had to be ordered in 1718. Thirty years later, only 150 were needed. But in 1760, 300, and in 1785, 400, were required. At that date, the congregation was established in the parish church of Saint-Alban and seems to have experienced a new prosperity.[23] In Mayence, Lucerne and

19 A. S. J. Rome, province of Champagne, 16, 17.
20 A. M. Epinal, GG 51.
21 Laborde, *Les Congrégations des Bourgeois*, pp. 43–4.
22 H. A. E. Cologne, parish of Saint-Martin, D II/35.
23 H. A. E. Cologne, parish of Saint-Alban, A II/42, register of the accounts of the congregation of the young artisans, 1715–98.

Soleure, the college diaries, preserved in part or complete (Soleure), show clearly the still considerable activity of the old and new sodalities.[24]

For not only did these last not experience irrevocable decline everywhere, but, in some regions at least, they proliferated. This was the case in Lorraine. The wave of foundations which had initially affected the towns, with the success we know of, spread, at the end of the seventeenth century, into the countryside. An account concerning Vézelise is enlightening on this score:

> When the Mission was held in the town of Vézelise in the last days of Lent and during the Easter fortnight of the present year 1695, Monsieur Verny, Curé and Dean of the said town, with the principals of the parish, inspired by God and filled with devotion for the Blessed Virgin, put to the missionary Fathers of the Society of Jesus the design they had formed to establish amongst them a Congregation of Our Lady, similar to those which were established in their houses. The thing seemed so edifying that without any delay they began to proceed to the accomplishment of this pious enterprise. In such a way that the Assembly being held in the parish Church of the town, it was decided that they should appeal to Monseigneur the Bishop and Count of Toul to obtain from him his agreement and the Institutions of the said Congregation and that they would then write to the Court at Rome to have the bulls which would confirm the union of the new and old Congregations and which would communicate the Indulgences and the ordinary privileges.

After which, they removed to the chapel of the hospital chosen for their meetings, the first officers were nominated and the curé was 'recognised as their perpetual director', and after him, his successors.[25]

The procedure was clearly spelled out and the link between the mission and the foundation of a sodality clearly established. The distribution of the saints of the month, the rule of life, and pious practices such as confession and frequent Communion, all happened as in the college. The work of the royal missions established in Nancy by King Stanislas (1738) made a considerable contribution to the spread of the institution in the countryside.[26] 'On the eve of the

[24] O. P. Munich, MSS, I, 17 (diary of the college of Mayence, 1753); Z. B. Soleure, S 3, 1, 2, 3 (diary of the college of Soleure, 1646–1830); S. A. Lucerne, cod. KK 240 (diary of the Jesuit church of Lucerne, 1722–70), cod. KK 250 and 260 (diary of the college of Lucerne, 1756–66, 1766–1826).

[25] A. D. Meurthe-et-Moselle, G 1219.

[26] Delattre, *Les Etablissements des jésuites*, vol. 3, cols. 756–68.

Revolution', according to one author, 'there were hardly any parishes in the diocese of Toul which had not at least their congregation of ladies, many of which survived during the Revolution.'[27]

Such initiatives were not confined to Lorraine. From the 1630s, rural missions organised in the kingdom of Naples resulted in the establishment of congregations. It was very probably the same with the great missions undertaken in 1715, and right up to the suppression of the Society, in Switzerland, in Southern Germany and the countries of the Rhine, with the effective assistance of the civil authorities.[28] Little by little, the villages of Italy, Bavaria, Swabia, the Swiss cantons, the Palatinate and Lorraine opened up to forms of association hitherto confined to the towns. The eighteenth century was the period of diffusion into the countryside of the devotional practices first introduced and implanted in the colleges and convents of the towns. Did the villages take the place of the declining towns? It sometimes seems that they did. But it must be said that in general the dynamism of the one resulted from the vitality of the other.

But in Paris, Rouen, Rheims and Antwerp, the crisis was a fact. It is even possible to establish a precise frontier, thanks to the statistics furnished by the Roman archives for the Jesuit province of Champagne (see figure 14, p. 204). On the one hand, there was irrevocable decline throughout the eighteenth century in Burgundy and Champagne; on the other, the excellent health of the Marian congregations of Alsace and Lorraine. When the Society was suppressed in France, more than two-thirds of the congregation members in the region studied were to be found in these two provinces. These large numbers were achieved less thanks to the colleges, in decline here as elsewhere, than to the bourgeois and artisan congregations. The difference is clear; but how should it be interpreted? Was it due to Jansenism and the campaign against the Jesuits and their works in France, where criticism was much less frequent and anti-Jesuit feeling less widespread further east and south? Perhaps; but it is also likely that the reasons go deeper. The divergent evolution of the congregations in neighbouring regions has the value of showing us, beyond Jesuits and Jansenism, beyond the measures of suppression and other events,

[27] Eugène Martin, *La Dévotion à la Sainte Vierge dans le diocèse de Toul* (Nancy, 1922), p. 80.

[28] B. H. Munich, Jesuits 564–78, accounts of the missions of the province of Upper Germany, 1718–72.

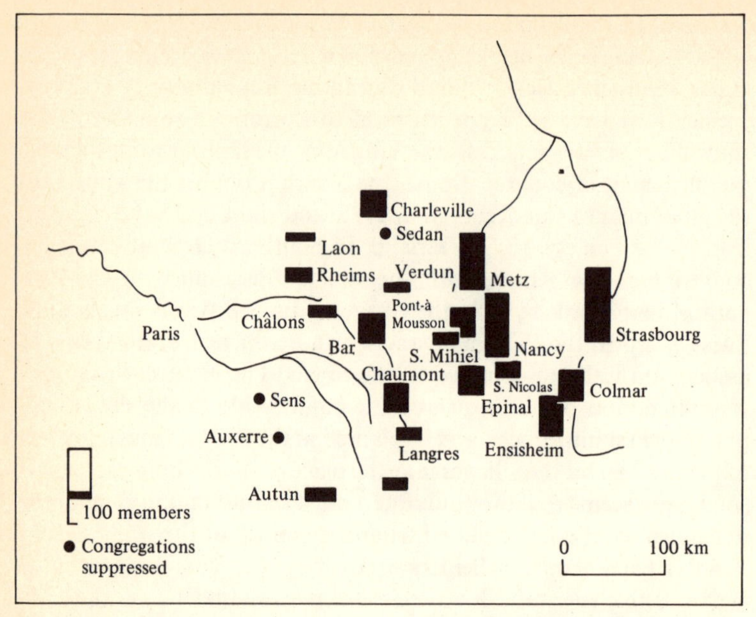

14. A frontier within Catholicism, *c.* 1750 (membership of bourgeois and artisan congregations in Eastern France)

how eighteenth-century Europe was divided into two very different camps as far as the practice, the sensibility and even the conception of Catholicism was concerned.

NEW PRACTICES

But meanwhile, the ancient institution founded in the middle of the sixteenth century by Fathers Leunis and Coster had perhaps itself also changed. Alongside the traditional congregations, new associations were born.

One of the most celebrated was the confraternity of the Agony of Christ, more commonly called, in French-speaking countries, the confraternity of the Good Death (*de la Bonne Mort*). Established in Rome in 1648 by Father Vincent Carafa, seventh General, it spread very rapidly throughout Europe, enjoying immense success in the countries of Germany and the Rhineland in particular.[29] Was it the

[29] *Dictionnaire de spiritualité*, vol. 2, article 'Confréries' (Joseph Duhr), cols. 1469–79.

precedent of the devotion to the Five Wounds of Christ, so strongly implanted in these regions, which favoured its expansion? Had the practice of general Communion so common in the congregations prepared the way? Or are the reasons for its success to be sought in the aim which the congregation set itself and in the simplicity of its rules? To obtain a good death was the sole end. To join, there were no conditions of entry, no probationary stage, no payment of dues, no presentation by peers. Rich and poor, children and old people, men and women could all join. They were simply required to make a general confession followed by a Communion. After which, they were full members for life. Every day, the brethren had occasion to remember those of their brothers who were in their death agony; the bell tolled at regular intervals (5.30 in the morning, noon, 6.30 and 8.30 in the evening) to remind them. Every Friday, on the altar of the Agony of Christ, many Masses were said with the same intention.

At the entrance to the Church of Saint-Charles in Antwerp, there were two large tablets on which were inscribed the names of the dead and the dying so as to commend them to the prayers of visitors. The names were changed every month. Nevertheless, there were usually more than six hundred people listed.[30] This says much about the confraternity's popularity. 'There is no confraternity in the world which has enrolled so many members from all social categories', wrote the Antwerp annalist.[31] At the major festivals, the church was not big enough and there were not enough priests to distribute Communion. This throws new light on the collapse in the membership of the Marian congregations established here. It was not a matter of de-Christianisation, or even of Jansenist influence, but simply of the attraction exercised by a new association better adapted to the sensibility of the time and the needs of families.

Its success was equally great in Cologne, since in 1735 the chronicler claimed that the majority of families were enrolled.[32] The phenomenon was even more spectacular in the small towns. At Sélestat, in Middle Alsace, which had at most 3,000 inhabitants in the 1660s, 1,157 people were registered between 1654 (date of the foundation) and 1668. At the later date, then, one in three inhabitants were members of the confraternity of the Agony. It is clear that by 1670 it encompassed every family in the town. It might be thought

[30] A. P. B. M. Namur, Droeshout deposit 24,3, pp. 270–2, 24,4, pp. 656–63.
[31] *Ibid.*, Droeshout deposit 24,3, p. 270.
[32] H. A. S. Cologne, A 647, fo. 243v.

that after such beginnings, a certain loss of impetus would subsequently be experienced. The opposite happened. There were 3,504 enrolments between 1701 and 1720, and 4,914 between 1741 and 1760. At Haguenau in Lower Alsace, which experienced many difficulties at the end of the seventeenth century, the movement hardly really got under way till well on in the following century – 2,836 entries between 1741 and 1760, against 719 between 1681 and 1700. As for Ottersweier, a village in the Baden region, its confraternity of the Good Death knew its greatest period of growth only after 1750 – 2,176 new enrolments in the period 1751–70 alone (see figure 15).[33]

At the same time, the recruitment changed. Women, who constituted two-thirds of the initial entry, to the point where the editor of the annals of the college referred to the 'sodality of mothers', lost ground, gradually, and especially beyond the Rhine, to men. The young became more numerous at the end of the seventeenth century. In Sélestat, the majority of those enrolled in the period 1692–1707 were under twenty, and, for the most part, under sixteen (51.9 % of the men, 56.9 % of the women),[34] as if the custom of solemn entry to the confraternity soon after First Communion was being established, a custom which survived in Alsace well into the twentieth century.[35]

Above all, from the 1700s, the association extended its influence. At Sélestat, the neighbouring villages accounted for 31.44 % of those enrolled between 1692 and 1707, but for 56.8 % after 1740. At Ottersweier, the inhabitants of the neighbouring Black Forest valleys seem to have sought admission very early. Describing the ceremonies for the festival of the name day at Molsheim in 1737, the editor of the *Annual Letters* said that they had been attended by whole families from more than twenty villages, near and far.[36] Initially, village inhabitants had travelled to participate in the exercises held at the nearest college. Later, the confraternity went to the villages. In the diocese of Strasbourg, the wave of foundations in the rural parishes between 1750 and 1789 consisted for the most part of confraternities of the Agony, which had been founded following the numerous Jesuit

[33] Châtellier, *Tradition chrétienne et renouveau catholique*, p. 430.

[34] From the calculations of Annik Schon, *Recherches sur une confrérie religieuse aux XVIIe et XVIIIe siècles*, Masters thesis, University of Strasbourg II (1976).

[35] Colette Ottmann, *Les Pèlerinages ruraux d'Ancien Régime du Kochersberg et du pays de Marmoutier*, Masters thesis, University of Strasbourg II (1980), p. 211.

[36] Châtellier, *Tradition chrétienne et renouveau catholique*, p. 481.

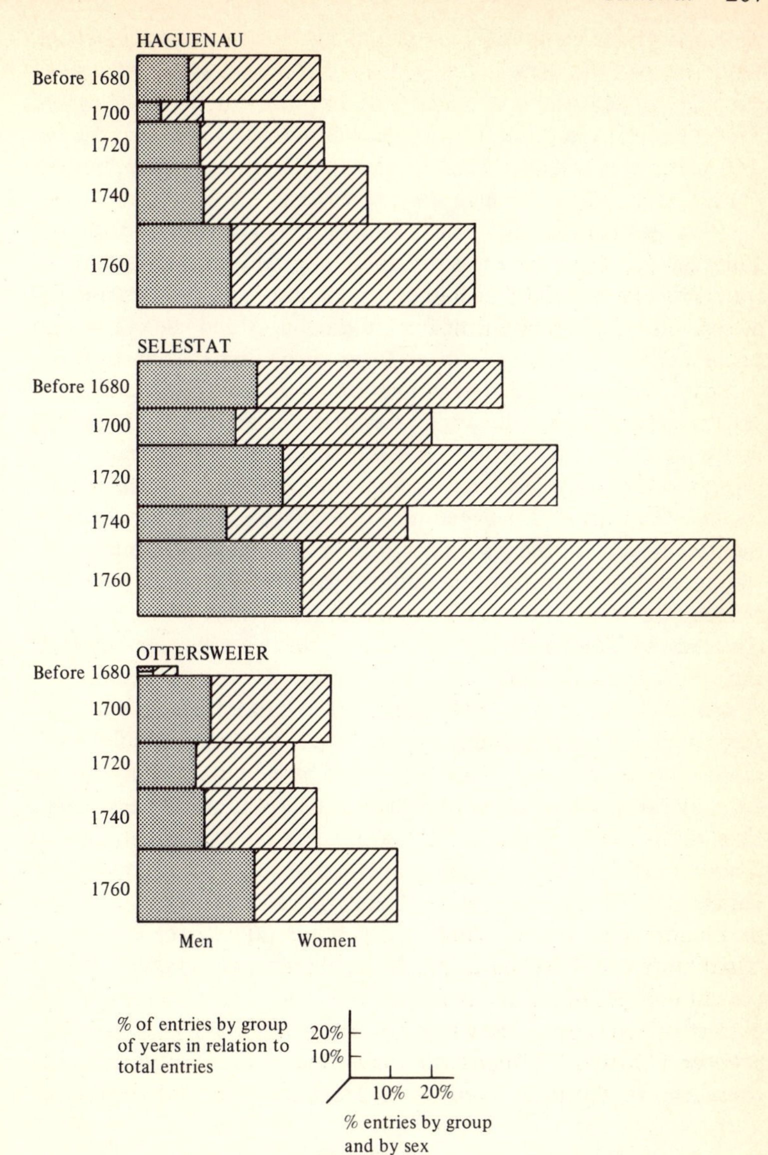

15. Three confraternities of the Good Death in the seventeenth and eighteenth centuries

missions of the eighteenth century.[37] It was a twofold movement, then: not only did these new associations spawned by the colleges of the Society reach a growing number of the faithful in the towns as well as in the countryside, but they also took root there. From adolescence to old age, they kept Christians company. They gave them, in their youth, habits of piety which they never lost.

Other groups emerged which also rather overshadowed the old congregations. One such was the Bond of St Aloysius (of Gonzaga), founded about 1750 in Southern Germany and Switzerland. It brought together young men from the colleges and the crafts who promised to follow the example of their patron, in particular as far as chastity was concerned. The obligations were very light, consisting solely of saying a Hail Mary every day when the bell tolled. In 1760, as many as 78,000 boys from those regions alone had joined.[38] The novena of St Francis Xavier, though not new, since it was already practised in Naples at the beginning of the seventeenth century, with the title 'novena of the graces', enjoyed a great success in the Age of Enlightenment. Crowds of the faithful gathered for the period 4–12 March (the date of the saint's canonisation) in most of the Society's churches. In Naples, the devotees of St Francis Xavier, on the eve of their nine days of prayer, processed through the town, wearing cloaks, satchels on their backs, and staff in hand. Instead of a shell, they wore a crucifix round their necks. They were called 'the pilgrims'.[39] In Antwerp, as in Naples and Strasbourg, the practice of the ten Fridays in honour of St Francis Xavier was quickly associated with the novena. Thus a confraternity was born, with its specific practices, its own prayers, its canticles and its devotees, male and female, coming from all over and from every social category.[40] When they met, they too, as in Cologne in the middle of the eighteenth century, found it was sometimes impossible for everybody to fit into the church, despite its great size.[41]

Further, the Spiritual Exercises long reserved for priests and seminarists were assimilated into the normal practices of the various sodalities, to the point where they sometimes became their chief purpose. In Turin, Chambéry, Naples and Lyons, and in many other places, a special building was constructed with the Exercises in mind,

[37] *Ibid.*, pp. 440–1. [38] S. A. Lucerne, KK 25/2, p. 307.

[39] A. S. J. Rome, province of Naples, 76^{II}, fo. 359.

[40] B. G. S. Strasbourg, MSS, 157, register of the confraternity of Saint-Francis Xavier, founded in 1756. [41] H. A. S. Cologne, A 644^{2}, fo. 366 (1706).

evidence of the place occupied by the annual retreat in the life of the congregations. Those for the nobles and the Gentlemen came first, then, not long after, those for the burgesses, the artisans, the journeymen, and the Agony of Christ. In Toulouse, the workers had adopted the habit of an annual retreat of three days at the beginning of the eighteenth century.[42] In Grenoble, 1,200 artisans made a retreat in 1750.[43] By this date, in effect, the Exercises had ceased to be performed only within the sodalities. They had become public, open to all the inhabitants of the town, as for example, at Molsheim in 1733, at Louvain in 1739, at Antwerp a year later, and at Naples at the same period.[44] Gradually, the retreats became the high points of the religious life in Jesuit colleges.

The old congregations themselves changed. A pious custom at first confined to priests spread widely to become, in the second half of the eighteenth century, the essential function of many sodalities: the Pactum Marianum. This took the form of a stronger union between the members of a sodality who each undertook to say (when they were priests), or to have said, a Mass when one of them died. In other words, there were to be as many Masses for the deceased brother as there were members. It was at Lucerne, it seems, in the middle of the seventeenth century, that the Pact was adopted. From there it was quickly taken up at Ingolstadt, Eichstätt, Fribourg and Molsheim.[45] From the academics, the custom spread to the ordinary burgesses and even to the artisans; those in Lyons had practised an agreement of this type since 1685.[46] The number of Masses required by two, three, even four hundred members was impossible. Waiting lists lengthened, and strict age limits were imposed to exclude candidates considered to be too old.

The congregations had become, in the apposite expression applied by Gabriel Le Bras to medieval confraternities, *mutualités spirituelles* (spiritual friendly societies).[47] Services for the dead constituted their

[42] *Les Saints Exercices de l'artisan chrétien*, pp. 126–7.

[43] Pra, *Les Jésuites à Grenoble*, p. 341.

[44] A. P. B. M. Namur, Droeshout deposit 24,6, pp. 38–44 (Antwerp, Louvain); A. B. R., Parish Archives deposit, Molsheim 7, pp. 91–2 (Molsheim).

[45] B. H. Munich, Jesuits 89/5; S. A. Lucerne, KK 25/1, pp. 278, 288–9; N. Paulus, 'La Grande Congrégation académique de Molsheim', *Revue catholique d'Alsace* (1886), pp. 94–102.

[46] A. D. Rhône, Galle deposit, *Heures à l'usage de la congrégation des artisans*, p. 61.

[47] Gabriel Le Bras, 'Les confréries chrétiennes', in *Etudes de sociologie religieuse*, 2 vols. (Paris, 1955–6), vol. 2, pp. 423–62.

main preoccupation. When, in 1749, the 'German burgesses' of Strasbourg decided to make a Pact, two hundred of them at once gave their names. Five years later, they numbered 452, that is 75 % of the total membership of the congregation (600).[48] But their wives and mothers, and even the women of the town who knew about the foundation, were reluctant to be excluded from these benefits. They constituted, like the men, an association intended to assure them, at death, a sung Requiem and fifty Low Masses and already numbered 467 in 1753. Their association had no specific name, except by reference to the male sodality to which, in a way, they belonged.[49]

A NEW SPIRIT

The introduction of the Pactum Marianum and other practices into the Marian congregations or alongside them brought about changes not only in their structures but also in their social composition and even in their purpose.

These new associations were not, in fact, intended for particular social or age groups to the exclusion of others, but, on the contrary, had bringing people together as a vocation. The editor of the annals of the Cologne college said that, from 1681, membership of the confraternity of the Agony was mixed: people of the highest rank registered alongside the poorest.[50] On the two large tablets hung at the entrance to the Church of Saint-Charles in Antwerp, the ranks of the dead were as jumbled as in a charnel house.[51] And the Pact lists anticipated this ultimate condition by recording the participants in alphabetical order without distinguishing the 'illustrious' or even the Domini. It was as if death, having become the *raison d'être* of many of those groupings of the faithful in the eighteenth century, already imposed on those here below an absolute equality.

Not only were women authorised to enrol in the confraternities of the Agony, but they soon became a preponderant element. From

[48] Louis Châtellier, 'Enquête sur la formation de la société catholique strasbourgeoise au XVIIIe siècle: le cas de la congrégation des "bourgeois allemands" ', in *Annuaire de la Société des amis du vieux Strasbourg* (1982), pp. 29–36.

[49] B. N. U. Strasbourg, *Nahmen-Register der Vier-Hundert und sechzig Frauen und Jungfrauen in Strassburg, welche sich in eine löbliche Gemeinschafft der fünffzig heiligen Seelen-messen sambt einem hohen Seelen-Amt, für eine jede aus Ihnen nach ihrem Absterben lesen zu lassen einverleibt haben* (Strasbourg, 1753).

[50] H. A. S. Cologne, A 642, fo. 127v.

[51] A. P. B. M. Namur, Droeshout deposit 24,4, p. 660.

1707, in Naples, a group of mothers performed the Spiritual Exercises under the direction of the Jesuit fathers.[52] In the years that followed, they had their time marked out over the year so that they could make them in the same way as the men. Thanks to the Pactum Marianum, finally, they entered the Marian congregations which had hitherto been closed to them. The separation of the sexes imposed in religious practice tended, little by little, to disappear.

There could now no longer be any question of a rule of life closely tailored to each person's condition. The diversity of people was too great. The novena of St Francis Xavier or the Exercises of St Ignatius for some, the annual meeting of all parties to the Pact in the Major for the others, were often, at the end of the eighteenth century, the chief elements in practices which were no longer exactly onerous. The monthly meeting of the brethren of the Good Death was held on the occasion of a Mass intended primarily for them. Festivals were few. The commemoration of the founding of the confraternity and, most of all, the Requiem Mass on the last Sunday in October were the two high points, to which were often added the feast of St Joseph, frequently chosen as second patron.[53].

The most imposing ceremonies took place at burials. According to a chronicler from Sélestat at the very end of the eighteenth century:

> The rule in use for interments is excellent. The men wear black cloaks. They march two by two in a long line. For a child, you often get more than two hundred people . . . Banners, torches, coats of arms, as well as all the distinctive signs of the confraternities, contribute to giving to burials a real processional character with singing and prayers.[54]

The whole family united and an overriding concern for the dead seem to be the features characterising sodalities at the end of the eighteenth century.

This evolution may appear to conform to what has been observed in the domain of manners. 'One should not forget', wrote Philippe Ariès, 'the great transformations in the family which resulted, in the eighteenth century, in new relationships based on sentiment and affection.'[55] This consolidation of ties within the tight-knit family was visible not only in daily life, but, above all, at the moment of

[52] A. S. J. Rome, province of Naples, 76^{II}, fo. 368.
[53] A. P. B. M. Namur, Droeshout deposit 24,4, p. 61.
[54] Châtellier, *Tradition chrétienne et renouveau catholique*, p. 425.
[55] Philippe Ariès, *Essais sur l'histoire de la mort en Occident du Moyen Age à nos jours* (Paris, 1975), p. 51.

death. The death of another – that of a wife, a husband or a child – became unbearable. For the beloved dead came baroque funeral pomp, many services, Requiem Masses, and fervent, day-long prayers to the sound of church bells tolling, then the erection of those imposing monuments surviving in our cemeteries, which bear vivid witness to the grief of those left behind.[56] But to what extent had this new sensibility which emerged in the West in the 1750s been widespread, before that, in families formed in the school of the congregation? As early as 1650, Father Cordier, whose work has been described above, guided those under his direction to adopt very similar behaviour.

Also, the spiritual teaching of the Jesuits changed little from one century to the next. What did change were their methods of apostleship. The great missions organised by the Society in Naples, Strasbourg, Nancy or Prague were destined to leave lasting traces. The very poorest inhabitants, the recent immigrants, coming from the country and still eking out a precarious existence in the suburbs of Naples, were the objects of the special attention of Father Francis de Geronimo, whilst Father Aloysius of Mutiis, whose death was attended by miracles, showed particular concern for soap workers and the poor.[57] The fishermen and the poorest families of the waterside were gathered into a confraternity at the college of St Joseph in mid-century. They performed all the required devotions as well as the Spiritual Exercises.[58] In town and country alike, the confraternity became a continuation of the mission and, as such, borrowed from it many of its features. Intended for the masses, who were often illiterate, it had to have conversion as its prime function.

Father Onofrio Paradiso was well aware of this when he created a confraternity of the Holy Sacrament at Lecce in the 1740s, whose members were divided into four sections, as many as there were parishes in the town. When the doors of a church opened to reveal the priest bearing the Host to a dying man, the *sodales*, young and old, rich and poor, were to be seen leaving their houses, each carrying a torch and providing an escort of light for the Holy Sacrament.[59] The new foundations appear clearly here in their double character: popular and communal. To say that they were popular is not to say

[56] *Ibid.*, p. 53; Michel Vovelle, *La Mort et l'Occident de 1300 à nos jours* (Paris, 1983).
[57] A. S. J. Rome, province of Naples, 76^{II}, fos. 424, 580; *Dictionnaire d'Histoire et de Géographie ecclésiastiques*, vol. 18, cols. 719–21. (Francis of Geronimo).
[58] A. S. J. Rome, province of Naples, 76^{II}, fo. 634. [59] *Ibid.*, fos. 621v–622.

that they were designed only for the ordinary people of town and country, but rather, as the chroniclers repeated, that they were composed of the faithful 'of all conditions'.[60]

It was the mix of classes, already visible in certain congregations at the end of the seventeenth century, but which became systematic and willed, which gave the Jesuit associations of the eighteenth century their special character. Was it necessitated by fear of social unrest? Or was it rather the consequence of a desire to make men in the here and now reflect on their equality before God? (In a very different spirit, certainly, from that adopted by the revolutionaries of a few years later.) One may, at all events, wonder whether the new orientations assumed by the different sodalities did not, in a sense, share the spirit of the century, or even whether they did not contribute, without the knowledge, obviously, of their directors, to its diffusion, in an original form, amongst faithful Catholics. The disquiet displayed by certain adversaries of the Jesuits, who saw in their institutions destined for the laity potential instruments for the subversion of the social order, may well make better sense when looked at in this light.

VIGOUR REDISCOVERED

In any case, the evolution of these ancient sodalities perhaps explains why so many of them survived the crises of the late eighteenth century unharmed. It is perhaps hardly surprising to learn that in Cologne, as we have shown for Munich, life for the unmarried journeymen or the married men of the Bürgersaal went on in 1800 as before, with the same calendar, the same festivals, and similar, still frequent, meetings.[61] Much more significant was the restoration of the congregation in Paris in 1801. Initially modest, at the time of Father Delpuits, it soon grew, and by the quality of both its members and its activities, disquieted the Imperial power. In Lyons and Toulouse, the old associations were re-established and immediately experienced a new vigour.[62] It was as if the traditional strong points of the map of Jesuit establishments emerged once again, the better to demonstrate the

[60] *Ibid.*, fo. 622.

[61] H. A. E. Cologne, Saint-Martin deposit D/II 35 (sodality of the bourgeois, 1801); B. H. Munich, GL fasc. 2708/559 (congregation of the unmarried men, 1804); Pichler, *Die Marianische deutsche Kongregation der Herren*, pp. 91–97 (congregation of the bourgeois, jubilee of 1810).

[62] Geoffroy de Grandmaison, *La Congrégation (1801–30)* (Paris, 1890).

continuity between the old congregations of artisans and Gentlemen and the new institutions. In Strasbourg, the congregation of Our Lady, an exact continuation of the eighteenth-century sodality of the German burgesses, no longer had as its sole function the emulation of the religious life. It added in 1847 a mutual benefit fund.[63] In Paris, from 1822, the famous congregation inspired a Society of St Joseph whose aim was to give moral and religious principles to the working class. An association of St Nicholas intended for apprentices extended this activity. For intellectuals there were the Société des Bonnes Etudes and the Société Catholique des Bons Livres.[64] In Toulouse, the reactivated Aas undertook similar activities.[65]

The congregations of the nineteenth century extended their activities well beyond the limits fixed by their founders. Were they still, strictly speaking, sodalities? Names such as 'society' and 'institution' often hide or even cast doubt on their real identity. Above all, the distinction between the surviving old and the new institutions is difficult to draw. The Society of St Vincent de Paul, founded in 1833 by Frédéric Ozanam, had as its purpose the strengthening of the faith of its members by the common practice of charity. As in the past, the main intention was to 'spread amongst youth the spirit of Catholicism'.[66] The whole organisation, its calendar and the regular holding of meetings conformed to the structures of the old sodalities. And its members had come from or been active in their youth in societies which depended on them. The Society of St Francis Xavier founded several years later by the Jesuits was inspired by similar principles. Intended, as the Brussels statutes show, to form true Christians ready to work for the conversion of sinners, it was open to all adult workers. The members, divided into *dizaines*, were directed by inspectors, or *chefs bu banc*, and had to meet on the second Sunday in the month. In Belgium, each group had its chapel, where from time to time communal Communions were held. At set dates, with their wives and children, they set off on pilgrimages to nearby long-venerated sanctuaries. If mutual assistance, savings banks and sickness funds, assumed ever greater importance, the religious vocation of the institution was by no means abandoned.

[63] Jean-Baptiste Duroselle, *Les Débuts du catholicisme social en France (1822–1870)* (Paris, 1951), p. 541.
[64] Grandmaison, *La Congrégation (1801–30)*, pp. 215–16.
[65] See below, chapter 13.
[66] Duroselle, *Les Débuts du catholicisme*, p. 174.

In Liège and the Walloon countries, the Society of St Joseph had the same function.[67] In Cologne, finally, and soon throughout the Germanic world, it was the *Gesellenvereine*, founded in 1845 by Abbot Adolf Kolping, which came to the fore. Intended for journeymen making their tour round Germany, these associations had as their purpose to arm these men against the evil influences to which they risked exposure during their itinerant life, as well as aiming to provide them with material comfort and aid. The statutes said:

A member of the *Verein* will be a good Christian, and, in consequence, will faithfully and conscientiously perform his religious duties. You should confess your faith bravely and observe its precepts. You need religion in life and in death. It takes more courage to be a good Christian than to be a bad Christian. Sanctify Sundays and feast days, as the divine law wishes. The best profession of faith is a life which conforms to the precepts of the Ten Commandments. Attend the offices of the *Verein* regularly to edify yourself and to set a good example to your brothers.[68]

One could well be reading the rules of a congregation of artisans under the Ancien Régime. The same precise details are found with regard to the apportionment of time during the week, even the day; with the difference always that the *Gesellenverein* also supervised the worker's leisure, his rest and his food. The house of the association became the house of the journeyman, and the *Verein* his true family.

The congregations did not go so far. But it is surely impossible not to see their continuation in these various institutions as characteristic of the social Catholicism which spread over Catholic Europe in the middle of the nineteenth century. When it is remembered that at Kolping's death in 1865 there were already more than 400 *Gesellenvereine*, that the arch-confraternity of St Francis Xavier alone counted in Belgium, in 1879, 83,000 members divided into 342 circles, that in Paris, in 1845, it numbered 15,000 workers, and that in 1848, there existed in Europe 388 Societies of St Vincent de Paul, 282 of them in France, the importance of the movement can be appreciated.[69]

[67] Rudolf Rezsohazy, *Origines et formation du catholicisme social en Belgique, 1842–1909*, University of Louvain, Recueils de Travaux d'Histoire et de Philologie, 4th ser., fasc. 13 (Louvain, 1958), pp. 51–8; Duroselle, *Les Débuts du catholicisme*, pp. 245–6.

[68] A. Kannengieser, *Catholiques allemands* (Paris, 1892), p. 158.

[69] *Ibid.*, p. 168; Rezsohazy, *Origines et formation du catholicisme social en Belgique*, p. 54; Duroselle, *Les Débuts du catholicisme*, pp. 253, 284.

Certainly, the congregations as such were no longer pre-eminent amongst the many nineteenth-century institutions of this type. But it seems as if, having prepared the ground over such a long period, having forged institutions, practices and habits of life on the anvil of time, they in some sense merged into new institutions which were better adapted to the needs of the moment, not without giving them inspiration and bequeathing them men of action trained by their attentions.

Far from showing signs of decline, the Jesuit sodalities in the period 1750–1850 often demonstrated a new vitality. They established themselves in the countryside in areas hitherto barely affected, they aimed firmly at the family, and no longer only at men, they gradually concerned themselves with every aspect of the Christian life (from the spiritual retreat to a man's last hours), they even went beyond the purely religious domain to participate, in the nineteenth century, in social action. To the point where, observing them in action and developing during this troubled period, one may wonder if they were not one of those forces capable of keeping alive those Catholic communities which were subjected to harsh trials; unless – and we tend rather to this view – their success constituted one sign, among many others, of how deep-rooted the Christian life had become in villages and in the hearts of men during this key period, a period which also saw parish life being definitively organised in the countryside.[70] The renewal of the congregations at the turn of the eighteenth and nineteenth centuries calls into question a received idea, that of the de-Christianisation at work in the Europe of the Enlightenment.

[70] Châtellier, *Tradition chrétienne et renouveau catholique*, vol. 3.

12. *The transformation of society*

Did the congregations transform society? This is a crucial question, to which we have endeavoured above to provide the elements of a reply; it is now time, after two centuries of history, to attempt an overall assessment. It is a difficult question, because of the lack of a series of sufficiently continuous archives and, most of all, because of the impossibility for a single researcher to analyse it as a function of the development of a town over several centuries; all the more so since it is clear that what is at issue is a long and obscure progress which did not result in the complete overthrow of the structures of society. One suspects, nevertheless, that everything which has been described and analysed above has had its consequences for how Catholics behave, even in their everyday life.

THE FORMATION OF A NEW ÉLITE

The vigilant guardians of tradition protested, but to no avail. In Toulouse, Molsheim and Munich, the congregations of Gentlemen and academics were invaded by simple burgesses. 'Persons of low condition', it still said in the rules of the sodality of the Gentlemen of Toulouse, 'are never admitted, however virtuous they may be.'[1] But they were fighting a losing battle.

Figure 16 shows that the lay members of the Major of Molsheim at the end of the eighteenth century were for the most part estate receivers, bailiffs, or even simple village *greffiers*. Over half the ecclesiastical members (57.87% exactly in 1790), meanwhile, were simple country curés, many of them poor *curés royaux* living on a pension in a parish with a Protestant majority.[2] There was an enormous gulf between the pretensions of the association, and even

[1] *Règles, Coutumes et Prières de la Congrégation des Messieurs érigée à Toulouse dans la Maison Professe des Pères de la Compagnie de Jésus* (Avignon, 1760), p. 7.

[2] B. M. Colmar, Chauffour collection, no. 1997 (year 1790); A. H. R., Parish Archives deposit, Saint-Hippolyte (year 1762).

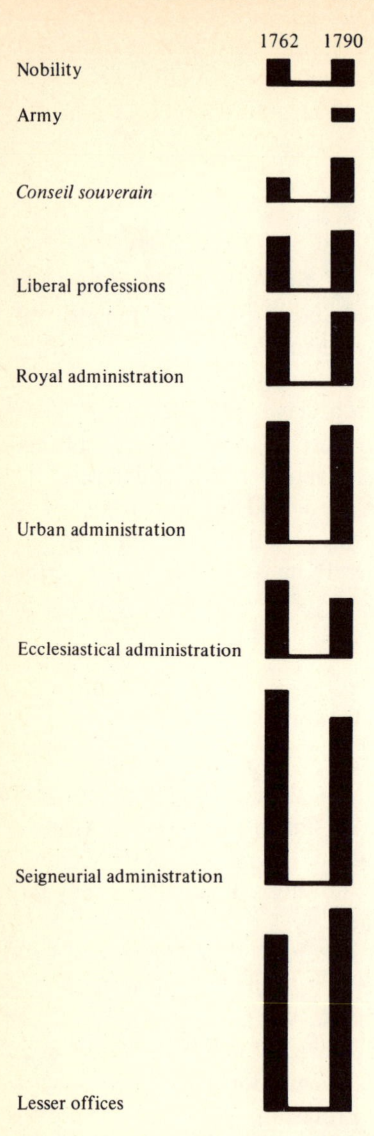

16. The academic congregation of Molsheim: socio-professional structure of lay membership

the regard in which it was held throughout Alsace and beyond, and reality. One can understand the pride mingled with embarrassment of its officers when two canons of the great chapter, both from highly prestigious families, the princes Jules de Rohan and Guillaume de Salm, having nothing better to do one fine day in 1785, decided to enrol.[3] Such an unexpected infusion of blue blood caused a minor sensation in this association intended to bring together the representatives of the most illustrious Catholic families in the region, but reduced, over time, to a decidedly popular recruitment.

In Munich, the princes, accompanied by their wives, never ceased to frequent the congregation of the Annunciation throughout the eighteenth century. The court, naturally, did the same. Thus its representatives and officials employed in ducal service maintained a stable presence from one century to the next: 41.52% in 1673 as against 41.03% in 1766 (figure 20 pp. 233–5). But artisans and tradesmen, non-existent in 1673, constituted over 10% (85 out of 831) of the lay members a century later.

The evolution of the clerical element was even more striking. In the seventeenth century, country curés and vicars were almost non-existent. By 1727, they were present in significant numbers, to the point where they constituted 43.23% of the clerical membership (358 out of 828). Forty years later, they were joined by the regular clergy. There were 176 of these in 1727, and 475 in 1766, 43.85% of all ecclesiastics – almost half. Another important change, not apparent from these figures, was that the Benedictines of the great Bavarian abbeys, long the sole representatives of the regular clergy, were now joined by members of the mendicant orders. These last, along with the hermits to be found in Bavaria as elsewhere in the eighteenth century, totalled 227, that is almost half (47.78%) of the regulars of the Major. Within this general trend, the Capuchins made spectacular progress. There were only 3 of them in 1727, but 83 in 1766. In the interim, the great rural missions had taken place in Southern Germany, and the Jesuits had become more familiar with the sons of St Francis, who had, in fact, often preceded them.[4] This fact, taken in the context of the entry of artisans and tradesmen into the prestigious

[3] A. B. R., Parish Archives deposit, Molsheim 7, proceedings of the assemblies, 5 April 1785.

[4] B. S. Munich, *Album Marianum* 1673; *Album Marianum* 1727; O. P. Munich, C VI 46, *Album Marianum* 1766. For an example of a mission, see Louis Châtellier, 'Mission et conversion dans l'espace rhénan et germanique à la fin du XVIIe siècle', in *Les Réveils missionaires en France du Moyen Age à nos jours (XIIe–XXe siècle)* (Paris, 1984), pp. 119–27.

sodality, shows clearly its tendency to assume an almost popular character during the course of the eighteenth century. The sharp decline in the number of nobles as a proportion of the whole (falling from 16% to 8% in a century) confirms this.

The implicit establishment of quotas for the different categories perhaps obeyed the same intention. Almost everywhere, Mayence, Molsheim and Munich included, there were two-thirds clerics to one-third laymen. The socio-professional distribution of the latter, in the short run at least, seemed to obey strict rules. The very close similarity of the figures for the Major of Molsheim for 1762 and 1790 revealed by figure 16 (p. 218) is one illustration of this. For Munich, figures for the group constituted by the municipal administration, ecclesiastical and seigneurial administration, minor offices and the liberal professions demonstrated remarkable stability between 1673 and 1766, moving only from 21.05% to 23.34% of the laity (figure 20 pp. 233–5). Should we see in this stability, which was not free from fluctuations when society changed and new realities became apparent, a desire for equality among the groups represented? The complex system practised at Molsheim when the magistrates were re-elected was one application of this; two panels composed of ecclesiastics were succeeded by a third composed of laymen. A rotation was established to permit, as far as was possible, the various categories to be represented. In the case of the laymen, the nobility were succeeded by the *conseil souverain*, and then by the local administrators. In the case of the clergy, the offices rotated between the canons, the regulars and the curés. Certain accommodations had to be made because custom decreed that the prefect elected the previous year became, the year after, the first assistant of his successor. Thus Prince François-Camille de Lorraine, great Dean of the Cathedral of Strasbourg, was chosen in 1770 as assistant to the Curé of Osthouse.[5]

Were these illustrious and ancient associations won over by the spirit of the Enlightenment, and did they become, at the time of the *Social Contract*, true schools of democracy? The Gentlemen of Toulouse, for their part, seemed hardly enthusiastic about introducing complete equality into their ranks. Their rules for 1760 stated:

And although in a Body whose members are all alike servants of the Holy Virgin, perfect model of humility, no one should affect rank or pre-eminence,

[5] A. B. R., Parish Archives deposit, Molsheim 7, proceedings of the assemblies, 8 December 1770.

it is fitting, nevertheless, that, when making their choice, the Electors should have regard both for the quality of the persons and for the rank which they occupy in the world. This is particularly so with regard to those who are to fill the three first Places.[6]

And were any brethren to forget these principles, the Aa, still active, and still recruiting in the middle of the French Revolution, was there to remind them.[7]

In towns without an Aa, the Pact took its place, as in Munich and Molsheim, and constituted a true congregation within what was called the 'external' one. Nevertheless, the academic sodalities, once so closed, by thus opening wide their doors, both revealed a major change in ways of thinking and contributed to their evolution. This was so above all, it seems, in the Rhenish and Germanic worlds. What did the 2,188 people who were members of the Munich Major in 1766 have in common? The distance between the village curé and the prince of the Church, the small-town doctor or apothecary and the chancellor of the Elector, the Capuchin father and the Abbot of Ottobeuren, appears vast. Nevertheless, all, according to their condition, had authority over people, in town or country, or were in daily contact with them. Perhaps the concept of service to the inhabitants of the duchy was more important than the concept of authority, which might explain the presence in large numbers of Capuchins, curés and apothecaries. The change in a century and a half was enormous. It was no longer a matter of restoring the court and staffing the administration of the prince with loyal men, but of concern for the people, country people for the most part, in this vast rural region, and the wish to give them a firm base.

The education of the *sodales* was more than ever a priority. The academic sodality of Molsheim was, especially in the eighteenth century, primarily a publishing house, producing every year, with extreme care, a presentation book received by all its members. Meditations for every day of the year, like those of Father François Nepveu, and the other simple books of spirituality of the beginning of the century, were succeeded, from the 1770s, by the solid doctrine of the Church Fathers, editions of the Bible, and Church history.[8] It was as if, anticipating the great storm, the directors wanted to provide the rural clergy and, in particular, laity, with the elements of a response,

[6] *Règles, Coutumes et Prières*, pp. 57–8.
[7] A. P. Toulouse, CA 102 ('Livre d'or').
[8] Châtellier, *Tradition chrétienne et renouveau catholique*, pp. 390–2.

or perhaps even the means to assume new responsibilities if this should prove necessary. This advanced knowledge was dispensed in the same terms to both ecclesiastics and laymen, and it constituted, with the practice of religious exercises, the strongest link between the brethren.

Thus, through the intermediary of the academic congregations, a new élite began to appear, in Germany at least, at the end of the eighteenth century. It was no longer characterised by service only to the prince, by wealth or by power, but by service to the people. It was no longer adherence to the same social group which gave it its cohesion, but participation in an identical culture, principally religious. An élite of Catholic service was in the process of formation within the Marian congregations. It was not slow to manifest itself.

THE FORMATION OF A MIDDLE CLASS

Addressing the brethren of the Good Death, assembled in plenary session in 1785, the preacher of Strasbourg Cathedral, Anton Jeanjean, declared: 'For, dear brethren, observe your trades; amongst the believers, there are few sages, few men of power, few nobles.'[9] No trace of bitterness should be seen in this reflection, which the pastor let slip as he contemplated his audience from the eminence of the pulpit. On the contrary, what these words reveal is the Church's secret preference at the end of the eighteenth century; was it not wary of the rich and learned whose indifference and sarcasms had often furnished ample pretexts to those fine spirits prone to doubt? 'All people of distinction, all enlightened people, think this way,' they would declare, 'it is only the simple and the stupid who believe what the preachers tell them.'[10] No, indeed, in Strasbourg as in Toulouse, it was wise to keep one's distance from people of 'distinguished and transcendent talents'.[11] It was the humble, in contrast, who constituted the true Christians.

It was not, it must be made plain, a matter of those owning nothing and compelled to live off charity, but of:

> the poor man according to the Scriptures, that is he who is of lowly origin, who comes from the common people, who enjoys no esteem, who is a prey to

[9] Anton Jeanjean, *Predigten*, 5 vols. (Strasbourg, 1830), vol. 1, p. 31.
[10] *Ibid.*, p. 32.
[11] Begouen, *Une société secrète émule de la Compagnie du Saint-Sacrement*, p. 83.

every anxiety, who is disdained by the great and powerful of this world, and who has to bear the weight of daily labour.[12]

It was thus not so much the poor as the representatives of the middle class, of the *Mittelstand*, as the preacher, Anton Jeanjean, called them. And for them he opened his pastor's heart:

Come, all you who belong to this middle class, you who have never tasted the abundance of goods and honours which raise some above others, you who have never known the extremities of need of poverty and wretchedness, you who live from your daily labour, from the product of your efforts in your common lot, and support your families![13]

It was, in fact, just such people who thronged to the meetings in large numbers at the end of the eighteenth century. In Strasbourg, Colmar and Epinal, towns for which it has been possible to advance furthest the sociology of the congregations, artisans counted for at least two-thirds of the total membership. In Strasbourg, they amounted to 84.64 %. If they were less numerous at Colmar (72.19 %) and Epinal (60.78 %), it was because farmers, *vignerons* and simple day-labourers were well represented (see figure 17a, p. 224). Furthermore, it was not a matter of all artisans indiscriminately. The building trades (from carpenters to masons) and the clothing trades (from weavers to shoemakers) were everywhere predominant. The continuity is striking; a similar conclusion was drawn, on the basis of statistics for the seventeenth century, for the towns of Antwerp, Cologne and Lille.[14] However, the example of Strasbourg around 1750 shows that there was not always a relationship between the number of congregation members practising a trade and the real importance of that trade in the city (see figure 17b, p. 225). Were certain types of workers more attracted than others by the sodalities? The hypothesis cannot be ruled out, bearing in mind that many of them, carpenters, masons and stone-hewers in particular, were compelled to travel, and that the congregations, present in every large town, might serve as reception centres for them. All the more so since, in Lutheran Strasbourg, certain guilds were closed, or, at the very least barely open, to Catholics. This applied particularly in the case of the carpenters.[15]

[12] Jeanjean, *Predigten*, vol. 1, pp. 19–32.
[13] *Ibid.*, vol. 2, p. 61.
[14] See above, chapter 4.
[15] Bernard Vogler, 'La vie économique et les hiérarchies sociales', in Georges Livet and Francis Rapp, *Histoire de Strasbourg des origines à nos jours*, 4 vols. (Strasbourg, 1980–2), vol. 3, pp. 185–252.

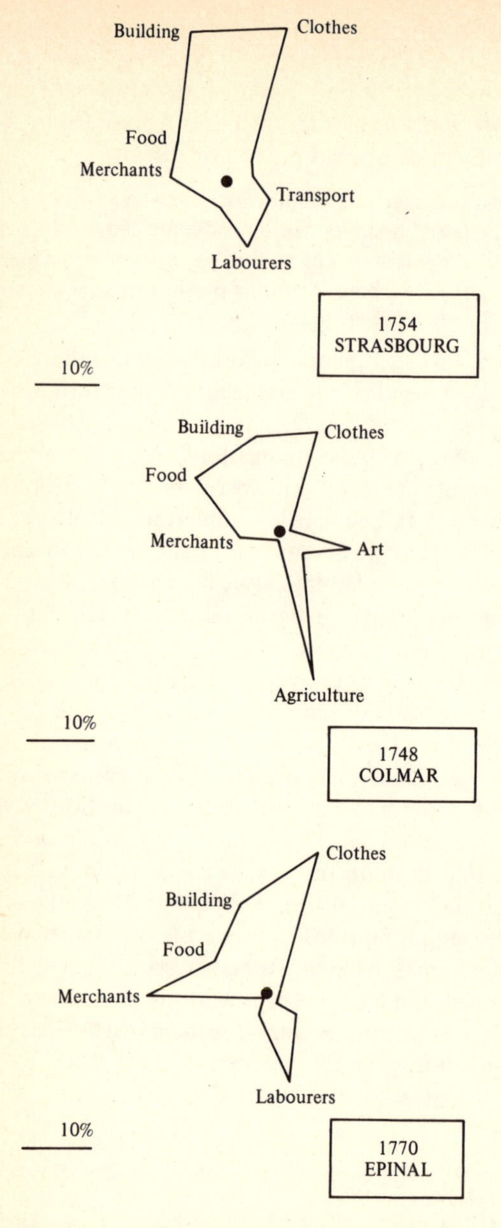

17. Congregation members in towns in the eighteenth century.
(a) Occupations

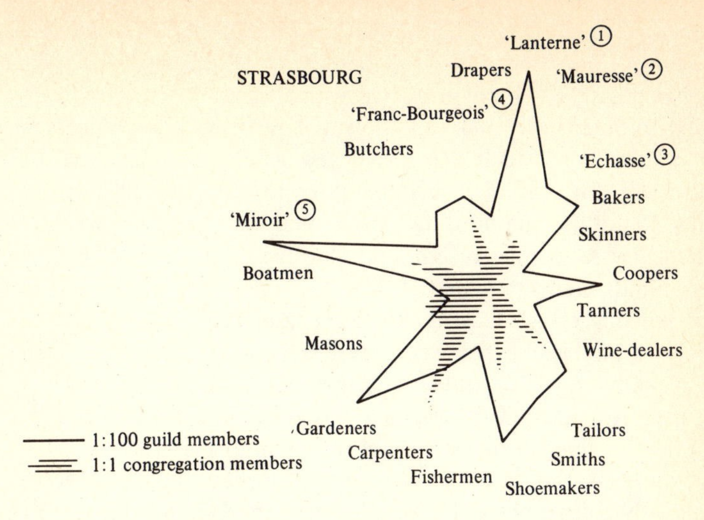

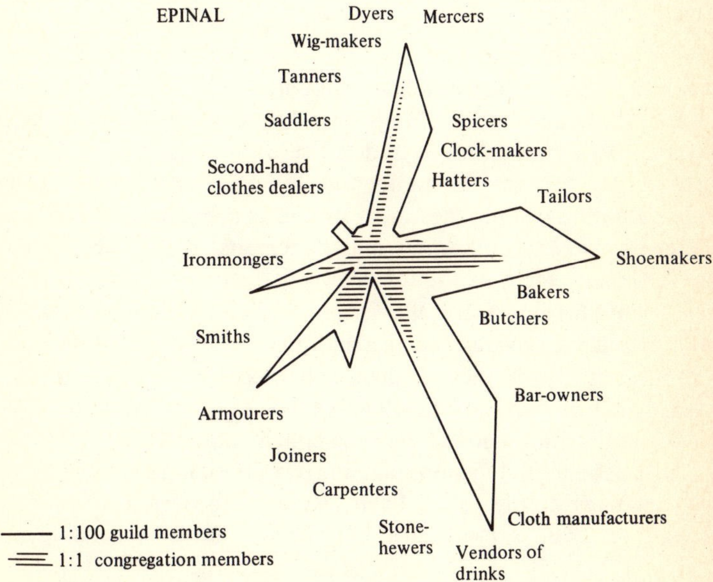

① Millers, plasterers and surgeons
② Vendors of salt goods, regrators and corders
③ Goldsmiths, painters, printers and binders
④ Innkeepers and bar-owners
⑤ Merchants

(b) Members within town guilds

But this is not a sufficient reason for the imbalance. The very small number of tradesmen, of general merchants, of innkeepers, butchers and bakers, in this commercial city, which enjoyed a constant traffic thanks to the frontier and, especially, the garrison, poses a problem. So, in a region which was privileged as far as education was concerned, does the high level of illiterates. Out of 288 members invited to put their name at the foot of their marriage deed, 65 stated that they were unable to sign, and 65 others were content to trace their initials clumsily – that is 45 % were illiterate.[16] In brief, the 'German burgesses', lacking education and money, were, for the most part, unable to exercise those trades which required capital, and which alone were capable of bringing, along with substantial revenues, respectability. They were independent artisans, certainly, but they remained at the bottom of the complex hierarchy of guilds, and amongst the poorest. It may be argued that Strasbourg, completely Lutheran until 1681, and with the Catholic presence of recent date, was an extreme case. Did the group of members reflect the profile of the recent immigrants, still poorly integrated into the town, like the whole Catholic community in 1750?

In Colmar and Epinal, things were different.[17] There was a better balance between the various trades. There was a much more coherent relationship between the numbers of artisans in the town and their representation within the ranks of the congregation. There were butchers, bakers, innkeepers and merchants in the congregation. Nevertheless, some of the features which were so apparent in the society of Strasbourg are still visible in Epinal. Shoemakers, tailors, joiners and masons were still in a majority. Does this show the power of tradition? Or was there, in the case of those professional categories regarded as mobile and difficult to control, a definite plan on the part of the authorities who directed the congregations?

In Strasbourg in 1754, only a minority of the congregation (37.9 %) were natives of the town. Even less numerous were the sons of burgesses: 22.38 % (see figure 18). This is hardly surprising in a

[16] Châtellier, 'Enquête sur la formation de la société catholique strasbourgeoise', p. 33.

[17] Sources: A. P. Saint-Martin, Colmar, registers of the congregation of the bourgeois, from 1748; Jean Bachschmidt, *Le Livre des bourgeois de Colmar, 1660–1789* (Colmar, 1985); A. M. Epinal, GG 51 (lists of members of the Parish Association of Epinal, 1767–77), Abbé Henri Barotte, *Les Corps de métiers d'Epinal* (Saint-Dié, 1899). The identification of the members of the association and the reconstitution of family ties has been done by Mlle Marguerite Frientz.

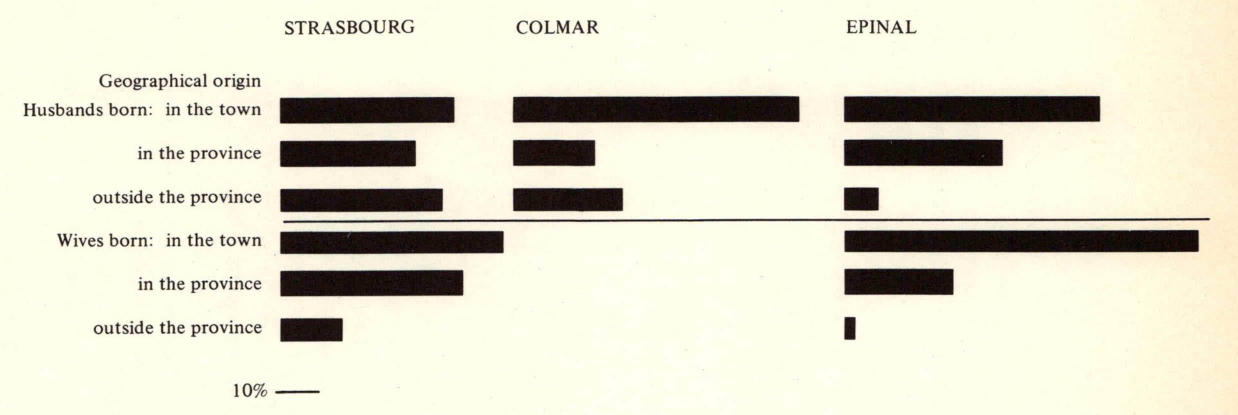

18. Origins of congregation members and their wives (eighteenth century)

town where Catholics were only recently established.[18] In Colmar at the same period, the situation was quite different. Half the members of the congregation of men were sons of burgesses. If sons of simple inhabitants are included, 60.69 % were natives of the town in 1748. The distribution by guild reveals, however, that there were still few coopers and innkeepers (*Au Géant*) or merchants (*A la Fidélité*) amongst the members. Masons, joiners and carpenters (*Au Sureau*), shoemakers (*A la Bonne Vie*) and weavers (*A l'Aigle*) were, on the other hand, very numerous. At Epinal in 1770, it is not so much the number of brethren born in the town which is striking (56.47 %), as the number of mercers (83.33 % of those established in the town) and general merchants (61.22 %). Out of 631 craftsmen listed for Epinal in 1779, 298, that is 47.22 %, belonged to the congregation (see figure 17b, p. 225).[19] These included shoemakers and carpenters as well as mercers and spicers. The settlement had been successful. The congregation had become a power in the town.

This entrenchment had been achieved gradually. Its progress can be traced through a study of the parish registers. Among the 'German burgesses' of Strasbourg in mid-century, natives of Strasbourg were few, whilst Alsatians were already in a majority. Two-thirds (66.06 %) of the immigrants had not come far – from the province or the diocese. What is more, once established on the banks of the Ill, they married, half of them (47.28 %) a girl from Strasbourg itself, the rest (86.04 %) a girl from nearby.[20] At Epinal, 266 (56.47 %) of the congregation members in 1770 had been born in the town, 165 (35.03 %) came from different parts of Lorraine. Less than 40 were from outside the province. Of the wives, 372 (77.17 %) came from Epinal. The phenomenon which can be seen emerging in Strasbourg, in a town where the congregation, like Catholicism, was a recent implant, appeared in full flow at Epinal at the end of the eighteenth century. Roots were put down by marriage, and even more by marriage to a local girl.

What part did the congregations, in particular those of young artisans, play in this process of integration? That they had a role is certain, though its importance is difficult to measure. The influence of the directors during more than two centuries of preaching, counsel

[18] Châtellier, 'Enquête sur la formation de la société catholique strasbourgeoise', p. 32.

[19] A. M. Epinal, GG 51; Barotte, *Les Corps de métiers d'Epinal.*

[20] Châtellier, 'Enquête sur la formation de la société catholique strasbourgeoise', pp. 32, 34.

and confession should not be underestimated. But most of all, behind the instruction dispensed, lay a structure. The organisation of the congregations, based on that of the guilds, and the effective presence of *sodales* in all of the latter (see figures 17a and b for Strasbourg, Colmar and Epinal) – even when it was almost symbolic, as in the case of Strasbourg – was not only a response to the desire for apostleship. It also facilitated support for the new arrivals and their integration into the various guilds. Further, as a connection existed everywhere between the latter and the right to become a burgess, it was no less than the status of burgess of the town which the sodality was often in a position to obtain for its members, at least when they were judged worthy. This was particularly the case, obviously, in towns such as Colmar and Epinal where the congregations were in a large majority in certain trades, even in the guilds as a whole. At Epinal at the end of the eighteenth century, it must have been difficult to open a workshop without being in a congregation, just as in other towns it was advisable to be a *sodalis* if you wanted to practise the trade of tailor, shoemaker or mason. It was very probably the same at Molsheim, Eichstätt, Ingolstadt and Munich. Without it ever being said, it seems clear that in the eighteenth century the congregation constituted for the young craftsmen who travelled the best hope of being able to settle down, and perhaps even to achieve social promotion.

It was among the devotees of Mary, and nowhere else, that the young Bavarian or Swiss journeyman who arrived in Strasbourg could meet the only Catholic craftsmen who counted in the town. He might impress one or other of them, and gain his patronage, in order either to receive rights of burgesship or to be accepted by a good master. This was what happened in the case of Jean-Pierre Brancour, originally a simple stonemason, who later became a painter on porcelain in the celebrated factory of Paul-Antoine Hannong. The new arrival might also so insinuate himself into the favours of one of the congregation members that he joined the family. Jean-François Apfel, recently arrived from Mayence, was a barber's assistant, like so many others in Strasbourg, until he married the daughter of André Eckert, from a powerful family of boatmen, and himself a magistrate. André Eckert's brother, Jean-Philippe, gave his daughter to another congregation member, Jean Frantz, who had come from Ribeauvillé to practise the trade of cabinet-maker in the Alsatian metropolis.[21] The marriage of Jean-Nicolas Claudel, son of a merchant of La

[21] A. M. Strasbourg, Catholic parish registers (marriages).

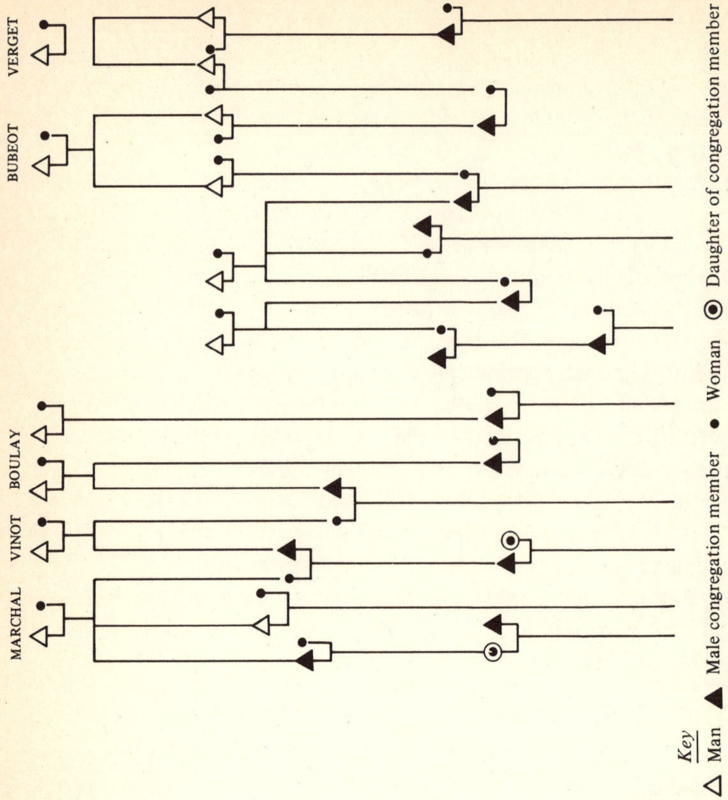

VERGET BUBEOT BOULAY VINOT MARCHAL

Key

△ Man ▲ Male congregation member • Woman ⦿ Daughter of congregation member

19(a) The formation of Catholic families: Epinal at the end of the eighteenth century

Bresse, to the daughter of a judge in the bailiwick of Epinal opened up to him the career of *avocat*, soon capped with the lucrative post of receiver of the Chapter of Saint-Goery.[22]

This was quite normal in a Catholic town. Fathers in Luxembourg refused to give their daughters to suitors who were not members of a congregation.[23] In Epinal, family reconstitution reveals clusters of men of the same generation linked by marriage. Figure 19(a)

[22] A. M. Epinal, parish registers, researched by Mlle Marguerite Frientz.

[23] Villaret, *Les Congrégations mariales*, p. 294.

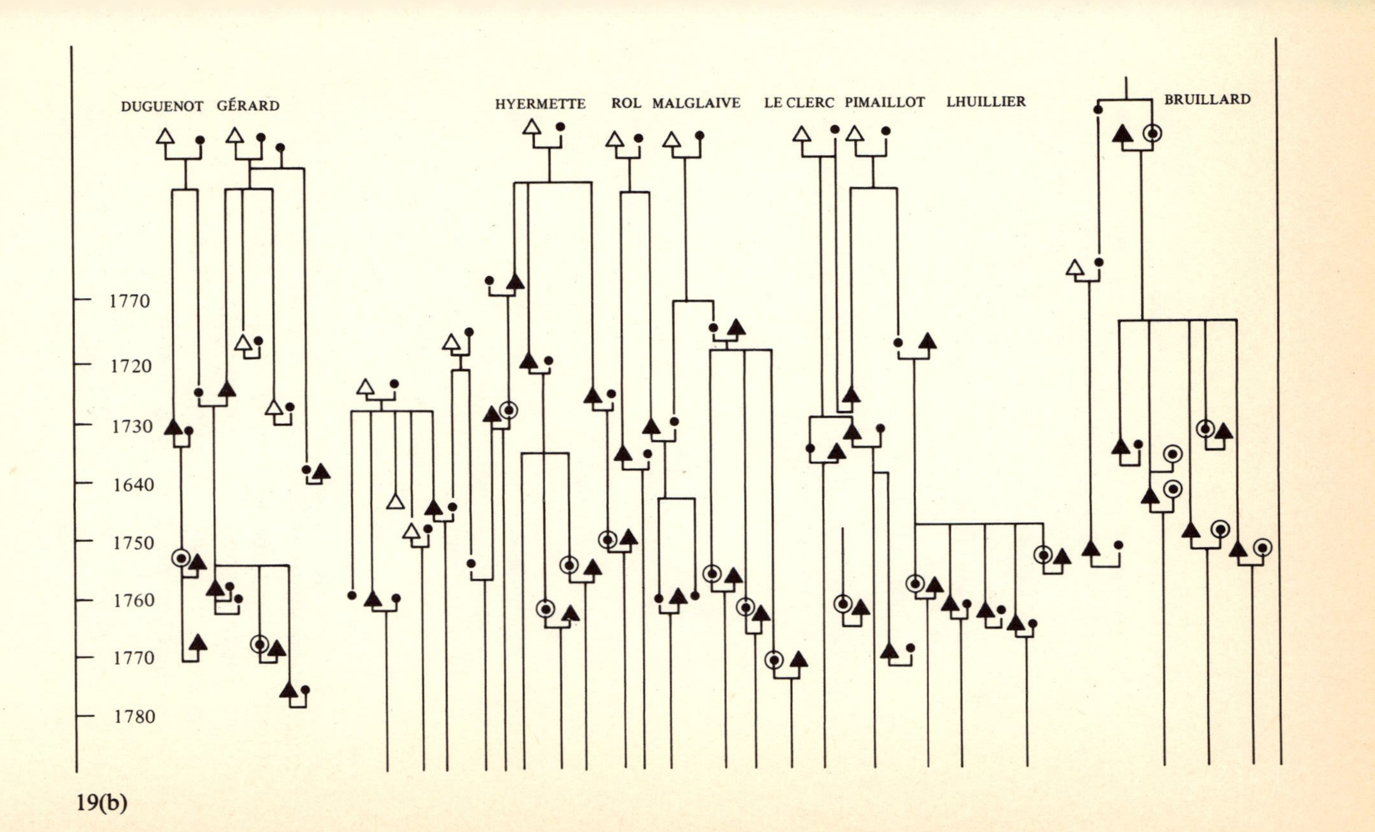
DUGUENOT
GÉRARD
HYERMETTE
ROL
MALGLAIVE
LE CLERC
PIMAILLOT
LHUILLIER
BRUILLARD
1770
1720
1730
1640
1750
1760
1770
1780

19(b)

shows the number of alliances between congregation members within one generation. Should we see this as an illustration of the role occupied by the association as a substitute for the companies of the young or *bachelleries*, with brothers marrying their sisters to other *sodales*?[24] It is tempting to do so. Figure 19(b), which covers two generations, demonstrates another phenomenon. It makes it possible to follow the strategies of families as diverse as the Bruillard (royal notary), Gérard (farrier), Lhullier (innkeeper), Hyermette (launderer, mason) and Duguenot (master edge-tool maker). It was always the same: sons followed their fathers into the congregation, and daughters invariably married members. Was this the consequence of paternal authority or the influence of their environment? However that may be, the trend is clear. After the new arrivals had married the sisters and cousins of their brethren, the next generation saw their sons enter office in the congregation, where their daughters continued to find husbands.

The aim was to establish Christian families. Already at the end of the sixteenth century, in Cologne as in Antwerp, the first directors had been anxious to prepare those under their direction for the tasks they would need to accomplish with regard to their wives and children. Fathers Caussin and Cordier later returned to this question and dealt with it in enormous detail. In the eighteenth century, it was the fathers of families who were the major preoccupation. Hence the importance of the first step – marriage. Was the very frequent presence of congregation members amongst the witnesses to marriages a sign of the importance the congregation accorded to this sacrament? Was it a way of manifesting its presence in an act which involved an individual but, at the same time, the whole Catholic community? Was it, in the last analysis, a form of control? Or was it, more simply, an extension of the sociability felt amongst the young men within the association?

However that may be, among the 'German burgesses' of Strasbourg, it was the custom right from the beginning to call on one or two brethren as witnesses. More than 52 % of the deeds of marriage or remarriage of *sodales* registered in 1754 were signed by one or more

[24] On this question, see Nicole Pellegrin, *Les Bachelleries: organisation et fêtes de la jeunesse dans le Centre-Ouest, XVe–XVIIIe siècle* (Poitiers, 1982); Nicolas Rétif de La Bretonne, *La Paysanne pervertie ou les dangers de la ville* (Paris, 1972), ed. Béatrice Didier, book 1, letter 2, pp. 53–6.

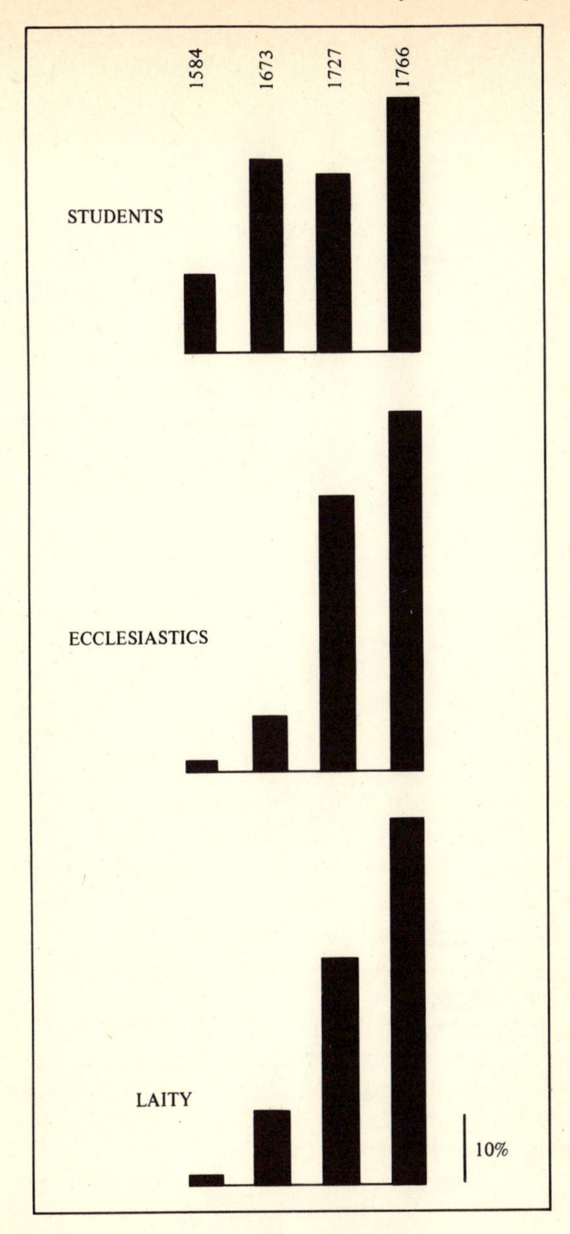

20(a) The Major of Munich, 1584–1766

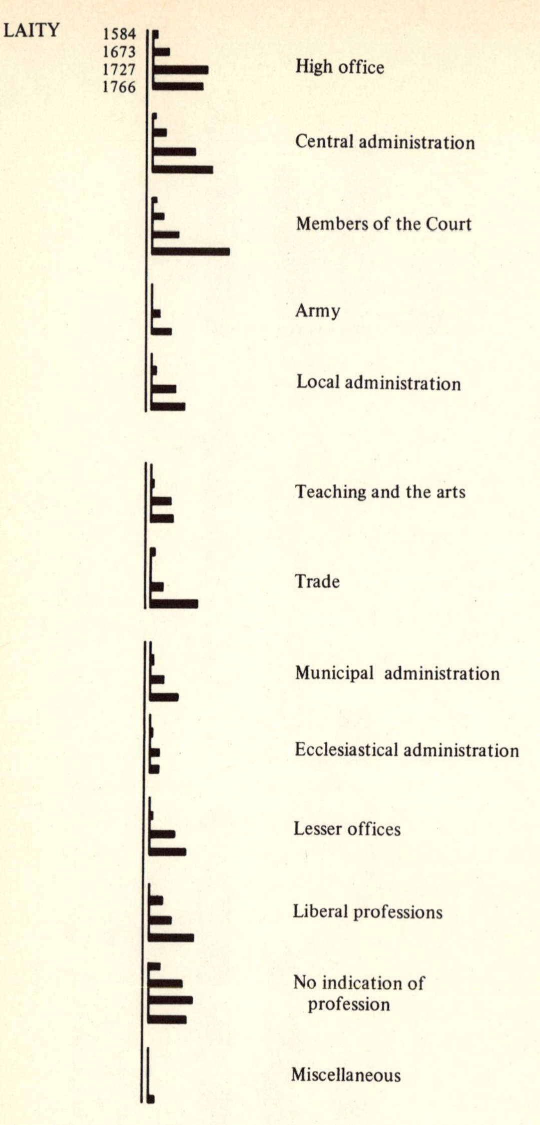

20(b) The Major of Munich, 1584–1766

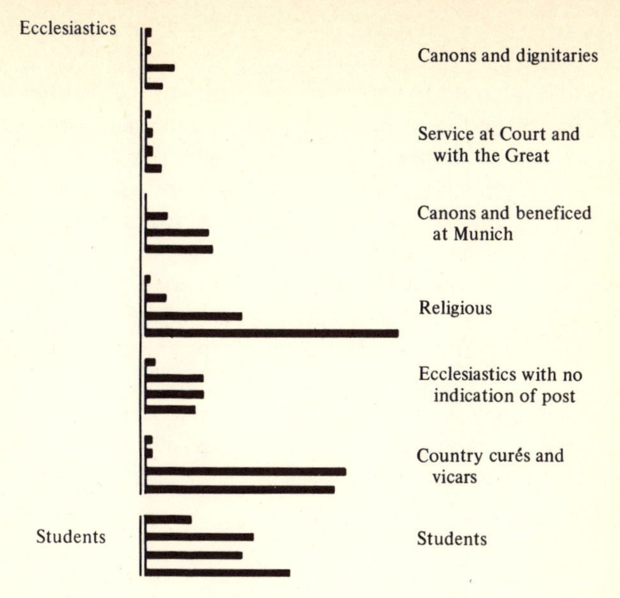

20(c) The Major of Munich, 1584–1766

members of the association.[25] This may have been a precaution appropriate to a Lutheran town where it was always wise to make absolutely certain of the religion of the men and women contracting marriage.[26] In Epinal, however, a wholly Catholic town, the proportion of deeds signed by one or more congregation members rose in 1770, for the group examined, to over 78 %. The congregation was everywhere. It was even present when children were born. More than 80 % of congregation members chose brethren as godfathers to their children at least once (and usually much more often).[27]

There can no longer, in such cases, be any question of control on the part of the congregation. The high proportion of godparents almost always chosen from amongst the family was a result of family structure. The families of this small town in southern Lorraine at the end of the eighteenth century were large. To be precise, since the very frequent deaths in the first years of life have to be taken into account,

[25] Châtellier, 'Enquête sur la formation de la société catholique strasbourgeoise', p. 35.

[26] Châtellier, *Tradition chrétienne et renouveau catholique*, pp. 348–59.

[27] Researched by Mlle Marguerite Frientz.

there was a very high birthrate. Of 487 congregation members in the 1770s and subsequent years who had children, 277 (56.87%) had 6 or more. In fact, as many as 122 (25.04%) had 10 children or more, whilst 14 had more than 16! In practice, these families soon shrank, with only a limited number of children reaching marriageable age.

We should perhaps see in these networks of associates, firmly rooted in the various stratas of society, the strong points of resistance to de-Christianisation. It is in this family structure, and its continuous links with the venerable institution founded in the sixteenth century, that the reasons for the permanence of the devotion to the faith still so widely found in Lorraine, Alsace and Bavaria must be sought.

Thus integration into existing families was succeeded by their consolidation. A new society was in the process of formation, with its own pious practices, ways of life, specific behaviour, and even its own demography.

THE CHRISTIAN WORKER

The individual was not, however, neglected. He had never, on the contrary, so preoccupied those in charge of the congregations, especially if he was a young worker. In the archives of the canton of Lucerne, there is a booklet dating from 1806 intended for the young men of the sodality of unmarried men. Entitled *A Hundred Instructions for the Journeyman to Take on his Travels*, it was very probably written by the father director.[28] This little work, meant to be slipped into the traveller's bag to accompany him on his travels, is of exceptional interest. It reveals, in its own way, the evolution in behaviour taking place within the congregations, at the end of the eighteenth and very beginning of the nineteenth centuries, with regard to work and working conditions. Many of its directions can be likened to a code of good conduct and they tell us, in their way, about the life of the journeyman travelling round Germany or Europe.

When travelling, it says, he should be on his guard: he should not bestow his confidence on just anyone. He should be very economical with his money, wear clothes appropriate to his condition in life, stay as little as possible in hotels and remember that sleeping on straw was

[28] S. A. Lucerne, cod. KK 720, *Hundert väterliche Lehren den wandernden Handwerksgesellen auf die Reise mitzugeben. Ein Andenken von der Congregation der ledigen Mannspersonen in Luzern ihren Mitgliedern gewidmet* (Lucerne, 1806).

far better for the health than a dirty bed in an inn, which might infect him with deadly diseases.[29] In the workshop, he should not be one of those who said 'That's good enough.' Nothing was ever good enough. The least job ought to be done to last for ever. And above all, nothing should be wasted, for that would be to rob the master or the customers. The poor master should be honoured as much as the rich, and both served with the same loyalty. He should work with the same zeal, whether his master was there or not. He should be even more exacting and zealous if he entered the service of a widow. He should look on the good master as a father, and his wife and daughters as a mother and sisters. As for the bad master, he would be well advised to flee him as quickly as possible, for fear that his bad reputation might injure him.[30]

He should choose his friends with care. He should be very circumspect if someone asked to borrow money, and even more so if someone wanted to give him a present, especially if they were of the opposite sex. He should beware of taking Mondays off (*lundis bleus*): there were quite enough holidays already without adding working days. Anyone who took frequent *lundis bleus* must expect to spend many days hungry.[31] Grave dangers lay in wait for the journeyman, of which he should be warned: indelicacy, conspiracy and demonstrations against the masters or the authorities of the country, enlisters who made men into soldiers after a drink, gaming, disagreements and conflicts with other journeymen, and, lastly, drink, which was worse than the plague.[32] To keep out of danger, he should watch his tongue, and remember that the less said, the better, especially when it was a matter of politics, military affairs or religion.[33] As far as possible, he should keep to the house of his pious master, the church, and the congregation, if there was one in the town where he was staying.[34]

But, alongside these recommendations, there were others which dealt with the professional training of the young artisan. 'Go to those regions where your trade is practised best', advised the author, 'because he who sees nothing better considers the bad to be good and remains limited all his life.'[35] And, 'do not be content with villages and small towns, because in the large towns better and finer work is

[29] *Ibid.*, instruction 23, p. 13.

[30] *Ibid.*, instructions 28–35, pp. 14–17.

[31] *Ibid.*, instruction 46, p. 22. This fear of Mondays taken as holidays is frequently expressed in contemporary episcopal ordinances.

[32] *Ibid.*, instructions 44–75, pp. 21–34.

[33] *Ibid.*, instructions 50–8, pp. 23–7.

[34] *Ibid.*, instructions 42, 79, pp. 20, 36–7.

[35] *Ibid.*, instruction 9, p. 8.

done because the work there is better paid'.[36] That said, it would be foolish for a beginner to rush headlong to a capital before he had acquired sufficient skill. 'You would be the laughing stock of your companions and you would receive a lesser salary.'[37] Another important piece of advice:

Do not cling to the past, profit by anything you see which is good and new; if your master does excellent work, learn from him; if you see journeymen practising new methods with skill, work without counting your time at their side; in your free time, read works dealing with your trade in order to improve yourself.[38]

It was no longer so much a matter of saving the young man, of putting him on his guard against evil, as of encouraging him to make the best use of his 'years of apprenticeship'. The main objective appears to have been to make him first into a qualified worker, and then a competent master, aware of modern techniques. Alongside the undeniable concern for apostleship in the world of work appeared a new desire to encourage Catholic workers to compel respect through their qualification in their various trades. Was this, in a country divided by religion, a response to the widely recognised pre-eminence of Protestant artisans and tradesmen? Was it a new form of apostleship adapted to the modern world where the values of competence, efficiency and success were highly prized and had to be possessed by anyone who wanted to act as a model and influence others? What is important is that the virtues of the good workman and those of the Christian were assimilated. If the former was not necessarily a good Catholic, it went without saying that the Catholic must be amongst the best in his profession. Religion and a work ethic came together.

Thus the *Hundred Instructions* intended for the young artisans of Lucerne seems to anticipate, more than half a century in advance, the ideas and principles of the social Catholics of the mid-nineteenth century. In a guide intended for his *Vereine*, Abbot Adolf Kolping wrote in 1849:

The worker who wants to go on his tour must have sound principles and a solid character, without which he will soon come to grief. Laxity ruins most

[36] *Ibid.*, instruction 11, p. 9. [37] *Ibid.*, instruction 10, p. 8.
[38] *Ibid.*, instructions 83–5, pp. 40–1.

young people. While on his travels, he must be polite to everyone, modest, prudent, and avoid all dubious society. As far as possible, the journeyman will not set out on his travels unless he has some funds in reserve. Wherever he arrives, he will address himself first of all to the *Gesellenverein* if there is one, if not he will endeavour to lodge in a suitable inn.[39]

In Paris, the men behind the institutions of patronage, who owed much to Kolping, declared in 1859:

If we wish to make the workshop Christian, it is necessary that the young men who leave our Institutes obtain, by their professional skill, an influence in the workshop which they can make serve the cause of religion.[40]

The author of the *Hundred Instructions*, however, emphasised that while travelling was necessary, it was not an end in itself. The aim was to return home once competence was acquired. *Das Vaterland*! What a moving speech this provoked on the part of this patriotic director! If only the young worker could restrict his travels to his native region, how much better it would be.

Thus you might perhaps find in the capital or towns of your native land what you seek in vain elsewhere. Because one's native land is, after all, one's native land, and it is it which you should know first.[41]

But the author corrects himself; it was necessary for the young artisan to go to learn his trade alongside the best masters in the big cities. Let him go, therefore, but let him think constantly of home, let him write to his parents, to his priest, to his old schoolmaster. And finally, once trained, let him return home without delay. He will joyfully rediscover his father and mother, his brothers and sisters, and it is at home that he should settle down, and win respect by his skill and his zeal.[42]

The vocation of the Christian worker, thus, did not lie in his travels, but in his establishment back home, where he would contribute, in his turn, to the consolidation of the Christian family.

At the end of the eighteenth century, we begin to see emerge, in certain European countries, the outlines of a specific Catholic society.

[39] Kannengieser, *Catholiques allemands*, p. 165.
[40] Duroselle, *Les Débuts du catholicisme*, p. 583.
[41] *Hundert väterliche Lehren*, instruction 8, p. 8.
[42] *Ibid.*, instructions 90–100, pp. 43–8.

This society had its elites, whose common features, on the cultural plane at least, stand out clearly. It had its mass of small men who, in the large towns, lost their heterogeneity and their mobility and began to put down roots. It had its own values and rules, according to which its members led their professional lives, and whose sound basis they, for the most part, recognised. At the heart of the old Christianity, a Catholic society was born, in whose formation the Marian congregations had played a major role.

13. *The origins of a Catholic ideology*

At a time of major upheaval, when first the Enlightenment, then the French Revolution, and lastly the Industrial Revolution and the growth of towns, were transforming Europe, would the congregations and the associations which derived from them appear as the upholders of traditional values? And might this defence not become, in some cases, their principal *raison d'être*? This is the impression often given by reading the instructions of the directors of sodalities in the eighteenth and early nineteenth centuries. The conviction is strengthened when one observes the actions and the interventions in public life of many *sodales* at the time when, in France, the famous Congregation assumed an important role in politics. However, it was at the very moment when the ancient institution of Fathers Coster and Leunis appeared as a counter-revolutionary force that both within it and, even more, in the activities it inspired, the first signs heralding Christian syndicalism and Christian democracy were visible. This was the ambiguity of an institution which was both of its time, and yet had had its own dynamic since the distant century of its birth. And, in the long term, it is perhaps rather these indications of modernity which dominate and which have greater significance for the future.

THE ROLE OF THE CLERGY

For all that, those running the congregations at the beginning of the eighteenth century seem to have wished to inspire in their troops only sentiments of resignation and submission to authority of whatever sort. The author of the *Saints Exercices de l'artisan chrétien* began his text with a hymn which clearly reveals the spirit which was intended to inspire the congregation member who worked with his hands:

> Vivants portraits de Dieu qui meurt dans les supplices,
> Que votre sort me paroît doux!

Dieu sait vôtre bonheur, vous faites ses délices.
Les Rois sont moins heureux que vous.

Au milieu du mépris vostre gloire est extrême,
Vous ressemblez tous à Jésus:
Bien qu'en proie aux douleurs, vous l'aimez, il vous aime,
Que peut-on désirer de plus.

Sans crainte, sans désir, vous passez votre vie
Ne recherchant que la vertu,
Ainsi vivoit Jesus, ainsi vivoit Marie,
Vous vivez comme ils ont vécu.

Accablez de travaux, toujours dans la misère,
Jamais vous ne fûtes chagrins,
Charmez de voir Joseph, Jesus, sa Sainte Mere
Vivre du travail de leurs mains.[1]

'Sans crainte, sans désir' was to be the attitude of those who worked just as Jesus had worked for thirty years without faltering. The good father who commissioned these verses was not only urging his readers to be resigned, he wanted to persuade them to regard this condition as the ideal, as that of the Christian *par excellence*. 'Remember that Jesus chose the hard lot of the Artisan', he wrote a little further on, 'in preference to that of Kings.'[2] But what was to be done when a congregation member could not manage to feed his family with the fruits of his labour? The director of the confraternity of the Good Death in Strasbourg at the end of the century offered such unhappy men this answer: 'Above all, do not complain, do not blaspheme, but, like St Peter after his long night of vain effort, put your faith in Jesus and get on with your work.'[3] Even the poor hired labourer, who 'can barely earn the coarse bread which his famished

[1] Living portraits of God who die in torment, how sweet your lot seems to me! God knows your happiness, you are his delight. Kings are less happy than you.

Though despised, your glory is great. You are like Jesus: though prey to sorrows, you love him and he loves you; what more could you want.

Without fear, without desires, you spend your life seeking only virtue. As Jesus lived, as Mary lived, you live as they did.

Worn out with work, always poor, you are never downcast, happy to see Joseph, Jesus and his Holy Mother live by the labour of their hands.

Les Saints Exercices de l'artisan chrétien, introduction, not paginated.

[2] *Ibid.*, p. 16.

[3] Jeanjean, *Predigten*, vol. 1, pp. 74–97 (sermons for the 4th and 9th Sundays after Pentecost, on work, 1781).

children snatch from his mouth', should not resort to violence. 'Ah! raise your lamentations to the Father who is in Heaven! Suffer, weep, but make no complaint.'[4] Peter, after all, toiled all night, what had they done? And when did success come to him? When Jesus was with him.[5] They should do likewise. Nor should they forget, once they had been paid, to behave like the disciple. He called the other fishermen to help lighten his boat; and they, if they earned a good living, should think of their workers, and see that they benefited.[6] A man who had a wife and family should take as his model Jesus providing food for the multitude in the desert. He should be wise, generous and thrifty, and remember that misery never penetrated a house where this last virtue was practised.[7]

Man might be meant to live in society, but he should not take it into his head to reform it. To each his place. He should hold to that in which Providence had placed him and find salvation by fulfilling the obligations of his position. As for authority, it comes from God. The Christian should imitate Christ and demonstrate submission. He should not complain, or, even worse, resort to violence against his master or the merchants or the magistrates or the prince who governs. Not mincing his words, Abbé Jeanjean put the troublemakers firmly in their place.

> Who gave you, who are subjects, the right to examine the actions of your superiors? You speak of things you do not understand; you criticise ordinances without understanding the reasons for them. Insolent people! Fine presumptuous spirits! You cannot even manage to run your workshop, you do not even know how to earn your living by your trade, you cannot support your family, and yet you want to run the country and its people?[8]

But there were some who said they couldn't pay their taxes. A fine argument! Wage-earners and journeymen were not so stingy when it was a matter of going to the inn. 'Prodigal with your pleasures, you are suddenly parsimonious when it comes to giving to the King, or to Authority, what they ask of you.'[9]

If the workers, 'Living portraits of God', were put on a pedestal, it was the better to make them conform to the model they represented on earth. What was wanted of them was sacrifice, silence, obedience, all virtues practised by Christ, to whom they were freely compared.

[4] *Ibid.*, p. 78. [5] *Ibid.*, pp. 81–93. [6] *Ibid.*, pp. 87–91.
[7] *Ibid.*, pp. 131–44 (sermon for the 6th Sunday after Pentecost, on the duties of fathers, 1785). [8] *Ibid.*, p. 48. [9] *Ibid.*, p. 49.

THE CONSEQUENCES OF THE REVOLUTION

In the early days of the Revolution, nevertheless, a few dissenting voices were heard. The tone employed by Abbé Anton Jeanjean to address the artisans of Strasbourg showed that by the 1770s the virtues of humility and of submission to authority were perhaps no longer, in spite of the example of Jesus the carpenter, universally admired or practised. In Pau, twenty years later, the director of the congregation used very different language to speak to his workers, most of them weavers suffering from competition from cotton, and disinclined to listen to the language of resignation and obedience.[10] Many of them would be found, not many months later, amongst the most active revolutionaries; to the point where, long afterwards, some members of the congregation demanded a purge of those who had demonstrated 'an excess of irreligion and misconduct'.[11]

In Epinal and Colmar, towns for which the membership lists survive from after 1770, a good number of brethren joined the Jacobin club. At Colmar, there were several among the founder-members.[12] Some, it is true, were struck off during the course of the spring of 1794, like the locksmith, François-Ignace Arles, guilty of 'having fanaticised the people', or the tailor, Jean-Baptiste Kastner, who was amongst those who, moved 'by antiquated prejudices, celebrated Sunday'.[13] More prudent were those who, having joined in the enthusiasm of the early days of the Revolution, faded discreetly away by the end of 1791.

But others were faithful to the club to the end and appeared unembarrassed by its radicalisation or the anti-religious measures it adopted. It was to a congregation member, the joiner François-Augustin Peclet, that the municipality of Epinal entrusted the mission of travelling to Paris in the summer of 1793 to seek the stone from the Bastille on which was carved the Declaration of the Rights of Man which the Convention assigned to the department of Vosges.[14] One of the heroes of the Revolution at Colmar was a longstanding congregation member, the boatman, Martin Stockmeyer. It was he, who, at the head of a troop armed with cudgels,

[10] Laborde, *Les Congrégations des Bourgeois*, pp. 90–110. [11] *Ibid.*, p. 135.

[12] Paul Leuilliot, *Les Jacobins de Colmar: procès-verbaux des séances de la société populaire (1791–1795)*, (Strasbourg, 1923).

[13] *Ibid.*, p. 167, note 8, p. 201, note 1.

[14] A. M. Epinal. Based on the research of Mlle Marguerite Frientz.

came, on 4 February 1791, to the rescue of the royal commissioners who were threatened by an angry mob following the secularisation of the town's convents.[15] The blows with which Stockmeyer cleared a space through the crowd won him fame throughout the whole of the province. Engravings represented 'the Hercules of Colmar' in the thick of the action, and the Jacobin club honoured him some years later with the flattering title of 'Father of the *Sans-Culottes*' – an unlikely triumph for a devotee of Mary![16]

Even more surprising was the case of the members of the Pact within the academic sodality of Molsheim, which brought together the Catholic élite of all Alsace. Though the sub-delegate, Jean-Amable Doyen, perished in the September massacres, and though the receiver of the great chapter, François-Louis Frischelt, and his wife were imprisoned in May 1794, charged with being 'aristocrats and fanatics', others of them occupied important administrative posts and seem to have had no difficulty in accommodating to the new régime. Thus Joseph-Armand d'Elvert, member of a family employed in the service of the Prince-Bishop, was *président* of the regency in Saverne in 1790. He became president of the criminal court of the Lower Rhine in September of the same year, and still held this post at his death at the end of 1796. Jean-Guillaume Liechtlé, inspector and *juge de la Monnaie* before the Revolution, was quickly accepted as a member of the Society of Friends of the Constitution. He was then appointed administrator of the Directory for the district, and, in 1798, became commissioner at the Mint in Strasbourg.[17] As for Jean-Thomas d'Aquin Laquiante, apostolic and royal notary at Strasbourg in 1790, he was in the same year founder-member of the Society of the Revolution, and soon president of the civil court, a post he still held in 1800. One has to admire the rapidity with which these representatives of the great Catholic families of Alsace managed, as early as 1790, their conversion into notables under the new régime. One may suspect opportunism, and the case of a Laquiante may appear to support this. A man of the Enlightenment, founder of one of the first learned societies in eighteenth-century Strasbourg, he was also a convinced mason, and an original member of the Beaux-Arts

[15] *Histoire de Colmar*, under the direction of Georges Livet (Toulouse, 1983), pp. 134–5.

[16] Leuilliot, *Les Jacobins de Colmar*, p. 7, note 3, p. 169, note 4.

[17] E. Barth, *Notes biographiques sur les hommes de la Révolution à Strasbourg et dans les environs* (Strasbourg, 1885).

lodge.[18] Mason and congregation member is a surprising combination, but one which was not in fact all that uncommon.

In the light of all this, the invective of Abbé Jeanjean acquires a new significance, and one cannot think without amusement of the indifferent air affected by Monsieur Laquiante while the good cleric thundered from the pulpit, or of the embarrassed demeanour of the 'brave' Stockmeyer contemplating his stick while the preacher forcefully reminded his audience of their duties of submission and humility. Such a contrast between teaching and practice was perhaps a manifestation of the crisis experienced by the sodalities at the end of the eighteenth century. But it is by no means certain that the individuals concerned felt that they were being unfaithful to their act of consecration to the Virgin. When he entered the Beaux-Arts, Laquiante found there eminent members of the Catholic society of Strasbourg, the military, administrators and jurists, with whom he was in constant contact. There were ecclesiastics among the most active and prestigious members of the mother lodge, the Candeur including canon-counts of the great chapter. And we know that the Prince-Bishop, Cardinal Louis-René de Rohan-Guémené, was well-disposed towards this type of assembly.[19]

And, in any case, they called each other 'brother', as in the congregation. The members of the Jacobins of Colmar were also 'brothers', and behaved as such. At the meeting on 22 prairial year III (22 May 1795), the society decided to depute officers for the sick with duties similar to those of the *infirmiers* among the artisans.[20] Why should Stockmeyer feel out of place? These were, for the most part, the same men, engaged in the same activities. We should remember that in the Age of Enlightenment, which gave such a major role to sociability in all domains of thought and action, the congregations had both a head start and vast experience. That many of them should feel an immediate affinity with numerous creations specific to this century, and, at Colmar at least, be amongst the founder-members of the Jacobins, need come as no surprise.

18 Louis Châtellier, 'En prélude aux Lumières, les activités d'une société de lecture de journaux à Strasbourg au milieu du XVIIIe siècle', in *Modèles et moyens de la réflexion politique au XVIIIe siècle*, 3 vols. (Lille, 1977), vol. 1, pp. 287–308; Bertrand Diringer, *Franc-maçonnerie et société à Strasbourg au XVIIIe siècle*, Master's thesis, University of Strasbourg II (1980).

19 Châtellier, *Tradition chrétienne et renouveau catholique*, p. 399; Diringer, *Franc-maçonnerie et société à Strasbourg au XVIIIe siècle.*

20 Leuilliot, *Les Jacobins de Colmar*, p. 240.

All the same, the more time passed, the less frequent were such manifestations of sympathy towards the Revolution. In the end, they disappeared altogether, swept aside by the powerful current flowing in the opposite direction. Was the message constantly repeated by the clergy for a century suddenly heard, as a result of the persecution they later suffered? Did the anti-religious measures taken by the Convention and the Directory give force and reality to the warnings and counsel dispensed for so long from the pulpit? Did the determined action of certain congregation members of new or recent vintage (Liebermann, Bertier de Sauvigny, Mathieu de Montmorency) or of persons close to the congregations (Vicomte de Bonald) suddenly turn them in a counter-revolutionary direction?[21] Father Delpuits, founder in 1801 of the famous Congregation of Paris, explained with great clarity the reasons which led him to found a new, rather than restore an old, institution. 'The best-taught young man', he wrote in 1799:

when today he arrives in Paris, and sees, what has never been seen, a Government without Religion, when he hears, what has never been heard of, atheism, materialism and libertinage established as principles and taught in tones of the deepest conviction by men who, in certain respects, merit esteem, who even, by their simple and modest habits, by the gravity of age, by a profound erudition, and for reasons in general sufficiently proper, seem to combine everything which attracts confidence; this young man, I say, cannot avoid some unease.[22]

Thus he wanted to come to his aid by making better known and propagating more widely the solid principles contained in the *Théorie du pouvoir politique et religieux* of Vicomte de Bonald. Some people, perhaps, found more than an affinity between the idea of the social man, which the famous ultra theoretician opposed to the individual man born of the Enlightenment, and the ideal defended by the old Jesuit associations. However that may be, this was what lay behind

[21] René Epp, 'Bruno François Léopold Liebermann', *Annuaire de la société d'histoire et d'archéologie de Molsheim et environs* (1975, pp. 91–7, (1976), pp. 43–9, (1977), pp. 113–16 (Liebermann); Guillaume de Bertier de Sauvigny, *Un type d'ultra-royaliste, le comte Ferdinand de Bertier (1782–1864) et l'énigme de la Congrégation* (Paris, 1948) (Bertier de Sauvigny and Mathieu de Montmorency); de Grandmaison, *La Congrégation (1801–30*, pp. 210–11 (de Bonald). Though the Vicomte de Bonald did not belong to the Congregation, he was an active member of a society instigated and inspired by it, the Société des Bonnes Oeuvres.

[22] Archives of the Paris Jesuits, Chantilly, 'Congrégation du père Delpuits' deposit, vol. 2, doc. 4092, piece 1.

the project which was to lead to the foundation of the Congregation.[23]

Ideological preoccupations were not so pressing amongst the provincial artisans, it is true, but at Pau as at Colmar, their ranks were discreetly purged.[24] In Colmar, the congregation of artisans, which had provided numerous recruits for the Jacobin club, became, at the time of the Restoration, the vigilant guardian of the rights of the monarchy. If some of them still used their fists, it was for a good cause, for the defence of the throne and the altar when these were threatened by the liberals, such as the partisans of General Foy.[25]

It was as if, consequent on the Revolution, the congregations had become counter-revolutionary societies and their members agents of ultra politics.

FROM PATRONAGE TO EMANCIPATION

This impression is strengthened by the fact that the traditional organisation of these old associations appears to have been overthrown. Artisans and apprentices lost their independence and passed under the control of the Gentlemen, who organised, directed, controlled and alone held the initiative. The patronage of the rich became everywhere the rule. This is how the Toulouse Aa, under the July Monarchy, set about keeping the societies of Catholic workers in their place:

> One of our venerable brethren, Monsieur de Lartigue, vicar of St Sernin, with the authorisation of Mgr the Archbishop, founded a society of good Christian masters of workshops, with whom one could confidently place as apprentices poor children who had just made their First Communion, so as to rescue them from the multifarious dangers which threaten their innocence, especially in a large town. The society has existed for some years and has already had the happiest results. To encourage these children, and at the same time to strengthen the zeal of the masters, our brother had the idea of establishing a society of patrons modelled on that in Bordeaux; a society whose members, coming from the families most distinguished by their social rank, could, by providing them with work, or by furnishing them with some

[23] See de Grandmaison, *La Congrégation (1801–30)*.

[24] For the purging of the congregation of the artisans of Pau after the Revolution, see Laborde, *Les Congrégations des Bourgeois*, p. 135.

[25] De Grandmaison, *La Congrégation (1801–30)*, pp. 253–4 (picturesque account reproduced from the Memoirs of the Prefect).

pecuniary resources, or by visiting them from time to time, inspire them to persevere in their good intentions.[26]

The initiative came from above. It was these Gentlemen from 'the most distinguished families who not only protected the young apprentices, but also supported, and discreetly controlled, the 'good Christian masters of workshops'.[27] For the control operated by the Gentlemen over the lower classes, regarded as potentially the 'dangerous classes', appears as one of the chief aims of the operation. The first worker institute of the nineteenth century, the Society of Saint-Joseph created by the Congregation of Paris in 1822, had as its purpose the protection of young workers from all the evil influences to which they might fall prey. Lodged and fed in the institution house, they also found there distraction for their free time and encouragement, on Sundays, to perform their religious duties. According to the director:

In this way, we make safe the most dangerous time for the workers, who, if they have neither heat nor light, are forced, in the winter months, to take refuge in houses they know nothing about, where they risk losing their virtue, their health and the fruits of their labour.[28]

In Germany, however, the congregations preserved their traditional character and organisation far better than in France. One may even wonder if it was not of them that Mgr von Ketteler was thinking when he wrote, in *La Question ouvrière et le christianisme*:

The future of the movement on the corporate level thus belongs to Christianity. The old Christian organisations have been dissolved, and the concern today is to get rid of the last vestiges, the last stone of that admirable edifice; the intention is to build another. But it is a wretched shack, a building constructed on sand. Christianity has to build afresh, and restore to the workers' societies their proper value, their true vitality and utility.[29]

The re-establishment of the ancient corporations, which he longed for as the sole means of restoring to the workman his dignity and his Christian base in the world of work, may have been suggested to him by observation of the old congregations of artisans, numerous in the

[26] A. P. Toulouse, CA 101, vol. 7, pp. 75–6.

[27] Paul Droulers, S. J., *Action pastorale et problèmes sociaux sous la monarchie de Juillet chez Mgr d'Astros, archevêque de Toulouse, censeur de La Mennais* (Paris, 1954), pp. 320–3.

[28] Duroselle, *Les Déburs du catholicisme*, pp. 29–36.

[29] Quoted by Georges Goyau, *Ketteler* (Paris, 1907), p. 188.

Rhineland, which had preserved echoes of the old craft organisation in their inherited structures and customs. It was, once again, in the name of restoration that the help of the worker sodalities was sought. They were expected to provide protection against triumphant liberalism, and against the rise of socialism, and counted on for the reconstruction of the old Christian social order.[30] Thus, in east and west, the congregations were first and foremost hailed as the guarantors of tradition, even as useful instruments for restoring the old order.

But those who lived day after day at the heart of the sodalities discovered other realities. Involved in good works, they learned to know the working world. They were led to admit, some of them at least, that the noble ideas which had inspired them had to be called into question. The poverty of the workers was on an altogether different scale from what they had imagined. Charity was inadequate, inappropriate and increasingly ill-received. The action of individuals or groups, however committed, was no longer sufficient. The state must intervene. It was no longer a question of charity, but of justice. Two years before the publication of the encyclical *Rerum novarum* of Pope Leo XIII, Comte Albert de Mun, hardly a man to be suspected of sympathy towards democratic ideas, urged the congregations to a new type of activity. 'Catholics, having learned from experience', he wrote in 1899:

and trained by a century of struggle, perceive, in its full extent, the vast field open to their efforts. They know that, in modern society, the people are the supreme arbiters of the fate of nations, and that it is necessary not only to animate their intelligence by education, and conquer their hearts by charity, but to secure their trust by justice. Social action is, and will increasingly be, the chief end which will incite their ardour and devotion. They will also find there, in the young, in the associations which conserve their faith and their morals, which stimulate their zeal, which keep them firmly united, the main focus for their efforts, their field of action, and the cadres which will enable their leaders to guide them to victory. The congregations will thus remain the principal strength of their army and the indispensable element in their success in the struggles which the next century has in store.[31]

30 *Handbuch der Kirchengeschichte*, ed. Hubert Jedin (Freiburg in Breisgau, 1970), vol. 6, 1, p. 760 (Ketteler's political and social thought); Franz Schnabel, *Deutsche Geschichte im neunzehnten Jahrhundert*, 4 vols. (Freiburg in Breisgau, 1951), vol. 4, pp. 208–10 (Kolping and the restoration of the guilds).

31 De Grandmaison, pp. xxiii–xxiv (preface by Comte Albert de Mun).

The word 'justice' had been spoken. A major change was apparent, even if Albert de Mun, and doubtless many of those to whom he spoke, were not ready to appreciate all the consequences of these new ideas. For some years now, in Germany and in Belgium, small groups had been forming within the existing Christian associations. They questioned patronage, called for the right of the working class to self-government and elaborated the principles of what would become Christian democracy.[32]

For their part, the workers, as in the seventeenth century, found in the congregations and the various societies the means to an education. They learned about social problems, compared their points of view, and learned, when the grip of patronage was relaxed, to administer and direct an association. Catholic institutions were thus schools for workers on two levels: they enabled them to appreciate more clearly their position and their solidarity with their fellow workers, and at the same time they provided the chance to assume responsibility. This would be the training of many syndicalists, especially in Germany, Belgium and Northern and Eastern France. As Rudolf Rezsohazy wrote, 'the Christian worker-unions sprang from the stock of a worker circle, a guild, a study circle or a friendly society'.[33] It was hardly surprising, therefore, that it was in Flanders, birthplace of the first congregations of artisans and journeymen, that the first Christian worker-union appeared. Founded in Ghent in 1886 among the cloth workers, it consisted of 'brothers' who actively practised mutual aid. They had a fund for the relief of the sick, who were visited regularly. Besides the meetings of the officers, there was in addition a full plenary session once a month.[34] The rhythm of activities, the organisation, even the spirit, of the young union recall the older associations which, although established with a very different purpose, had perhaps made possible its birth.

The role of the congregations between 1750 and 1880 may seem paradoxical. Initially active supporters of the union of throne and altar, they subsequently became places where the future defenders of Christian democracy, and also the militants of social and worker action, were trained. But was the contradiction as great as it appears? Concern for the propagation of the faith and for the defence of the

[32] Rezsohazy, *Origines et formation du catholicisme social en Belgique*, pp. 79–98.
[33] *Ibid.*, p. 158. [34] *Ibid.*, p. 159.

Church had always been the aim of the institution from the beginning. On the other hand, the desire manifested since the sixteenth century to reach all social groups in the towns predisposed it to take an interest, on more than only a spiritual level, in the lot of the artisans and workers. The two major aspects of its vocation were successively revealed during the course of the nineteenth century. It had by no means been the only institution to experience this evolution.[35] The study of the congregations has the merit of showing how the process was accomplished. It also shows how a Catholic ideology was established. Caught between two demands, the defence of the Church and the fight for justice on behalf of the deprived, the actions of Catholics trained in this school could not but be delicate. If they favoured one or other duty according to circumstances, they soon ran into criticism. But, in this too, were they not sharing the lot which had been that of the *sodales* of the seventeenth century?

In 1750, even before the suppression of the Society of Jesus, the Europe of the *dévots* had practically ceased to exist. But this disappearance did not signify the dislocation of the Catholic world. It corresponded rather to the establishment of an entirely new situation, characterised, on the one hand, by the adaptation of the institutions and devotional groups to the transformations of society, and, on the other, by the diffusion into the countryside and the suburbs, into families in large and small towns, amongst workers and notables, of mentalities and habits of life formerly reserved for the congregations alone. The *dévots* of the past were succeeded by a Catholic society. But although this was widespread, it was more firmly established and more solidly maintained in places like Flanders, Alsace, Bavaria, Switzerland, Austria and Italy, where the congregations had been well established since the beginning of the seventeenth century. In spite of major changes, the idea of a continuity is inescapable.

[35] Jean-Marie Mayeur, *Catholicisme social et démocratie chrétienne: principes romains, expériences françaises* (Paris, 1986), p. 12.

Conclusion

The project conceived after the Council of Trent by devout men eager to found a Christian, or rather a Catholic, Europe had thus indeed been realised. This was not, it must be said, always according to the forms and within the time scale originally envisaged. The constitution of the Christian State and the union of princes were soon revealed as Utopian dreams. The reform of morals on a country-wide scale and the transformation of the whole of France into a true City of God, through the medium of the Society of the Holy Sacrament, failed; so, by arousing such sustained hatred and distrust, did the project conceived two centuries later to reconcile the French people with the king and religion, if necessary by force. These last had, in any case, often been less than enthusiastic about a plan conceived in Rome and principally supported by the Society of Jesus, an order which had always encountered opposition in the State of the Most Christian King. The suppression of the Jesuits by Pope Clement XIV in 1773 seemed to put an end to these experiments and condemn the project to oblivion.

But if one looks beyond appearances and dramatic events, and examines men and their behaviour within society or with regard to religion, the results are very different. The study of several congregations as they evolved over nearly three centuries enables us to appreciate the nature of the changes experienced and the manner in which they were effected.

To reform the world, it was necessary to adapt to it. It was not so much by the preaching and teaching of clerics that the doctrine of the Council of Trent and the principles of Catholic reform were diffused amongst the mass of simple faithful; it was by the example and the word of others – husband, son, fellow student, workmate, neighbour or friend who were members of and formed by the congregation. Like preached to like. In this way alone was it possible to find the right words to convince and to assure a constant presence by the side of the new convert. It was no longer appropriate for the Church to speak a different language from that used in the family or at the workplace.

At this point there emerged, thanks to the congregations of Gentlemen, burgesses, artisans and journeymen, the first attempts at a pastoral activity adapted to its surroundings. Within the various groups, men capable of bringing relief to the sick, of assisting the fathers in their missions in town or village, or of influencing their brethren by their natural authority, soon came forward. It was not long before they were called on not only to speak in public, but also to direct, within the churches, the pious exercises of the meeting. There had been a real promotion of the laity, at a period when there emerged from time to time, from within the mass of German and Flemish artisans affected by Anabaptism, some shoemaker or tailor preaching revolt and hope. It was soon not only young men and adults, but also children and, above all, women, who became the privileged intermediaries. The whole of society was involved. It was no longer so much the individual taken in isolation who was the target, it was no longer he alone who must be changed, it was the family which became the principal object of apostleship, just as it moved to the forefront of eighteenth-century preoccupations.

Thus were acquired the religious habits which have marked the behaviour of the populations of Catholic countries down to our own times. The morning prayer, the nightly examination of conscience, confession every fortnight and frequent Communion became, with the passage of time, the accepted practice within families. How to follow the Mass, how to order one's meditations during Lent and how to pray at the stations of the Cross on Good Friday were all taught to congregation members from an early age, like the canticles and prayers which are with a person for life and which are sung or recited together every Sunday. Sensibility was also moulded by the paintings contemplated during the week in the oratory and by the pictures received at the distribution of the saints of the month, especially when the painters of the former were called Van Dyck or Seghers and the engravers of the latter Rubens or Jacques Callot. The pilgrimages to the Virgin at nearby sanctuaries, novenas and the annual retreat gradually became family traditions. To begin with, only certain towns were affected by the chance foundation of colleges; then the mission fields, every town and soon even villages, were influenced. This was particularly the case in regions such as Flanders, the Rhineland, Lorraine, Alsace, Switzerland, Bavaria, Austria and Italy, where the Jesuits were strongly established in the sixteenth century and where their activities, soon firmly based, demonstrated great vitality. It is hardly surprising if these are the regions which resist most strongly, even today, the process of de-Christianisation which has been visible elsewhere since the end of the eighteenth century.

In adapting to society, the congregations also contributed to its transformation. The model presented to Christian families from the middle of the seventeenth century diverged considerably from that of the patriarchal family. It was even its exact opposite. The direction of the household belonged to the father and mother jointly. The role of the latter, in particular, was considerably elevated, even, as regards the education of young children, exalted. The father was no longer the all-powerful repository of authority. He and his spouse together ought to take account of the legitimate aspirations of their sons and daughters, their choice as to vocation, trade and marriage. Relationships based on love took the place of the old relationships based on authority. Similarly, if the rigid barriers separating the different social groups (Gentlemen, burgesses, artisans and journeymen) began to weaken during the eighteenth century, it was perhaps not only because of the development of the economy, but also because of the wishes of the Catholic associations which had sprung from the congregations. The family came before the individual, the Christian community of the parish was preferred to the old socio-professional hierarchy. And already a new society seemed in the process of formation. An élite much larger than before, and much more mixed in its social origins and functions, emerged. It was primarily characterised by the culture and support which it afforded to the Church, and the service which it rendered to others. Amongst shopkeepers, artisans and journeymen, groups which were mobile, unstable, and often excluded from burgesship in towns, the congregation helped to weave solid ties, to establish men, to consolidate families, and to give them roots within a region. There is no doubt that, at the dawn of the contemporary period, quietly, and slowly but surely, it contributed to the formation of the middle class.

The congregations, by their widely diffused teaching, and the instructions and warnings of their directors, gave this newly constituted society the elements of an ideology. Preaching submission, and calling on workers to follow the example of Christ, the Jesuits and their successors appeared as men of order, just as their sodalities may appear as veritable antidotes to *compagnonnage*. This was particularly the case after the great urban revolts of the middle of the seventeenth century and even more at the time of the French Revolution. But the very structure of the institution, the responsibilities given to lay members, the poorest and the youngest included, and the charitable preoccupations manifested from the beginning facilitated the participation of the *sodales*, or of some of them at least, in social and even political action. When they intervened in political life or when they defended the religious rights and the lot of the workers, the Catholics of the nineteenth century were only continuing, by adapting to circumstances, a type of activity for which they had already been prepared by their fathers or their predecessors in the congregations. Little by little, the old *sodalis* became a militant. A continuity is visible between the youth associations, even Christian syndicalism, and the ancient institution founded in the sixteenth century. Further, the failure of the union of Christian princes did not prevent the congregations, which had been united from the beginning by the ties of prayer, from demonstrating a common bond. The men they had taught over the centuries had been taught according to the same principles in the different Catholic countries, and with the same books translated into different languages. The new élites which they had contributed to establishing had been formed in the same manner whether in Flanders, Alsace or Bavaria. How could these regions, marked by the centuries-long activity of the Marian congregations, not be more sensible than others to the European ideal?

Careful to preserve tradition, in its religious components above all, but nevertheless open to the ideas of the modern world, and to the preoccupations of others, rich and poor, near or far, the members of the congregations of the late eighteenth and early nineteenth centuries were conservatives of a very special type. We may perhaps see in their ideas, and in the choices they made at decisive moments, the heralds of what would later be called Christian democracy.

Thus it can be argued that, in part at least, modern Europe was prepared within the Europe of the devout.

Index of people and places

Index of topics

Past and Present Publications

General Editor: PAUL SLACK *Exeter College, Oxford.*

Family and Inheritance: Rural Society in Western Europe 1200–1800, edited by Jack Goody, Joan Thirsk and E. P. Thompson*

French Society and the Revolution, edited by Douglas Johnson

Peasants, Knights and Heretics: Studies in Medieval English Social History, edited by R. H. Hilton*

Towns in Societies: Essays in Economic History and Historical Sociology, edited by Philip Abrams and E. A. Wrigley*

Desolation of a City: Coventry and the Urban Crisis of the Late Middle Ages, Charles Phythian-Adams

Puritanism and Theatre: Thomas Middleton and Opposition Drama under The Early Stuarts, Margot Heinemann*

Lords and Peasants in a Changing Society: The Estates of the Bishopric of Worcester 680–1540, Christopher Dyer

Life, Marriage and Death in a Medieval Parish: Economy, Society and Demography in Halesowen 1270–1400, Zvi Razi

Biology, Medicine and Society 1840–1940, edited by Charles Webster

The Invention of Tradition, edited by Eric Hobsbawm and Terence Ranger*

Industrialization before Industrialization: Rural Industry and the Genesis of Capitalism, Peter Kriedte, Hans Medick and Jürgen Schlumbohm*†

The Republic in the Village: The People of the Var from the French Revolution to the Second Republic, Maurice Agulhon†

Social Relations and Ideas: Essays in Honour of R. H. Hilton, edited by T. H. Aston, P. R. Cross, Christopher Dyer and Joan Thirsk

A Medieval Society: The West Midlands at the End of the Thirteenth Century, R. H. Hilton

Winstanley: 'The Law of Freedom' and Other Writings, edited by Christopher Hill

Crime in Seventeenth-Century England: A County Study, J. A. Sharpe†

The Crisis of Feudalims: Economy and Society in Eastern Normandy c. 1300–1500, Guy Bois†

The Development of the Family and Marriage in Europe, Jack Goody*

Disputes and Settlements: Law and Human Relations in the West, edited by John Bossy

Rebellion, Popular Protest and the Society Order in Early Modern England, edited by Paul Slack

Studies on Byzantine Literature of the Eleventh and Twelfth Centuries, Alexander Kazhdan in collaboration with Simon Franklin†

The English Rising of 1381, edited by R. H. Hilton and T. H. Aston*

Praise and Paradox: Merchants and Craftsmen in Elizabethan Popular Literature, Laura Caroline Stevenson

The Brenner Debate: Agrarian Class Structure and Economic Development in Pre-Industrial Europe, edited by T. H. Aston and C. H. E. Philpin*

Eternal Victory: Triumphal Rulership in Late Antiquity, Byzantium, and the Early Medieval West, Michael McCormick†

East-Central Europe in Transition: From the Fourteenth to the Seventeenth Century, edited by Antoni Mączak. Henryk Samsonowicz and Peter Burke†

Small Books and Pleasant Histories: Popular Fiction and its Readership in Seventeenth-Century England, Margaret Spufford**

Society, Politics and Culture: Studies in Early Modern England, Mervyn James*

Horses, Oxen and Technological Innovation: The Use of Draught Animals in English Farming 1066–1500, John Langdon

Nationalism and Popular Protest in Ireland, edited by C. H. E. Philpin

Rituals of Royalty: Power and Ceremonial in Traditional Societies, edited by David Cannadine and Simon Price

The Margins of Society in Late Medieval Paris, Bronislaw Geremek†

Landlords, Peasants and Politics in Medieval England, edited by T. H. Aston

Geography, Technology, and War: Studies in the Maritime History of the Mediterranean, 649–1571, John H. Pryor

Church Courts, Sex and Marriage in England, 1570–1640, Martin Ingram

Searches for an Imaginary Kingdom: The Legend of the Kingdom of Prester John, L. N. Gumilev

Crowds and History: Mass Phenomena in English Towns, 1780–1835, Mark Harrison

Concepts of Cleanliness: Changing Attitudes in France since the Middle Ages, Georges Vigarello†

The First Modern Society: Essays in English History in Honour of Lawrence Stone, edited by A. L. Beier, David Cannadine and James M. Rosenheim

The Europe of the Devout: The Catholic Reformation and the Formation of a New Society, Louis Châtellier†

*Published also as a paperback

** Published only as a paperback

† Co-published with the Maison des Sciences de l'Homme, Paris